The Revised and Expanded Book of Raccoon Circles

A Facilitator's Guide to Building Unity,
Community, Connection and Teamwork
Through Active Learning

Dr. Jim Cain
Teamwork & Teamplay

Dr. Tom Smith
The Raccoon Institute

KENDALL/HUNT PUBLISHING COMPANY
4050 Westmark Drive   Dubuque, Iowa 52002

Inquiries for copy permission should be addressed to:
Jim Cain, Ph.D.
Teamwork & Teamplay
468 Salmon Creek Road
Brockport, NY 14420 USA
Phone (585) 637-0328
Email: jimcain@teamworkandteamplay.com
Website: www.teamworkandteamplay.com

or

Tom Smith, Ph.D.
The Raccoon Institute
N2020 Cty. H South #570
Lake Geneva, Wisconsin 53147 USA
Phone (262) 248-3750
Email: tsraccoon@earthlink.net

Copyright © 2002, 2007 by Jim Cain and Tom Smith
ISBN 13: 978-0-7575-3265-8

Kendall / Hunt Publishing Company
4050 Westmark Drive
P.O. Box 1840
Dubuque, Iowa 52004 USA
Phone   1-800-228-0810 or (563) 589-1000
Fax   1-800-772-9165 or (563) 589-1046
www.kendallhunt.com

Printed in the United States of America

10 9 8 7 6 5 4 3

Contents

iii

Foreword to the Revised & Expanded Edition

In the past decade, Raccoon Circles have grown from the imagination of Tom Smith and the gracious internet sharing of activities by Jim Cain, to a worldwide team and community building phenomenon. With the first printing of *The Book on Raccoon Circles* and downloaded Raccoon Circle activity guides, there are more than 20,000 copies of Raccoon Circle activities in circulation around the world. If you have ever participated in a teambuilding event, you have no doubt experienced some Raccoon Circle activities.

At the 2005 International Convention of the Association for Experiential Education (AEE), the Raccoon Circle was honored when Tom Smith was presented with The Karl Rohnke Creativity Award. In his acceptance speech, Tom mentioned:

> *"It was a great honor to receive the AEE Kurt Hahn award in 1996, but this is an even greater joy. I knew of Kurt Hahn, but I did not know Kurt Hahn. Karl Rohnke is my friend! I wish I could say that I invented the circle—but I cannot! I wish I could say that I created most of the activities that can be facilitated with a web loop circle—but I cannot! I can't even take credit for naming the Raccoon Circle—Karl Rohnke did that! Karl also wrote an introduction for the original Book on Raccoon Circles that Jim Cain and I put together a few years ago. He said, "Tom Smith has been fooling around with tied loops of webbing for years." He was half right, for I had been exploring circle activities for many years. But he was half wrong, too—because I wasn't "fooling around." I am quite serious about the symbolic, ritualistic, and programmatic possibilities of circles of connection. I believe it is in the message of circles that humankind may find a way out of the darkness, the loneliness, the confusion, and the angst that stifles growth and transcendence to a higher order of humanbeingness for the 21st Century. I believe that circles of connection may be our salvation. I believe that Raccoon Circles are good medicine wheels. The circle is the message. . . . I am just the messenger."*

We are indeed messengers. The wisdom of the circle has become apparent to many others who work with small groups. When we first collaborated to combine our knowledge of ritual, ceremony, history and philosophy with team and community building activities, the result was a modest book on Raccoon Circles. In the four years since the printing of that book, facilitators, trainers, authors, counselors, teachers and friends have continued to share their experiences with Raccoon Circles. It became obvious that another edition of the book was needed to contain all the new ideas, activities, stories, photographs and other recent additions to this wonderful circle of connection.

This revised and expanded edition of *The Book of Raccoon Circles* is the result of the generosity of the adventure-based learning community in general, together with some careful editing, refinement and clarification by the authors themselves. We hope you enjoy the fresh new information presented here, along with the historical, and sometimes hysterical, favorites from the past.

Jim Cain and Tom Smith

Introduction

by Karl Rohnke

Tom Smith has been fooling around with tied loops of webbing for years, and getting some good experiential mileage from their applications to various games and initiative scenarios. During a T.E.A.M conference in Chicago some years ago I casually mentioned, based on Tom's business card rubric *The Raccoon Institute,* that the webbing circles he was using in a workshop looked to me like "Raccoon Circles." I blurted out this appellation spontaneously *(Watch out what you think, thoughts can become words at any moment),* with no intention of naming anything and certainly not anticipating that it would stick, but stick it did and now adorns the title of a book. Very cool!

A few years ago Tom and I were working together in South Africa. We were traveling from Cape Town to a game preserve north of town and had stopped at a roadside pull out to stretch our legs and look around. During that time Tom, because of some personal atavistic aura, attracted the attention of a fairly large and inquisitive baboon. During that brief period of joint introspection, Tom, at some level, connected with the primate. Tom commented about and processed at length that simian contact for the remainder of the drive. Do you anticipate what's coming? Baboon/Raccoon! I, of course, suggested that the heretofore Raccoon Circles might be more appropriately called, what else, *Baboon Circles.* It was a toss up for awhile, but Raccoon Circles it remains and rightly so. Except in South Africa, of course, where *Baboon Circles* still get the nod.

Jim Cain, well known for authoring the teambuilding activity book *Teamwork & Teamplay,* and Tom have expositorily teamed up to record the history, philosophy, ceremony and surprisingly numerous activities that can be attempted using just a piece of webbing, resulting in this reference book you were wise enough to purchase.

Having trouble hauling around a heavy and burdensome bag of tricks? Reduce your load and angst by trying some Raccoon Circle activities. No Props—No Problem!

Karl

The History of Raccoon Circles

My first experience with the Raccoon Circle came during a workshop conducted by Dr. Tom Smith at the Bradford Woods Institute in the fall of 1995. I even have a few photographs of the events that day. Tom managed to lead an entire morning session, nearly 4 hours of programming, using only a few segments of tubular webbing. Needless to say, I was pretty impressed. So were the 20 or so other participants that day. For many of us now, that day lives in our memories as a wonderful piece of our own history. We had the chance to be there at the start.

In the years that followed, I've had many opportunities to share and use Raccoon Circle activities with audiences ranging from elementary school children to the management teams of major corporations, and from staff training sessions for youth-at-risk counselors to some of the most progressive colleges and universities on three continents. In every case, the invitation to 'connect up' has created some wonderful moments.

When Tom first invited us to 'connect up,' his invitation did not stop merely with the activity, but was an invitation to truly join the Raccoon Circle. I have visited quite a few adventure-education centers and challenge courses in the past decade, and more than a few of them have multigenerational copies of Tom's original Raccoon Circles document. Over the years, I've encouraged a few of my friends and associates to contact Tom personally, when they wanted to make copies of his information for conferences or workshops. When I spoke with them later, they always mentioned what a kind and generous soul Tom Smith is.

So it is not surprising that today, as I write this, I again feel blessed to be a part of the Raccoon Circle family. And like any good family member, I'd like to share the rich experience that comes from being a part of the circle. I hope you enjoy what so many have shared.

When I asked Tom Smith about the birth and history of the Raccoon Circle, he, like most of us, pondered about the exact dates when this or that happened. But to the best of his, and my recollection, here is what we remember.

After several decades of utilizing adventure-based activities in therapeutic settings, Tom Smith had acquired a rather extensive knowledge of group work skills, and he used these to the benefit of the many organizations that he assisted in the heartland of the United States. Often, his adventure-based programs would involve the use of climbing rope, which Tom found to be as useful in climbing and rappelling, as for other initiatives at ground level.

At the Heartland Association for Experiential Education conference in the spring of 1992, Tom pulled out a climbing rope to lead some large group activities. A year later, in 1993, Tom again used this rope with about 60 participants as part of the closing ceremony, performing yurt circles, energy waves and stretching. But large conference gatherings were not that typical for Tom, and he needed to find a way to do such activities with smaller groups. At the 1994 T.E.A.M. conference in Chicago, Tom brought along his dependable climbing rope and the standard collection of webbing that rock climbers and outdoor educators always seem to have on hand. Tom looked over the 200 or so participants and realized that he would most likely have to cut one of his possessions so that some small group activities could occur. So the choice was, should he cut a viable climbing rope, or the less expensive webbing that he carried. So now you know the rationale. It was not out of comfort or style or some higher logic, but simply a matter of financial economy that the circles Tom first used, were made of tubular nylon webbing. Surprisingly enough, there is a photograph of that first historic T.E.A.M.'s conference where the webbing loop circles first appeared.

From a balcony position, Karl Rohnke looked down upon Tom's activities with amusement. When he asked Tom what he called those pieces of webbing, tied with a knot, Tom mentioned that he didn't call them anything, just 'webbing circles.' Karl, knowing that Tom's given Native American (Ho Chunk) name was 'Raccoon' suggested that, "they ought to be called Raccoon Circles."

Tom went on to continue his use of Raccoon Circles with the audiences he encountered. At the AEE international conference in Vermont, Raccoon Circles again made an appearance. By now, Tom's idea had begun to circle the globe. Awards, accolades and appreciation for the circle flooded in. But during this time, Tom remained humbled by such expressions, and quietly continued his life's work of inviting people to 'connect up.'

Kirk Weisler of Utah heard of Tom's work, and borrowed a copy of his Raccoon Circle publication, and added some fancy new graphics to it, including the cover artwork for this book. Kirk's friend, Mike Cottom, enjoyed the idea of the Raccoon Circle so much that he published a series of activities that his students participated in as part of a social skill building event. Mike called the circles 'Freedom Circles' so that students could use them to be free from isolation, poor decisions and life choices, and a host of other social ills. He incorporated American Indian medicine wheels, Ute and Navajo drum circles, Australian Aboriginal circle art, the Taoist circle of balance and other circular symbols and rituals.

In 1997 Karl Rohnke and Tom Smith journeyed to South Africa to lead some workshops for the Play for Peace organization. After Tom had a special encountered with a baboon, Karl and Tom came to understand that in South Africa, the web loops should be called 'Baboon Circles!'

I included some Raccoon Circle activities in the book, *Teamwork & Teamplay.* I also took webbing loops to Japan as part of my work in Nagano, and shared them with camp counselors there. When the first year students of Hobart and William Smith Colleges finished their orientation session in 1998, all 700 of them were holding onto two giant circles (in school colors) made from the individual Raccoon Circles they had been using all day to build community. They 'connected up' in a very spectacular way.

More recently, I began to create some files on the Teamwork & Teamplay website so that others could experience and share the Raccoon Circle. I was on my computer finishing the first Raccoon Circle document the morning of September 11, 2001. As I listened to the radio that day (the camp I was at had no TV sets), I knew that what I was writing was exactly what was needed. Later that week, and in the months since, I've used Raccoon Circles and invited folks to 'connect up,' and always with great success. The creation of 'connection' and community is not specific to our region either. In the months following the posting of the Raccoon Circle documents to the internet, more than 15,000 downloads occurred, in 30 different countries. Horizons magazine, published by the Institute for Outdoor Learning in the UK, published an eight page pull out feature of Raccoon Circle activities in their Spring 2003 edition. And after a request from Asia to translate the document into the local language, an email attachment was received with some Raccoon Circle activities translated into Taiwanese.

Tom Heck included the concept and spirit of the Raccoon Circle in his work on "Group Loop" activities. Chris Cavert has also added his voice to the choir with his "Lines and Loops" activities with a focus on building community. Michelle Cummings, Mike Anderson, Don Rogers, Tim Borton, Clare Marie Hannon and Alf Grigg have all done their part too. It is because of talented, creative and sharing folks like these that this publication is no longer just the few pages of Tom's first conference handout, but the treasure chest of information that you now hold in your hands.

For the first printing of *The Book on Raccoon Circles,* Tom and I worked with Sam Sikes and the folks at Learning Unlimited, in Tulsa, Oklahoma. 4400 books were originally printed and quickly sold to camp directors, challenge course facilitators, teachers and trainers. During this time, Tom and I continued to expand the activities we facilitated with Raccoon Circles, and friends and colleagues continued to share their latest innovations, activities and stories involving the Raccoon Circle. Tom continued to write articles related to working with groups and the power of using the Raccoon Circle. I continued to innovate and gather activities that could be performed with Raccoon Circles. Soon it became obvious that we had the critical mass necessary to either print a new publication, or substantially expand the first edition.

Given the choice, we decided to print this new edition, and place the very best teambuilding activities, stories, theory and practice within it. So now it is time for you to add your own part to the rich and growing history of the Raccoon Circle. Like never before, this book is our open invitation to you to 'connect up' and join the growing family circle.

Jim Cain

"When the Raccoon looks out from inside, the circle of connectedness of all things in the universe becomes quite evident."

Tom Smith

Section I

Raccoon Circle Activities

You'll find hundreds of activities in this section arranged in the following four categories:

Icebreakers, Introductions and Get-Acquainted Activities

Team Challenges, Active Learning and Adventure-Based Activities and Games

Exploring the Stages of Group Development with Raccoon Circle Activities

Processing, Debriefing, Reviewing, Reflection and Closing Activities

Some of these activities have been shared by other facilitators, trainers, teachers and friends, and their contributions are appreciated. You'll also find activities in some of the theoretical papers and stories found in other sections of this book.

In addition to those activities shown here, you'll find additional activities on the Teamwork & Teamplay website and in the new Ropework and Ropeplay Collection of Team Activities, also from Teamwork & Teamplay.

With each new printing of the *Book of Raccoon Circles,* you'll find the newest activities, stories, articles and ideas in the final chapter of this book, entitled Recent Additions. There is also space in this chapter for you to add your own Raccoon Circle ideas.

Icebreakers, Introductions and Get-Acquainted Activities Using Raccoon Circles

In this section of introductory Raccoon Circle activities, a collection of icebreakers, get acquainted activities, networking and community building ideas are presented. These activities are perfect for the start of a program, summer camp, college orientation session, corporate meeting, new employee orientation session, conference opening event, first day of school, family picnic or social gathering. The intimate size of a Raccoon Circle brings people closer together, which is a nice way to begin a program!

Number	Activity Name	Type of Activity
1	Believe It or Knot	Conversation, Discovery, and Disclosure
2	The Meter	Finding Your Place in the Group
3	The Bus	Finding Commonalities
3a	Which Side of the Road are You On?	Making Choices with Others
4	First Impressions	Getting Acquainted at a Deeper Level
5	A Long Line of Knots	Self Introduction and Disclosure
6	The Four Corners of the Earth	Finding Commonalities
7	The Time Capsule (Fortune Cookies)	Planting Memories for the Future
8	See Ya!	Conversation, Familiarity and Inclusion
9	A Circle of Four (In the Loop)	Conversation and Forming Groups
10	Taking Charge	An Invitation to Leadership
11	Geography	Identity, Knowledge of Others
12	Come Join Us!	Unity, Cooperation
13	Core Groups	Group Identity
14	The Shape of Things to Come	Group Identity
15	Commonalities	Finding Commonalities
16	Sign In Please	Group Identity, Unity, Belonging to the Group
17	Where Ya From? Where Ya Been?	Telling Your Personal Story
18	The Goal Line	Setting Goals and Milestones
19	Tie Us All Together	Individual and Group Identity, Unity
20	Painting the Future	Commitment, Creativity, Exploration, Unity
21	Outside In	An Invitation to Participate, Commitment
22	Jump!	Active Decision Making Just For Fun
23	The Story of Your Name	Conversation, Storytelling
24	My Life Line	Introduction, History Giving
25	My Life As A Circle	Introduction, History Giving

1. Believe It or Knot

Thanks to Mike Anderson for this excellent activity that is a simple variation of Two Truths and a Lie. With the entire group holding a Raccoon Circle (either seated or standing), the knot is used as a pointer to identify the person talking. Begin by passing the knot to the right around the group. Someone says "stop!" and when the knot stops the person nearest to the knot is invited to disclose some interesting fact about themselves, such as, "I have a twin sister!" It is now the discussion and responsibility of the rest of the participants to decide whether they believe that this information is true or false. Group members can ask the person speaking a total of three questions. After some discussion, the group gives their opinion of the validity or falseness of the disclosure, and then the person providing the comment tells the truth.

After a person has revealed the true nature of their comments (true or false), they say "left" or "right" and then "stop!" and a new person has the opportunity to disclose something to the group.

The level of disclosure to the group is often a measure of the closeness, unity and respect within the group. For example, a disclosure such as, "I have two dogs as pets," is a lower level of disclosure than "I repeated the seventh grade in school." Depending on the group setting, and the purpose of this activity for your group, different levels of information or disclosure are appropriate. As the group becomes more unified, this activity can bring out greater disclosure between members of the group, family members, members of a team, etc.

This is also the type of activity that can be performed again and again with the same group. Probably because there is an endless supply of comments that can be made. Enjoy!

2. The Meter

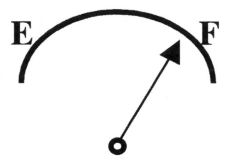

With one Raccoon Circle, make an arch shape like the one shown here. This is your fuel gauge, or any type of meter that you wish. Ask participants to stand outside the meter, at the position that best relates to them. For example, the amount of energy that you have right now could be just like a gas tank gauge (empty, half a tank, full). This activity acquaints participants with each other, indicates preferences and lets us find out about the other members of our group. This activity can also be used by a facilitator to gain useful knowledge about the participants in each group. For example, the number of hours spent working out each week-or-the number of books read in the past six months-or-the number of frequent flyer miles accumulated in the past year-or-the number of brothers and sisters in your family-or-the number of hours of sleep you had last night.

Thanks to Tom Heck and Roger Greenaway for sharing examples of this simple but powerful activity.

3. The Bus

One of the best ways to unify a group is to identify the commonalities shared by the members of that group. Chris Cavert says (with regard to some of his students) that, "the more they know about each other, the less likely they are to hurt each other." This means that the more students have in common with each other, the more they recognize their commonalities rather than their differences, the more likely they are to include each other, the more likely they are to be nice to each other, to protect each other, and the less likely they are to steal, injure or be mean to each other. To this end, our goal is to find out some of those commonalities that we have with each other. The more unusual and unique the commonality, the better. This activity from Tom Heck is perfect for finding some of those more unique commonalities.

The Bus requires two Raccoon Circle Lines, stretched parallel to each other. Have participants "get on the bus" by standing between these two lines. At the first stop, have folks get off the bus, according to what is there for them on the left or right sides of the bus. First stop, chocolate ice cream on the left side, vanilla ice cream on the right. Now look around you, you have something in common with those folks on your same side of the bus. Now back on the bus, next stop:

Cats		Dogs
Loud		Quiet
Running	the	Walking
Save Money	BUS	Spend Money
Bus Driver		Bus Rider
Sky Diving		Deep Sea Diving
Problem Solver		Problem Maker
Hamburgers or Hot-dogs		Chicken or Salad

The object here is to find interests, activities and events that folks have in common. Be careful to choose topics appropriately for the audience that you are serving. This activity can be used with even large audiences, provided that the folks on the bus can hear the bus driver!

3a. Which Side of the Road Are You On?

For corporate audiences, The Bus can be transformed into a corporate vehicle for making decisions. Which Side of the Road Are You On? invites participants to actively make decisions. The decisions to be made have been chosen specifically to meet the needs of the group. In this case, the more job related, the better.

Which Side of the Road are You On? requires a central gathering place and two boundary lines made from unknotted Raccoon Circles. Participants begin 'standing in the middle of the road.' As the first company truck comes barreling down the road, loaded with information for your project, team members must decide which side of the road they should be on. Some of the following decisions are fairly easy and the information content doesn't have severe consequences. Others may make or break the entire project. After choosing sides, give project team members a minute to see who is on the same side of the road with them, and to discuss why they chose this particular side.

PC		Macintosh
Loud		Quiet
Running	the	Walking
Fixed Salary	middle	Salary + Incentives
Fixed Schedule	of the	Flex Time
Group Decisions	road	Individual Contributor
Problem Solver		Problem Maker
Zero Travel Days per Year		Travel Far and Wide

The object here is to team members to make a fixed choice. Either / Or. Obviously team members can be on 'different sides of the road,' on some issues. These issues bear additional discussion. Be careful to choose topics appropriately for the audience that you are serving. This activity can be used with even large project teams, provided the folks in the middle of the road can hear when the truck is coming!

This activity also provides the opportunity for a bit of group discussion throughout the process. For example, were some folks left 'in the middle of the road' and only saved by another person pulling them to safety as the information truck came speeding towards them? Or did they become 'corporate roadkill?' Did some folks change their minds during a particular decision, and then change sides? Is there always a right and wrong side of the road, or more appropriately, two possible choices, both of which have merit? Does the entire project team need to be on the same side of a particular issue for the team to move forward successfully? How would you go about trying to get everyone on the team on the same side of the road for a key project decision?

In the book *Good to Great*, Jim Collins talks about 'getting the right people on the bus and the wrong people off the bus,' and then 'getting the right people into the right seats.' This activity can be used to explore where some members of your project team choose to be on specific team or management issues, but you might want to wait for the 'storming' stage of group formation to bring this up, rather than here in the safe environment of the 'forming' stage. Thanks to Tom Heck for sharing this activity.

Good to Great—Why Some Companies Make the Leap . . . and Others Don't, 2001, Jim Collins, Harper Collins, New York, NY USA ISBN 0-06-662099-6

4. First Impressions

Raccoon Circles bring people together in a variety of ways and this activity illustrates that point. First Impressions brings participants into a closer physical proximity to each, discovers commonalities between participants, allows participants to become acquainted at a deeper level, and provides the opportunity for participants to discuss how their instinctive guesses about others, especially those that they do not know very well, may or may not be accurate.

Begin by forming groups of three participants, seated on the floor within a Raccoon Circle. Why use a Raccoon Circle here? Because it brings participants into close proximity with each other.

Provide a copy of the following page and a pencil for each participant. The instructions for this activity are printed at the top of the following page. Just pass out copies of this page, and go.

First Impressions

Form a group of three with two other participants that you do not know very well, and have a seat. With the other members of your group, you are to guess the following traits and characteristics about your partners. This is not a conversation, just make your best guess about each of the following traits, for both of your partners and write your answers in the outer left and right margins of this page. When you and each of your partners are finished guessing the following eight traits, begin sharing your guesses with each other, writing in the true information when given. Keep track of how accurate your guesses have been.

Person on Your Left Side	The		Person on Your Right Side		
Your Guess	The True Story		Traits	The True Story	Your Guess
		Where were they raised? (Farm, city, suburbs, other country...)			
		Their favorite food?			
		What type of music do they listen to? (Rock, country, hiphop, folk, classical, etc.)			
		What would they consider a fun time on a Saturday night?			
		What would their ideal job be?			
		What would their ideal car be?			
		What hobbies do they have?			
		What do you have in common with these individuals?			

5. A Long Line of Knots

Begin by giving each person in the group an untied Raccoon Circle and asking them to tie as many knots in the webbing as they like. Next, the facilitator tells the group that the number of knots in each Raccoon Circle is equal to the number of pieces of information that each participant is invited to share. The facilitator then begins the sharing process, demonstrating both the number of pieces of information and also the type of information that is appropriate. For example, with seven knots in a Raccoon Circle, a participant could share where they are from, where they went to school or college, their occupation, the number of members in their family, their favorite pet, their favorite food or restaurant and how they spent their summer vacation.

As a variation to this activity, you can ask each participant to knot their Raccoon Circle and then trade their circle with others in the group, before telling them how the knots relate to the number of pieces of information they have a chance to share.

If time is short, you can also have a group tie knots in just one Raccoon Circle, and pass the knotted webbing around the group, which each person sharing something about themselves until all the knots have been removed.

6. The Four Corners of the Earth

There are two possibilities of Raccoon Circle arrangements for this activity. For large groups, as shown on the left, you can divide the floor space available with four unknotted Raccoon Circle webbing strips. For smaller groups, as shown on the right, you can create four Raccoon Circles separated by a small distance.

With the facilitator standing in the middle of the group, identify four distinct classifications, and ask participants to join the quadrant that they most identify with.

For example, if the classification is music, the four quadrants might be: rock, rap, country and classical. After participants join a group, ask the group to discuss why they chose this particular group. The facilitator can also ask the group to act out a song, or sing a line from a piece of music in their category. Additional classifications are shown below, along with suggestions for discussion and additional activities for each category. Thanks to Clare Marie Hannon for sharing this technique.

Sports (Basketball, Soccer, Volleyball, Gymnastics) Create a cheer for your sport.

Vacation Locations (Beach, Mountains, Big City, Ocean Cruise) Discuss what you'll bring along.

Food (Hamburgers, Chicken Salad, Tuna, Veggie Burger) or something a bit more unusual such as:

(Cous Cous, Sushi, Broccoli, Mountain Oysters) Discuss what goes along with each food.

Vehicles (pickup truck, sports car, mini van, limo) Discuss color, features and optional equipment.

Travel (North, East, South, West) Discuss what you would bring with you to these locations.

News (Newspaper, Radio, Television, Internet) Discuss recent events and issues.

7. The Time Capsule (Fortune Cookies)

One of the unique features of a Raccoon Circle made from tubular climbing webbing is that before the ends have been sealed, you can insert various items inside a Raccoon Circle, such as strips of paper with quotations, messages, comments, goals, beliefs and other personal wisdom, marbles, tiny metal bells, the type of fortune strips found in fortune cookies, a single long piece of ribbon with information written on it or any other safe and interesting object that fits. Use waterproof ink for any writings placed inside the Raccoon Circle.

If you have a group that will be meeting for an extended period of time, consider having participants place some personal wisdom or a goal within the Raccoon Circle before sealing the ends. You now have a very personal time capsule for the group. At the completion of your time together, open the end of the Raccoon Circle, remove the contents, and share them with the group.

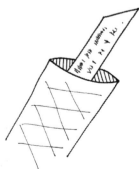

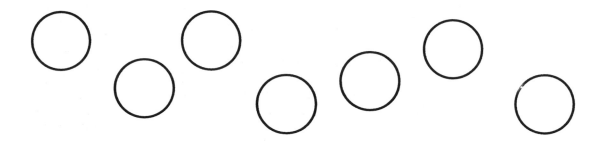

8. See Ya!

Thanks to Chris Cavert for this excellent get acquainted activity. And be sure to read the articles on connectedness and what's next in adventure-based learning in Section II of this book. These articles discuss the importance of creating unity and connection, and this activity is one of the best we know to reinforce this kind of community building.

Begin by spreading several Raccoon Circles around on the floor or ground (one for every four or five participants). The object here is to discuss some things that participants have in common and then to decide which person has the most (or least, or best, etc.) of these. For example, in each group of four or five participants, find out who has the most brothers and sisters. The facilitator should allow the group a few seconds for discussion, and then says loudly, "one, two three," and the rest of the group replies, "See Ya!" as they bid farewell to the person with the most brothers and sisters. This person then moves on to another circle.

Each circle has now lost a member of their group. Encourage them to attract a new member by yelling, "over here, over here, over here!" Once a new member joins a group, a new question is given to the group, such as, "who is wearing the most jewelry?" After a few minutes, "one, two, three. . . . See Ya!"

For additional time or to learn a bit more about the other folks in the group, the facilitator can have two questions for each encounter. The first should be a topic for discussion that the whole group can discuss and for which they are likely to have something in common. For example, what is the best deserts you have ever had? Then the second question can be a brief one, followed by "one, two, three. . . . See Ya!"

Here are some additional questions for "See Ya!"

Who has the most books in their personal library collection?

Who has watched the most videos or movies this month?

Who has traveled the farthest distance from here?

Who has the most living family members?

Who traveled the farthest distance today?

Who has the most unusual middle name?

Who is wearing the cleanest shoes?

Who is the tallest?

9. A Circle of Four (In the Loop)

Thanks to Rick French for sharing this interesting get acquainted, debriefing and/or closure activity. In a similar fashion to See Ya, spread a few Raccoon Circles around on the ground. Enough for the entire group, with about four people in each circle.

As a goal setting activity, ask the participants to share with the others in their circle the goals they have for themselves and for the group that day. After a few minutes, ask each circle to say to the whole group some of these goals. A facilitator should be available to write these goals down on a large piece of paper (you'll see why in a minute). Ask the participants to all go to a new circle, with four new people in it. Continue goal setting, or ask another goal oriented question, and record the responses.

For debriefing, this Circle of Four activity, which can easily be done with a different number of participants, allows simultaneous discussions, so that the whole group can have a chance to express their feelings. This may allow a debriefing process that takes a bit less time when a large group is involved, while not diminishing the need to share and discuss. After each topic of discussion, participants can be encouraged to join another new circle, with four new people.

As a closing activity, let the group reflect back on the original goals mentioned above, and evaluate whether those goals were met during the event. This format is also a nice way to say good-bye to a variety of folks, in small groups, using some discussion and a close proximity of participants to each other.

_____

_____

_____

_____

_____

_____

10. Taking Charge

This event is both a warm-up activity, and an opportunity for leadership within the group. Place a Raccoon Circle at the center of a group. As facilitator, begin the activity by standing in the center, and informing the group that the person standing in this position has the power to lead the group. The music "I've Got the Power" can be used, or some other motivational, athletic, or inspirational music. Begin with some stretching motions, such as arm circles, neck rolls, or leg stretches. Then progressively begin using more complicated motions, such as jumping jacks, where typically someone else will find the motivation to say "I've Got the Power," or "I'm Taking Charge!" and lead the group into another stretching movement. Continue for the length of the song, or until most group members have had a chance to lead the group.

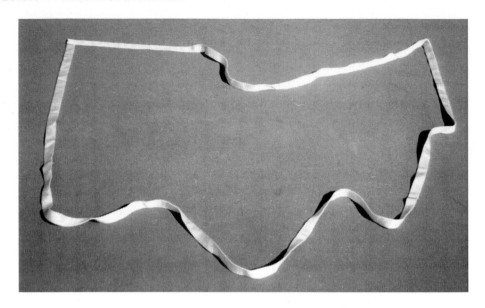

11. Geography

Use one or more Raccoon Circles to create the shape of the local town, county, state, nation, country or area, and then ask participants to stand relative to this shape, according to where they: were born, live now, work, would like to retire, would like to visit, would like to vacation, would like to go to college. For example, for a first year college orientation, with the Raccoon Circles in the shape of the country, have participants stand relative to where they were born. While most participants will likely be within the boundaries, some students may come from outside the borders of the country. This activity can open the door to discuss local customs, traditions and unique cultural differences and similarities between the members of the group. Use the space below to create your own categories and shapes.

_____

_____

_____

_____

_____

_____

_____

_____

12. Come Join Us!

Come Join Us is a large circle activity that brings participants in close proximity to each other, identifies some of the commonalities within the members of the group, and helps to unify the group. Begin with about a dozen knotted Raccoon Circle loops placed around the perimeter of the group, and ask the group to join one of the circles. At any time during this activity, the facilitator can take away any Raccoon Circles that are unoccupied. The activity begins as the facilitator provides various categories for moving to a new circle, such as, "anyone with tennis shoes on, move two circles clockwise." Additional categories are then presented to the group, and empty Raccoon Circles removed. Ultimately quite a few participants will be crowded into several of the circles, again bringing participants into close proximity and identifying commonalities with other group members.

In order to be within a circle, a participant must not be contacting any point outside the Raccoon Circle. The distance moved during each category is for the facilitator to decide. Additional categories, and room for adding your own are available below.

Has a picture of a family member in their pocket, wallet or purse.

Skipped breakfast this morning.

Owns a cat, dog, horse, or goldfish.

Has a unique email address or personal website.

Would go bungie jumping if the chance were available.

Has ridden a camel or a unicycle.

Has played a sport.

13. Core Groups

At the beginning of a conference, especially one with many participants, forming "core groups" will enable new and unfamiliar groups of people to find each other, especially if the next time they gather, everyone has changed clothes and forgotten who was in their group the day before.

Core groups are formed around a Raccoon Circle, typically with about 8-12 people. The job of the group is to create some large hand motion and a sound, so that when the facilitator yells, "CORE GROUPS!" everyone begins making their group's sound and hand motion to find the other members of their group. Amazingly enough, it is often easy to remember the core group signal and sound, and yet forget who was in the group.

For extremely large conferences, have each core group demonstrate their signal and sound prior to a break. This is to insure that no two groups have the same signal.

14. The Shape of Things to Come

This activity is especially useful for large gatherings of people.

At some point, it might become necessary to have individual groups take a break, or gather resources, or leave their Raccoon Circle, and then return. In order to have each group return to their "own" Raccoon Circle, let them create a symbol, shape or word using the webbing. Then when they return, they'll be sure to come back to the right location.

15. Commonalities

Begin with partners for this activity. This conversational activity has the goal of identifying unique and sometimes unusual events, activities and life experiences that we have in common with other members of our group. The two partners need to identify three unique items that they have in common. Encourage participants to dig deep for these items. For example, they may discover that they both like dogs, but under closer examination, they may also discover that they like the same breed of dog. Additionally, they may discover that they both enjoy reading, but by digging a bit deeper, they may discover that they have read the same book in the past 6 months or perhaps enjoy the same author.

After identifying three attributes that they have in common, these two partners raise their hands, and find another group of two ready to form a group of four. Now the challenge is to identify 2 items that they have in common. Again, look deep, and no fair using any of the attributes already identified.

Finally, after this group of four finds out what they have in common, they raise their hands and join another group of four, for a total of eight, now standing inside one of the Raccoon Circles spread around on the floor. The goal for these eight is to find ONE event, interest or activity that they have in common. Have each of these groups of eight tell the other groups what they have in common. Again, the more unique and unusual, the better (or at least the more interesting!)

16. Sign In Please

Tom Smith once mentioned that he often encouraged members of the group to write words of encouragement or significant phrases directly on the Raccoon Circle using a permanent marker or waterproof pen. He also encouraged them to sign their name. At the completion of their time together, he would cut the group's Raccoon Circle into small pieces, so that everyone in the group could take away some portion of the whole "spirit" of the group. Names and words will be most visible when you choose a dark color marker and a light color Raccoon Circle webbing (yellow, light gray, orange, etc.)

17. Where Ya From? Where Ya Been?

During one Raccoon Circle activity session, a member of our group mentioned that they were born in Scotland. Another member of the group was unfamiliar with this location, and so we formed the geographical outline of Scotland with our Raccoon Circle. Next, several group members told stories about their travels to Scotland, which led to the creation of the following activity.

Where Ya From? Where Ya Been? has become a great way for each person in the group to share 'their story.' One at a time, they create the outline of where they are from, or similarly someplace they have recently visited, and then tell stories about these important places in their lives.

At a recent leadership conference, one keynote speaker mentioned that there are three things that we each uniquely own: our name, our reputation and our story. Where Ya From? Where Ya Been? gives each member of the group a chance to tell their story.

18. The Goal Line

Place a single untied Raccoon Circle in front of each participant, with three overhand knots along the length. Where the participants are standing now is the beginning of the day. The first knot represents some event in the first half of the session (morning), the middle knot is the midday break (lunch), the third knot is an event in the second half of the session (afternoon), and the other end of the Raccoon Circle is the conclusion of the program.

Now invite participants to verbally plan their experience, using this knotted Raccoon Circle model. Where do they want to be at the end of the experience? Where do they want to be by the mid-point (lunchtime). What "events" need to happen to achieve their personal (or group) goals for the day?

Thanks to Roger Greenaway of the UK for sharing this simple idea for individual goal setting. You can find this and other creative ideas for introductory activities, processing, debriefing and reviewing at: www.reviewing.co.uk. You can also find other reviewing activities from Roger Greenaway in final chapter of this section.

19. Tie Us All Together

Thanks to Alf Grigg of Willowdale, Ontario, Canada for showing us how old ties (those men's ties that have gone seriously out of fashion) can be used to create community, and build teams. In fact, Alf has a brief book on the subject. You'll find his contact information in the resources section of this book.

In this case ties, or 3 foot (1 meter) long segments of Raccoon Circle webbing can be used to create groups. Begin with a collection of ties or short Raccoon Circle webbing segments. First group together with other participants holding the same color of webbing. Other suitable configurations include one participant of each color webbing. Next, the group can use a water knot to tie their webbing segments together (a simple overhand knot works for the ties). Participants can also sign their names, or write a quotation, inspirational phrase or goal on their segment of webbing.

This simple activity also works at the completion of a program, where all participants tie themselves together with the rest of the group.

20. Painting the Future

For those times when you introduce the Raccoon Circle at one time in the program, and then not need it again for a few hours, you can have the group decorate 'their' Raccoon Circle by finger painting it. This process is familiar to children, and interesting with adults. Begin with some light colored webbing, and choose some brightly colored finger paints (reds, orange, neon colors, sparkles, etc.). Encourage everyone in the group to 'add their mark' to the project. For some folks, this might mean simply a fingerprint, carefully placed. For others, they may jump in with both hands, in finger paint up to their elbows, and smear, doodle and decorate the entire length of the webbing. One of our favorite is simply to have each person place both hands in different color finger paints, and then 'connect up.' This will leave their hand prints on the webbing. The next time you 'connect up,' don't be surprised if folks tend to go to the location marked by their hand prints.

Allow adequate time for the paint to dry before using the Raccoon Circle.

21. Outside In

At the beginning of many teambuilding or adventure-based learning activities, many facilitators will incorporate some form of group commitment ceremony, or at the minimum some form of informed consent regarding the activities about to be performed. Choosing the level of challenge, contracting between facilitator and participant, and presenting an environment where participants can choose to join in, without being coerced, are a valuable part of the team's commitment, and the group process of enabling a collection of individuals to successfully work and play together.

To this end, Outside In is a brief activity where individuals make the conscious choice to "join" the group for the upcoming session. Place one or more Raccoon Circles on the ground, and have the group gather around the outside. After explaining the "contract" between a challenge course facilitator and the members of the group (i.e. choosing how to be a part of the challenge for the day, being fully present, listening to the other members of the group, keeping physical and emotional safety a priority, etc.), ask the group members to indicate their level of commitment to the event by approaching the Raccoon Circles, and entering a circle as far as their level of commitment. For some folks, this will mean standing at the center of one of the Raccoon Circles (fully committed). For others, this will mean standing within one of the Raccoon Circles (committed), or perhaps only one foot within a Raccoon Circle (partially committed). Finally, if the level of participation is a true option for your program, it is possible that some participants may initially be comfortable only when standing outside the commitment circle. While this may not be the desired or optimal situation, it does give you valuable feedback as a facilitator as to the whether your initial introduction to your program enables participants to make a commitment, or leave them slightly less than committed, given the information and contracting that you have presented.

Typically, most facilitators would like to have everyone within the commitment circle at the beginning of the program. There are however, at least two options available for the case where some participants are not yet there. First, you can thank the group for their input, and offer to revisit the team commitment later in the program (perhaps at the midpoint, and again at the end). Or you can discuss the level of commitment within the team, and request that in order to "begin" the event, you'll need to have everyone in contact with the Raccoon "commitment" Circle (either inside or outside). This, you can explain, is not a full commitment for anything that happens, but rather a commitment to begin the process of working as a team. If this second option is chosen, revisit the team commitment as the program continues (after a few more activities).

The purpose of Outside In is to provide a visual check of the commitment level of the entire group, before beginning a teambuilding or adventure-based learning program. The location of participants will give the facilitator an indication of the commitment level of the group, to each other, and to the program itself.

As an alternate approach to Outside In, the facilitator can place three Raccoon Circles (for example, a red, green and blue Raccoon Circle) on the ground, and ask participants to join one of the three circles. The red Raccoon "commitment" Circle signifies that the participants are ready to fully commit to the group and the team events that are about to begin. The green Raccoon "commitment" Circle signifies that the participants are willing to try, but will need some assistance and support from the group to be successful. The blue Raccoon "commitment" Circle signifies that the participants are basically willing to begin the process, but may have questions, concerns or comments that they would like to make before continuing.

A final variation of this alternate approach to Outside In, is to use three different sizes of Raccoon Circles to form a "target" on the ground. Where the inner circle represents the highest level of commitment (bullseye), the middle circle represents a medium level of commitment, and the outer circle represents the minimum level of commitment necessary to begin the program, presentation or process.

22. Jump!

Here is an introductory activity that provides plenty of action, and you can present it two different ways. For groups of twenty to thirty people, locate three tied Raccoon Circles on the ground. Designate one circle 'yes,' another circle 'no' and the third circle 'maybe.'

Next, ask the group a series of questions and ask them to quickly move to the location that best represents their choice of answer. Once each group has gathered, ask them to discuss their choice of answer and why they personally chose it.

For smaller groups, you can place a single tied Raccoon Circle on the ground and designate the inside 'yes,' the outside 'no' and the straddling the webbing (i.e. standing on both sides) as 'maybe.'

As a variation, consider a version of Jump! played like 'Simon Says.' In this case, the goal is to see who can follow directions correctly and quickly.

23. The Story of Your Name

Of the three things that each one of us uniquely owns (our name, our reputation and our 'story'), this activity incorporates two. Begin by placing a knotted Raccoon Circle on the floor and ask the members of the group to sit around the outside perimeter. In this case, the Raccoon Circle provides the perfect spacing so that everyone can hear the other members of the group.

Next invite each member of the group, to tell the story of how they were given their name. Were they named after a significant family member, friend of the family or famous personality? Why is this name important? Do they have a nickname? Do their parents or grandparents have other names they call them? What do they like most about their name? And finally, what would they like to be called? If they answer, "I'd like to be called Ted," everyone then says together, "Hi Ted!"

24. My Life Line

Here is a geometric way of measuring the length of a lifetime. Begin by laying an unknotted Raccoon Circle in a straight line on the floor. Group members walk along the line, from beginning to end, telling the story of their life, from birth to the present day. Invite them to mention key milestones (graduation from school, first job, birth of a child, etc.).

For a circular and musical version of this activity, see My Life As A Circle.

25. My Life As A Circle

Over the years, I've discovered that some of the best icebreakers and get-acquainted activities employ not only an element of conversation, but also some kinesthetic movement as well. Here is one of our newest get-acquainted activities, and one that is sure to keep the whole group in motion.

Begin by placing a knotted Raccoon Circle on the floor. One person stands on the outside of the Raccoon Circle, near the knot, and begins to tell the story of their life's journey. "I was born in Omaha, Nebraska on June 22nd. . . ." As the story continues, both the storyteller, and *all* the other members of the group rotate around the outside of the Raccoon Circle. This movement keeps everyone in the group active and engaged.

At some point along the journey, the storyteller will reach the present day. At this point, ask them to look forward to the things that are still waiting for them in their life. Goals they have. Opportunities they are hoping to find. Plans they are making. When they reach the knot, the next person in the group can tell the story of their life's circle.

As a musical accompaniment, try playing Harry Chapin's classic song, "All My Life's a Circle," from his *Greatest Hits Live* album.

Team Challenges, Active Learning and Adventure-Based Activities and Games

Number	Activity Name	Teachable Moment
1	2 B or KNOT 2 B	Group Problem Solving, Consensus Building
2	Not Knots	Group Problem Solving, Consensus Building
3	The Missing Link	Group Problem Solving, Consensus Building
4	Spaghetti	Group Problem Solving, Consensus Building
5	Moving Toward Extinction	Group Problem Solving, Adapting to Change
6	Inside Out	Group Problem Solving, Planning, Ethics
7	Tree of Knots	Group Problem Solving, Teamwork
8	Over the Fence	Group Problem Solving, Teamwork
9	A Window of Opportunity	Group Problem Solving, Teamwork
10	The Clock	Group Problem Solving, Working Together
11	Traffic Circle	Group Problem Solving
12	Turnstile (Community Jump Rope)	Kinesthetic Group Problem Solving
13	Target Specifications	Group Problem Solving, Communication
14	The Giant Texas Lizard Egg	Group Problem Solving
15	Knot Right Now	Group Problem Solving, Teamwork
15a	A Knot Between Us	Group Problem Solving, Teamwork
15b	Tie the Knot	Group Problem Solving, Teamwork
16	Far, Far Away	Individual and Group Problem Solving
17	Knot on the Phone	Customer Service, Communication
18	The Keys to Communication	Communication
19	Interference	Communication, Listening Skills
20	Minefield	Communication, Trust and Problem Solving
21	Yurt Circle (Team Balance)	Balance, Unity and Cooperation
22	The Wave	Cooperation and Groupwork
22a	Shaking Things Up	Breakdown and Group Limitations
23	Pass the Loop	Physical Warm Up and Problem Solving
24	Props	Creativity and Improvisation
24a	This is Not a Raccoon Circle	Creativity and Improvisation
25	Photo Finish	Timing, Cooperation, Unity, Problem Solving
26	Line Up	Communication and Problem Solving
27	Human Knot	Creativity and Problem Solving
28	Octopus	Creativity and Problem Solving
28a	Knot Our Problem	Creativity and Problem Solving
29	Surfing the Web	Multiple Creativity and Problem Solving
30	Cut the Cake	Group Puzzle, Creative Problem Solving
31	Zoom!	Creativity and Problem Solving
32	Raccoon Circle Bracelets (Handcuffs)	Creativity and Problem Solving

1. 2 B or KNOT 2 B

As a consensus building activity, 2B or KNOT 2B is terrific. For this activity, you will need five different colors of Raccoon Circles for the first level, and five identical colors for level two. With a water knot, tie four of the Raccoon Circles into separate loops, then tie the fifth Raccoon Circle through the other four. Now place all five of these circles on the ground, in such a way that it is not immediately obvious which one of the five Raccoon Circles is holding the other four together. The challenge of this activity is for the group to come to a consensus on which Raccoon Circle they believe is holding the other four together.

We recommend a strategy known as 'pairing and sharing' for this activity. Within the group, form subgroups of two or three participants. Partners are asked to analyze the collection of Raccoon Circles, without touching them, and to first come to agreement with their partner. Then, once consensus is reached for these two or three participants, other subgroups can be approached, until all groups are in agreement.

After completing this first level of 2B or KNOT 2B (with five different colors of webbing), invite the group to try level two, where all five Raccoon Circles are the same color. Again, the object is for the entire group to come to a consensus as to which one of the five Raccoon Circles is holding the other four together, without touching any of them during the decision process.

For some groups, the facilitator may need to explain what consensus means, and perhaps why it is important in a group to utilize consensus. Next, the facilitator may choose to assist the group

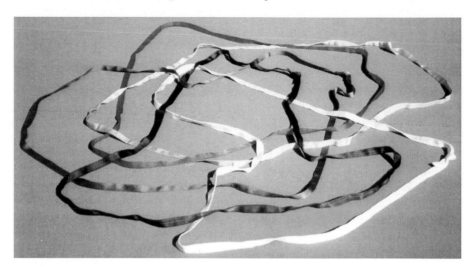

in coming to consensus, by asking how to check for consensus (visual sign, voting, verbal confirmation, etc.), partnering with others in the group, and asking pairs to vote on their choice, etc. Finally, after the group has achieved consensus, the facilitator may choose to investigate the various styles of problem solving used to successfully complete this task.

2. Not Knots

A natural consensus building activity to follow 2B or KNOT 2B is Not Knots. In this activity, which can be accomplished with a single piece of unknotted webbing, a "doodle" is constructed and the group is given the choice of whether this doodle will create a KNOT or NOT A KNOT, when the ends of the webbing are pulled.

The object here is to provide the group with some tools to use when they cannot easily form a consensus. Typically upon analysis, about half of the group thinks the doodle will form a knot and the other half a straight line. If this is the case, ask participants to partner with another person that has a different viewpoint (i.e. one partner from the KNOT side, and one partner from the NOT A KNOT side). By learning how to listen to a person with a different viewpoint, group members learn how to cooperate. They can also learn that they really believe in their convictions. Allow time for discussion and then ask participants to choose sides, with the KNOT decision folks on one side of the knot doodle, and the NOT A KNOT folks on the other side.

At this point, it is likely that there will still not be a complete consensus within the group. Prior to slowly pulling the ends of the knot doodle, let the members of the group know that you will pull the knot doodle slowly, and that they can change sides at any time during the unraveling of the knot doodle (this illustrates the ability to make an initial decision, but still be flexible as more information becomes available).

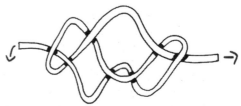

3. The Missing Link

The field of Topology, which is the study of surfaces, placement and position, or as some folks refer to it, "a lesson in bendable geometry," is a unique way of looking at objects that can alter their shapes, orientation and geometry. For this reason, classic knot theory actually has a real life usefulness here. The Missing Link can be presented with three levels of difficulty. For Level 1, you will need two Raccoon Circles of different colors, tied with water knots. These two circles can either be linked together (like links of chain), or entirely separated. Place both loops on the ground, in such a manner as it is difficult to tell whether the two loops are in face linked, or unlinked. Now assign the group the task of achieving a consensus as to whether the two loops are linked or unlinked, without touching the Raccoon Circles. For Level 2, use three Raccoon Circles, of different colors. In this case either all three circles are linked, or all three are unlinked. For Level 3, the highest difficulty level, use three Raccoon Circles of the same color. For this case, all circles may be unlinked, or two may be linked, or all three may be linked.

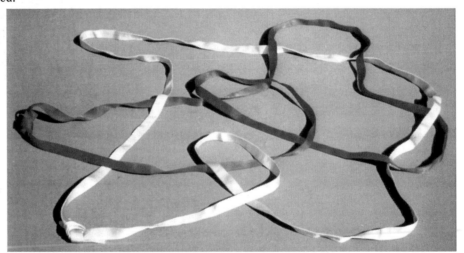

4. Spaghetti

Here is a consensus building activity that comes in three different levels. The challenge here is for the group to decide how many different untied or tied Raccoon Circles are present. Level One requires several different colors of webbing. This level of "challenge" is actually quite simple, this first level should be used to discuss how the group will know when they've reached consensus, how to solve a problem as a group, and how to listen to each member of the group. Level Two

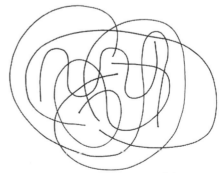

involves making a giant plate of spaghetti with several (about 5 to 8) Raccoon Circles of the same color. At this level, the various pieces of Raccoon Circle should still have each of their untied ends easily visible. Level Three Spaghetti should have a different number of Raccoon Circles of the same color, but this time the ends are hidden, knotted together, or otherwise more challenging to discover. The goal in each case is for the group to reach a correct consensus as to the true number of individual Raccoon Circles present in the spaghetti pile.

For each of these four consensus building and group problem solving activities, one technique that is particularly effective is to introduce the concept of 'pairing and sharing.' This method encouraged participants to first talk with one other member of the group, and form a consensus before approaching the rest of the group. This technique generally tends to increase the speed of the group in achieving consensus, and makes sure that all the voices have had a chance to be heard.

5. Moving Toward Extinction

This activity will require about a dozen Raccoon Circles, and works best for groups of 12 to 50 participants. The task is for each member of the group to find a "safe place" to be when a "shark" is spotted in the surrounding water.

Begin by spreading about a dozen Raccoon Circles around the floor. These represent islands of safety. Ask members of the group to swim, boat, jet ski or snorkel about in the surrounding waters, but be cautious. If the lifeguard (facilitator) should yell "shark" members of the group can become safe by placing their feet within the perimeter of the Raccoon Circle islands (illustrate this by having a facilitator standing within an island for visual clarity). After the first sighting of a shark, the facilitator removes one of the islands and the participants again venture into the murky waters.

Participants often keep trying the same methods of becoming safe, even though the amount of resources (islands) diminishing. Any person is safe when their FEET are within the perimeter of an island (hence it is possible to sit on the ground, with your feet within the Raccoon Circle, and be completely safe!)

If you begin this activity with the Raccoon Circle webbing untied, but simply placed in a circle-you will leave open the possibility for the participants to combine islands. This will produce a collaboration rather than a competition effect as the resources continue to diminish.

As the number of islands went from one to zero, one creative group placed their feet together in a circle. Satisfying their interpretation of the rules in a very collaborative way.

6. Inside Out

This is one of my favorite activities. It is not only a great initial problem solving activity, but one that allows a group to discuss some very serious corporate cultural issues, namely, ethical behavior in the workplace.

Begin with a Raccoon Circle on the floor. Have a group of five to seven participants step inside the circle. The task is now for this group to go from the inside of the circle to the outside, by going underneath the Raccoon Circle, without anyone in the group using their hands, arms or shoulders.

It is important to stress the group problem solving process in this activity. In order for other members of the group to assist in the completion of the task, they need to know the plan, and what their part is in the solution. To this end, encourage the group to "plan their work" and then "work their plan." This means that prior to ANY action, the group will need to plan their approach to solving this problem, and making sure that everyone in the group knows their part of the plan.

It is typical that participants do in fact use their arms, shoulders and hands during this activity. Not that they grasp the webbing with their hands, but often they will use hands to balance each other, to hold up their leg while completing the task, or to crawl on their hands and knees.

After completing the task, debriefing questions include asking the group if they had a plan, and did they change the plan during the completion of the activity, and if so, why? As a second part to this activity, you can also ask the group to go Outside In, again without using their hands, arms or shoulders . . . and see if they "plan their work" before "working their plan." Debriefing questions for this second version can include, "how long did you spend planning Inside Out compared to Outside In?" Why was there a difference? And finally, to introduce ethical issues, "how do you feel about following the guidelines of not using your arms, shoulders or hands? For example, did anyone crawl on the ground, using their knees and hands?"

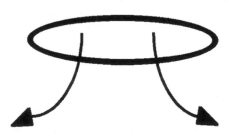

The ethical dilemma of group members using their arms, shoulders or hands, when specifically instructed not to, does not need to turn into a discussion about rules, but more about interpretation of such rules. For example, rather than asking why group members did not follow the rules, ask how the rules could have been better presented so that no interpretation errors would occur.

7. Tree of Knots

For this simple problem solving activity, you will need two Raccoon Circles, tied with a water knot behind a tree, pole or column. The task is for the group to tie a square knot at the front side of the tree, pole or column with the two sides of Raccoon Circle webbing shown. Participants are told that where they touch with their right hand must stay connected at that point throughout the activity, but they may use their left hand for guidance, and this hand may slide along the webbing or leave the webbing at any time if they wish. There is an opportunity to teach some basic knot tying skills prior to this activity, or you can provide a visual example of what a square knot looks like.

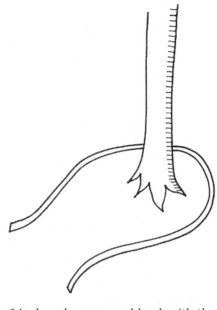

8. Over the Fence

Here is a simpler and improved version of the classic adventure activity, the Electric Fence. Begin with two participants holding a Raccoon Circle, approximately 6 inches above ground level, with the long parallel sides of the Raccoon Circle about 12 inches apart. Place half of the group on each side of the Raccoon Circle "fence." The first two persons (one from each side, one at a time) to cross the "fence" have the fence at 6 inches from the ground. The next two persons have the height increased to 12 inches, and so on. The maximum height, even for large groups is 4 feet (about 1.3 meters).

This version of the Electric Fence places spotters on both sides of the fence at all times. It also provides a changing level of challenge to the group. Even at the lowest levels, it is required that all participants crossing the fence, be in contact with at least 2 other participants at ALL times during the crossing. Allowing two participants to hold the Raccoon Circle also leaves an opportunity for a participant that may wish not to be passed over the fence. Or, if the holders do wish to pass over, they can rotate into and out of the holding positions with other team members during the event.

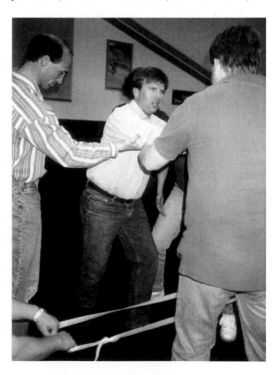

9. A Window of Opportunity

In a similar fashion to the Over the Fence initiative, a vertical "window" is created between two holders with a Raccoon Circle. The task is now for each half of the group to transfer through or over the window of opportunity, without touching the Raccoon Circle. Begin with a window approximately 12 inches (30.5 cm) tall and 6 feet (183 cm) wide. The size and location of the window, and the amount of challenge, can change with each participant. For example, for each person passing over the "window," the distance between the bottom of the window and the floor increases by 6 inches (15 cm).

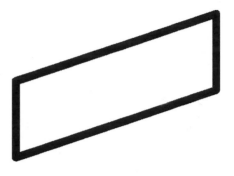

For each person passing through the "window," the width of the window decreases by 12 inches (30.5 cm) and the height increases by 12 inches (30.5 cm). This modification of the size of the opening is a great way of helping groups work with changing environments and working conditions. Planning also becomes important, so that each participant passes through the Window of Opportunity at the optimal time for their abilities, talents and size.

10. The Clock

There are two versions of this activity. The first involves a single Raccoon Circle, tied with a water knot. One person, holding the Raccoon Circle at the knot, becomes the hour hand of the clock, standing at the 12 noon position. The facilitator stands behind this person, to provide a visual location of 12 noon. Next, the facilitator calls out various times, and the entire group attempts to move with the Raccoon Circle so that the hour hand (the person with the knot) moves to the correct position. For example: 3 o'clock, 7 o'clock, 6 o'clock (clocks cannot move backward, only forwards), 10 o'clock, 10:45, 2:25 pm, 11pm, 12 o'clock and all's well.

A second version of this activity involves using a participant as the hour hand, supported by a Raccoon Circle made into a cradle (See the Trust Lift in Section 35 of this chapter, and Tom Smith's original explanation of this activity in the history chapter of this publication).

11. Traffic Circle

Traffic Circle uses a single Raccoon Circle, that has been overlapped to form an even smaller circle 2.5 feet (0.8 meters) in diameter, or roughly the size of a small hoola hoop. This circle is placed at the center of the group. The surprisingly simple task, is for each member of the group, and their opposite partner, to exchange places, by passing through the middle of the circle, each touching one body part (foot, hand, nose . . .) in the Raccoon Circle, at the same time, and then continuing on to stand in the place where their partner was. All this must be accomplished without touching their partner, or the Raccoon Circle, and both participants must be in contact with the ground inside the Raccoon Circle at the same time. The group should set a goal to perform this task as quickly as possible.

For a higher level of challenge consider adding a set mouse trap in the center of the traffic circle, or perhaps to exchange the traffic circle entirely with a circle of set mouse traps located in the center of the group. An interesting risk factor here. Be extra careful!

12. Turnstile (Community Jump Rope)

Turnstile, or the Community Jump Rope, is an activity where two participants (or facilitators) turn the Raccoon Circle webbing like a jump rope, and the participants must travel underneath the webbing in order until the entire group has successfully passed through. Variations include the direction that participants must travel (i.e. whether they must jump over the webbing during the passage, or merely travel under it as it swings around). Another variation is that once the first participant passes through the swinging webbing, every other participant in the group must pass through on successive swings (that is, there can be no revolution of the Raccoon Circle without at least one participant passing through). A final variation is that participants must pass through, single, then as a paired couple, then by fours, and finally the whole group within one revolution of the Raccoon Circle.

Raccoon Circles also make an interesting and colorful prop for Double Dutch jump roping (shown in the photograph).

Jumping rope is note necessarily an easy task for everyone. If you would like to scale the level of challenge for this activity, Tom Heck suggests the following stages:

Stage 1   Participants can go at any time, in any number. A good way to start.
Stage 2   Participants must go one at a time, for every turn of the webbing.

Stage 3   Participants must go through in pairs for every turn of the webbing.
Stage 4   Participants must go through in groups of four, for every turn of the webbing.
Stage 5   Participants must go though in pairs for every turn of the webbing. The first two
           pairs are carrying soft objects that must be passed to the last two pairs before they
           pass through.

Shawn Moriarty of YMCA Camp Lakewood suggests the 1,2,3,12 riddle to go along with this activity. The challenge for the group is to figure out how 1,2,3,12 is relevant to the turning of the webbing. The answer is to follow the following pattern: 1 person, 2 people, 3 people, for 12 revolutions of the webbing.

Debriefing topics for this activity include: Which stage was the most difficult, and why? Can the whole team be successful if even one member lacks the skill to move forward at the right time? Did the team allow time for practice?

13. Target Specifications

Here is an interesting activity in communication and team coordination. The challenge is for a single blindfolded participant (the "pitcher") to communicate with the remaining members of the team, and successfully throw an object through the Raccoon Circle they are holding (the "strike zone").

Begin by tying three Raccoon Circles that form different sized circles (i.e. you can either use different length webbing strips, or tie the Raccoon Circles with different length "tails"). You'll end up with a small circle 3 ft (1 meter) in diameter, a medium circle 4 feet (1.3 meters in diameter) and a large circle 5 feet (1.6 meters) in diameter.

Next, you'll need another tied Raccoon Circle to use as the "pitcher's mound." Any diameter will do. Place the pitcher inside the pitcher's mound, blindfolded, holding a series of soft throwable objects (foam balls, beach balls, a foam noodle, a flexible flying disc, stuffed animals, etc.).

Finally, use several untied Raccoon Circles to form an outer circle, approximately 15-20 feet (5-7 meters) away from the pitcher's mound (see the graphic below). The "strike zone" team now holds the largest Raccoon Circle, and chooses a position to stand outside the outer circle. They must now communicate to the pitcher their location, and instruct them how far to throw the object.

For a successful pitch (in the "strike zone"), the object needs to pass through the Raccoon Circle, without touching either the team or the Raccoon Circle, and without the team moving their feet.

For variation, the strike zone team can move to different positions, or even farther outside the outer circle, or team members and the pitcher can trade places, or different size Raccoon Circles can be used, or different objects can be tossed, and (my personal favorite), using a rubber chicken, the pitcher can toss the "chicken ball" for which the strike zone team can only make chicken sounds to communicate their location. You can find this activity with even more variations in the book Teamwork & Teamplay, Chapter 4, page 179.

14. The Giant Texas Lizard Egg

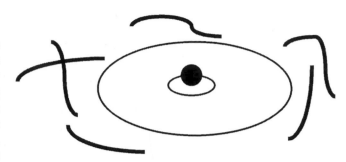

Thanks to Sam Sikes for this interesting activity, from his book "Feeding the Zircon Gorilla." For this unique problem solving activity, you'll need about a dozen untied Raccoon Circles, one regular size (tied) Raccoon Circle, four pieces of webbing tied into one large Raccoon Circle, and a Bowling Ball. An illustration of this setup is provided here.

Place the Giant Texas Lizard Egg (the bowling ball) in the center of the single knotted Raccoon Circle. The challenge is now for the participants to find a technique for removing the Giant Texas Lizard Egg from the central Raccoon Circle (the "nest"), completely outside the larger circle, without allowing the bowling ball to touch the ground in the space between the inner Raccoon Circle and the larger outer circle. The participants have a dozen untied Raccoon Circles as resources to accomplish this tasks.

Encourage the participants to be careful when transporting the Giant Texas Lizard Egg. As a consequence to dropping the Giant Texas Lizard Egg or allowing the bowling ball to touch the ground in the space between the central and outside circles, the participants can be asked to give up one untied Raccoon Circle resource for any "errors." For inclusion, the facilitator can also require that all participants must be touching (or connected or somehow attached) to the Raccoon Circles when lifting the Giant Texas Lizard Egg from the inner circle.

Typical solutions for this initiative include creating some sort of basket, ring or hoop with one Raccoon Circle, and attaching the remaining webbing as "handles" and/or forming a type of channel or bridge to transport the ball, and using another Raccoon Circle or two to roll the ball along this path.

15. Knot Right Now

This activity is a modification of the Group Loop activity from Tom Heck called Knot Now. Instruct the entire group (up to 8 participants per Raccoon Circle) to grab hold of the straight webbing. Wherever they hold with their right hand must stay there, however the left hand can move, slide, or let go as necessary to make movement easy. The task is for the group to tie a single overhand knot in the Raccoon Circle. A simple method is for one of the end person to use both hands to tie a knot at the end! Other similar activities include: A Knot Between Us and Tie the Knot.

If you like this activity, be sure to read the story entitled "Raccoon Circles in Texas—In Three Parts, in Section III of this book."

15a. A Knot Between Us

Using a section of Raccoon Circle between each person, tie and overhand knot loosely at the midpoint of each. Now instruct each member of the group to pick up one end of a Raccoon Circle with each hand, forming a horseshoe pattern (not a complete circle) with the entire group. The task is now for the group to untie each of the knots in the various pieces of Raccoon Circle webbing without letting go of the Raccoon Circles in their hands.

15b. Tie the Knot

Tie the Knot is just the opposite of A Knot Between Us. The object of this activity is for a U-shaped group of participants, each holding a Raccoon Circle between them, to tie an overhand knot at the middle of each Raccoon Circles, without letting go of the webbing they are holding in each hand. This activity is a more complicated version of Knot Right Now, and requires all group members to be active.

16. Far, Far Away

How far can you throw a raccoon circle?

Begin by giving each participant a single untied Raccoon Circle. The goal of this activity is to see how far a Raccoon Circle can be thrown. Participants are encouraged to individually create their own Raccoon Circle flying apparatus (such as tying the Raccoon Circle into a ball, or rolling the Raccoon Circle up into a tight circle or hoop, or simply swinging the Raccoon Circle and letting go). Measure the distance each Raccoon Circle travels from a throwing line, and add all measurements together for a group score. Would it be possible for 12 participants to throw their Raccoon Circles the combined length of a football or soccer field?

Next, allow participants to work together, combining their Raccoon Circles to form more complicated shapes and flying objects, and throw again. Typically, the distances traveled by combining Raccoon Circles is greater than when they are thrown individually. An interesting method of showing that the results of a team are often greater than the sum of its parts.

Don't be surprised if throwing isn't the only way to send your Raccoon Circle a long distance away. If you wind the Raccoon Circle into a tight spiral, and then tape the end, you can roll this little Raccoon disk (like a bowling ball) quite a distance, especially on a smooth surface. And, if you throw your Raccoon Circle into an envelope and throw this envelope into a mailbox, you can send your Raccoon Circle a very long distance (maybe to your best friend). Email us and let us know your distance records! jimcain@teamworkandteamplay.com tsraccoon@earthlink.net

17. Knot on the Phone

This activity uses the entire team at one time. Begin by asking for a volunteer to attend your "hardware training session" offsite. Take this person aside, and teach them how to tie a water knot. Verify that they can tie it by themselves, and then hand them the hardware center How-To Booklet on tying water knots in webbing. Ask this person to answer the phone at the help desk. Next provide various pieces of 1" tubular webbing to the rest of the team, who all have their backs to the help desk. Then "call in" to the help desk, and mention that you recently purchased a bunch of rope from their store, and have a whole bunch of youth group dads hanging around, trying to tie knots. Then have the help desk employee explain how to tie a water knot. Measure the group's success rate, by counting the number of correctly tied water knots at the end of the process.

Debriefing topics include: "What made this activity so hard, when it was so easy to learn this knot in the training class?" "Are there other training topics that are easy in class, and hard in real life—name a few?" "Which of the explanations used by the help desk operator was most helpful?" "What was the most unusual, interesting or critical question that you have ever answered?"

HOW-TO BOOKLET
The Water Knot

With tubular webbing it is often necessary to form a circle or loop. While a variety of knots can be used, the water knot is one of the strongest and best. The water knot is so named because river rafting guides use such a knot with flat webbing, so that even when wet, the knot can easily be removed. Shown below are two techniques for correctly tying a water knot.

The Teacher—Student Method

Start by tying a simple (but loose) overhand knot (Fig. 1) in one end of the Raccoon Circle webbing, with a short tail (less than 2 inches is fine). Because of the flat webbing, this overhand knot will remain very flat. This first knot is the "teacher" or "mentor" knot.

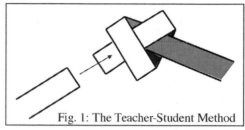

Fig. 1: The Teacher-Student Method

Next travel the length of the webbing, unwinding and untwisting the webbing as you go, and hold the opposite end of the webbing. This end is the "student" end of the webbing. The student does everything the teacher does, they just happen to do it backwards. This means that (first), the student looks directly at the teacher (each tail end of the webbing nearly touches). Next, the student "doubles" the teacher by following the same path as the teacher backwards. This involves following the webbing, and finally tucking the student end of the webbing into the teacher knot, leaving about a 1 or 2 inch long tail.

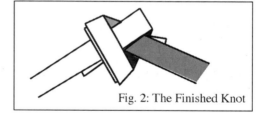

Fig. 2: The Finished Knot

Now simply pull the opposite sides of the knot to secure it. The finished knot is shown here (Fig. 2).

Created by Jim Cain of Teamwork & Teamplay www.teamworkandteamplay.com

18. The Keys to Communication

Thanks to Alf Grigg for sharing the original idea for this activity. This expanded version includes beginner, intermediate and advanced challenge levels, and was first used with a corporate team theme of 'unlocking the future.'

Round One. Begin by dividing the group into two teams. Two untied Raccoon Circle boundaries are established (see illustration), two blindfolds (for the active participants from each group), and a small object (in this case, keys and padlocks) is needed. The activity begins in the first round by placing the blindfolded participants at each end of the playing area. Next the facilitator shows each team what the objects are. Their teammates then attempt to verbally (only!) tell them how to find the keys and the lock, and then open the lock. Chaos is pretty likely in the

HOW-TO BOOKLET
The Water Knot

The Race Car Approach

Begin by tying the an overhand knot so that the black stitching typically found running down the middle of most colorful webbing can be easily seen (Fig. 3). This dashed line looks a bit like the line found running down the middle of many roads. The other end of the webbing is now seen as an automobile (or race car for faster knot makers) which simply needs to drive down the middle of the road to complete this knot.

Now simply pull the opposite sides of the knot to secure it. The finished knot is shown here (Fig. 4).

Created by Jim Cain of Teamwork & Teamplay
www.teamworkandteamplay.com

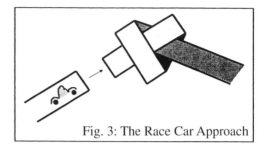
Fig. 3: The Race Car Approach

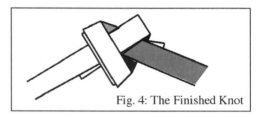
Fig. 4: The Finished Knot

keys dropped
somewhere in
this space

first round. Facilitators should stand between the two blindfolded participants to make sure that they don't bump into each other.

In round two, allow each team 3 minutes to form a strategy between their teammates and appoint a new blindfolded participant. Then repeat the activity, moving the keys and locks to a new, mostly central location.

Round three also allows for 3 minutes of strategy, but uses a combination lock instead of keys and padlocks. The combination numbers are given to the sighted team members of each group. Only the blindfolded participant can touch the object, but the combination locks can be brought to their teammates for additional visual assistance during the unlocking procedure.

A higher level variation of this activity would be to have the blindfolded participant find several objects, and then assemble them together, while still blindfolded. Possibilities include: plastic building blocks, a child's puzzle, Mr. Potato Head, tennis shoes and laces or several nuts and bolts.

Debriefing topics include: "what communication techniques were valuable during this activity?" "What were some of the unsuccessful techniques for communicating with the blindfolded teammate?" What additional, but untried suggestions were made during the strategy sessions?" "Were different techniques used for the combination locks, compared to the key and padlocks?"

19. Interference

Here is a communication challenge from Tom Heck that is loud and playful, but still carries a significant message about how we communicate. Using two untied Raccoon Circles as boundary lines, create the activity space shown below. In this space, the "senders" occupy the left "endzone," the "interferers" occupy the middle space, and the "receiver" occupies the right "endzone." The challenge is now for the senders to verbally or visually communicate a message to the receivers, while the interferers in the center region attempt to disrupt the message, distract the senders or receivers, and basically add a great deal of chaos, noise and confusion to the activity.

Senders   Interferers   Receivers

After 30 seconds, the receivers are asked for the message. Then the three distinct groups switch to new roles (interferers become receivers, receivers become senders, senders become interferers) and a new message is delivered. Typical messages might include:

In order to listen, you must first become quiet.
Somewhere in the forest, there is a tree, that longs to be a ship.
The best things in life, are not "THINGS."

20. Minefield

This activity requires a variety of Raccoon Circles, both tied and untied, and shorter web segments if available. Begin by placing four untied Raccoon Circles around the perimeter of the space. Next, place several Raccoon Circles within the space as forms of obstacles. The challenge of this activity is for a sighted partner to verbally guide a blindfolded (or eyes closed) partner through the space, without touching any of the obstacles littering the path. The activity can begin with the blindfolded partner looking at the minefield in advance, or perhaps never seeing the minefield until after crossing it. The Raccoon Circle in the center of the minefield can be a "vision restored" location, where the blindfolded partner can temporarily remove their blindfold to gain some perspective of their progress, and of the task ahead. Some of the web segments can be "treasure" that needs to be gathered along the way, or that can be used in barter in case a future object is "touched." This space can be used for only one set of partners, or multiple partners at the same time. The facilitator can change the obstacles when the sighted and blindfolded partners change places.

21. Yurt Circle (Team Balance)

This activity works for both small groups (using a single Raccoon Circle) and for incredibly large groups (by using multiple water knots to tie several Raccoon Circles together). Begin with the group holding the Raccoon Circle with both hands about a shoulder's width apart, and standing with their feet also about a shoulder's width apart. Next have the group pull the Raccoon Circle gently to form a complete circle, with some tension in the Raccoon Circle. Now by leaning outward from the circle (a small amount), the group should be able to balance the circle, and keep each other safely leaning outward. This is the first level of unity, calmness and balance, and is often referred to as a yurt circle.

For level two, ask participants to keep holding the Raccoon Circle, but to bend their knees and slowly and gently sit down, and then come back to a full standing but still leaning position. This motion is appropriate for those individuals whose knees allow for this type of motion, without giving out! We have discovered that the number of knee "clicks" increases with the age of the group (light group laughter here!). The next level, level three, is for the group to close their eyes and balance down and up twice while the facilitator gives the commands. Finally, the level four challenge is for the group to balance down and up twice, but this time with their eyes closed, and with no one talking. Calm music playing in the background is nice for this activity. It can also be performed as a closing ceremony using some of the music suggested in the last activity of this publication. This activity is also at the ideal height for both standing and seated participants to work together since both can hold the Raccoon Circle at about 3 feet (1 meter) off the ground.

For a variation, the group can make one sound when lowering and another sound on the way back up. This makes for interesting sound effects with large groups.

22. The Wave

As a simple stretching exercise, have the members of the groups each hold the Raccoon Circle with their hands and feet approximately shoulders width apart (for balance) in a standing position. Next, have one person bend their knees and sit, while keeping their hands in contact with the Raccoon Circle. As they begin to sit, the next person to their right (counterclockwise) should begin to sit. As this sitting "wave" is passed around the circle, each person to the right continues to sit.

When the sitting wave has reached the opposite side from the original person (person #1), person #1 stands, and the standing portion of the wave passes to the right. When the entire group is in motion, a balanced wave exists, and participants can stretch and move in a well connected flow.

Essentially, folks need to watch the person on their left, and when that person begins to sit or stand, they should be ready to do the same. Do not rush this activity. The objective is to stretch slowly and keep some balance within the group.

22a. Shaking Things Up

While the use of Raccoon Circles has usually been to create balance and harmony, a friend recently shared this lively variation. It is similar to a standing game of wrestling, where one opponent tries to off-balance the other while staying in balance. Have the group 'connect up' and give instructions that each person is to shake and move the web loop and try to off-balance others in the group, without moving their own feet.

Those with more upper body strength or greater range of movement may be independently successful. Others will consciously or unconsciously begin to cooperate with neighbors and succeed in off-balancing those across the circle. This exercise gets people in touch with their competitive and aggressive tendencies, but the activity is designed to create conflict between that tendency and their supportive, care taking tendency.

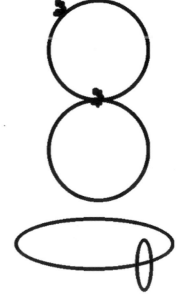

After the group has had some time with the instruction to try and off-balance others, introduce a second instruction. While working to off-balance others, everyone is to take responsibility for helping the person to their right stay in balance. Participants will often respond quite differently. Some will tend to put more energy on the goal of off-balancing others, while others will put great effort into the goal of helping their neighbor stay in balance. When most of the people emphasize the care taking goal, the whole group will shake and tug the web loop—but no one will be off-balanced.

23. Pass the Loop

This event is both a typical warm-up activity, and an opportunity for cooperation. With the entire group holding hands in a circle, ask them to pass a Raccoon Circle (like a hula hoop) completely around the circle, without letting go of the person next to them. Encourage participants that this is not a race (unless that is what you would like). After completing one full circle, the facilitator can add a second Raccoon Circle, perhaps a bit smaller, and ask that one Raccoon Circle move to the left (clockwise), while the second Raccoon Circle moves to the right (counterclockwise).

For an even higher level of cooperation, take a 15 foot long Raccoon Circle, and tie a knot at the midpoint so that there is now a figure-8 Raccoon Circle. Now the object is to pass the lower end of the 8 to the left, while the upper circle of the 8 goes to the right. This version will allow more participants to be involved at the same time.

Another version of pass the loop (or circle the circle) incorporates two Raccoon Circles. One large Raccoon Circle (made from 1 or more pieces of webbing), which the entire group holds on to. And a second Raccoon Circle linked to this first one. Participants must now pass the smaller Raccoon Circle around the group, while holding on to only the larger Raccoon Circle.

24. Props

This activity requires about three items to be placed in the center of a group of participants. Typical items include: an untied Raccoon Circle, an oven mitt or large glove, a tennis ball, a yardstick or broom handle. This activity is often used in Theater Sports or improvisation classes as a technique for improvising with common objects, as they become extraordinary props. For example, the oven mitt, stick and ball could become an imaginary baseball game, with a catcher's mitt, baseball and bat (which would need three people to create). The Raccoon Circle could become the throwing circle for a track and field discus thrower as they unwind a record-breaking throw. Use your imagination and have fun.

You can find additional games like this by searching the phrase 'theatre sports' at your local library or on the world wide web. One of the classic books on this subject was written by Viola Spolin.

24a. This is Not a Raccoon Circle, it is a . . .

I originally witnessed Mike Spiller leading this activity, using foam "noodles" at the Texas TERA conference in 2001. In this variation, participants stand in a large circle passing around both tied and untied Raccoon Circles. The goal is for participants to invent a new idea for the Raccoon Circle and tell their neighbor about this. For example (while showing my neighbor an untied Raccoon Circle), "this is not a Raccoon Circle, it is my belt, and I just lost 200 pounds!" Or perhaps, "this is not a Raccoon Circle, it is a climbing rope for my ascent of the shortest peak in Kansas!" The neighbor can then either pass on this same idea, or make up a new one.

25. Photo Finish

Thanks to Sam Sikes for this seemingly simple but yet complex activity. You can find this and other activities in his book, Executive Marbles.

Photo Finish (or the Finish Line) uses a long rope as a straight line. The task is for the members of a group to ALL cross the line at exactly the same time. You can additionally "stress" the group by minimizing the available space that they have to plan prior to crossing the finish line.

Tell the group that they have 15 minutes to make 5 attempts to cross the finish line at exactly the same time. This is a great opportunity to use a digital camera for instant feedback. Every time someone breaks the plane of the finish line, the facilitator yells, "Click!" even for the occasionally careless mistake.

This activity involves planning, communication, timing and occasionally the ability to deal with frustration.

26. Line Up

This activity is a modification of one shared by Chris Cavert. Begin by creating a straight line with an untied Raccoon Circle. Next, shuffle a deck of ordinary playing cards, and give one to each participant, face down. When told to begin, time the group with a stopwatch, as they attempt to line up in order, based on their playing card. This self directed work team will need to define what "in order" means, and how to complete the task. When completed, check for accuracy, and report the time to the group. Collect the cards, shuffle only these cards, and pass them out again to the group, and ask them to establish a new time goal to again complete the task (with the same cards, but potentially with a new person holding a different card).

The team does need to establish such order as where the Ace of Hearts goes. Does it go first, because a 1 is low, or first because Ace begins with an "A", or last because an Ace is the highest card in the deck?

Other cards that can be created from blank index cards include: animals (placed in order by name, size, weight), nouns (alphabetical order, size of the object they represent), vehicles (number of wheels, number of passengers they can carry, relative cost), or any other objects or items that have some natural order, rank or sequence (like hours of the day: 6:15am, 0700, 12 noon, 13:20, 5 pm and 2300 hours).

27. Human Knot

One technique for increasing the number of participants that are able to join hands for the human knot initiative, is to extend their reach via several pieces of webbing. This is a great idea if you just happen to have some short lengths of webbing around. It is also a useful method of extending the comfort level of participants by creating a bit more space between participants, and allowing a bit more freedom of movement with assuming difficult positions, or twisting the wrist of the person you are connected to. And finally, having multiple pieces of webbing with different colors assists the problem solving method by making it a bit more obvious which piece of webbing needs to be moved to help the group be successful.

It is possible to gather about 8-12 participants conveniently together to perform the Human Knot initiative when holding hands. Typically this will bring most groups snugly together, and shoulder to shoulder. By using short webbing strips between participants, the available space between participants is greatly increased.

It is also possible to set up this initiative in advance, before the participants arrive. This can be accomplished by placing one untied Raccoon Circle per participant on the ground, and then having participants approach this collection of Raccoon Circles and take hold of two separate pieces of webbing. Now the challenge of unwinding this mess and forming a circle can begin.

With or without webbing, the basic challenge of Human Knot is to have participants hold hands with a person across the circle from them (or be connected to them via the webbing), and then attempt to unwind and untangle the mess of crossed arms and tangled webbing.

For more complex, but similar initiatives, see 'The Octopus' and 'It's KNOT Our Problem' in Section 28.

28. Octopus

I first encountered this activity from some friends in Europe. It is an interesting problem solving activity, and an even more interesting method for finding a partner. The Octopus is a great big tangled mess of Raccoon Circles, and here is how you create this activity.

First, take two untied Raccoon Circle pieces of webbing, and (using one water knot) tie these two pieces together to form one long piece of webbing. These two pieces of webbing can be different colors, or the same color, but a collection of each style is best (i.e. some long pieces of webbing with different colors of webbing, some with the same color). You'll need one piece of webbing for each person in the group (or one long "joined" piece of webbing for every two participants).

Next, take several of these long (joined) pieces of webbing, and tangle, twist, spiral, loop and basically make spaghetti of them (be sure not to tie difficult to remove knots in this webbing mess), leaving about 1 foot (30 cm) of each piece of webbing visible outside the pile, so that participants have a place to grasp the webbing at the start of the activity.

The challenge is now for participants to work together to unravel this mess, without letting go of the piece of webbing that they are holding, and ultimately discover which person in the group is holding the other end of their piece of webbing. Untangling the rope is allowed, however untying the water knot joining the two pieces of webbing together is not allowed.

28a. KNOT Our Problem

Here is a fun variation of Octopus that members of the group can create for each other. Thanks to Mike Spiller for sharing this one.

Begin by giving each participant an untied Raccoon Circle. Next, have the entire group form smaller groups of 8-10 people. Each smaller group now has the task of twisting, winding, knotting and basically scrambling their Raccoon Circles together. Begin this task by having each person hold one end of their untied Raccoon Circle, and passing the other end to another person in their group. Now twist, tangle, stretch, twirl and basically make a huge knotted mess of these Raccoon Circles. Then place this "mess" on the floor, with the ends of each Raccoon Circle clearly visible. Each group now moves to a new location, and attempts to unwind the mess by first grasping the ends of a Raccoon Circles, and without letting go of the end, attempting to untangle them.

If you choose to time the groups as they attempt to complete this task, here is a hint . . . some knotted masses come apart more quickly if rather than grasping the ends of the webbing, participants start with only one end, and tug and untangle as they go. Some webbing strips might even slide completely out of the mess with a single tug!

29. Surfing the Web

Chris Cavert created this simple problem solving activity that challenges a group to find multiple techniques for solving the same problem. The challenge is as follows: using only an initially tied Raccoon Circle, teams of 4 participants are asked to cross over an area, marked by lines, boundaries, or untied Raccoon Circles, crossing as many times as possible in 5 minutes, using as many different styles to cross the area as they can. Any portion of a team member (hand, foot, etc.) may touch the ground within the area, provided that it is also touching a portion of the Raccoon Circle at the same time. For example, if the first group of four decides to use the Raccoon Circle loop like the tread of a bulldozer, they can step on the floor, provided that they always have the Raccoon Circle below at least a portion of their foot.

While many teams of 4 work independently on this task, some will see the opportunity to collaborate with neighboring teams, and work together. The typical spacing between the borders of the area is approximately 15-20 feet (5-6 meters). This is an interesting activity to see just how many possible solutions the entire group can find to the challenge. It also encourages groups to find more than one solution to a problem, to actively brainstorm without excessive evaluation, and to consider different points of view.

Planning Space   Surfing the Web Space   Planning Space

30. Cut the Cake

Thanks to Mike Anderson for sharing this creative problem solving puzzle that uses three untied Raccoon Circles. With sidewalk chalk or masking tape, create a large circle on the ground, about 10 feet (3 meters) in diameter. This is the outline of a giant cake. As shown in the illustration, place seven gumdrops on the cake (you can use gym spots, paper plates or any available round objects for these). The team uses the three untied Raccoon Circles to illustrate where three straight cuts can be made to the cake, creating seven pieces that each contain one gumdrop. The illustration to the right gives one possible solution.

As an alternative, make another large circle, and ask the team to use the three Raccoon Circles to create three lines that effectively cut the cake into eight pieces. No gumdrops this time. One solution requires one of the lines to be curved, rather than straight, as shown here.

If you enjoy puzzles as teambuilding challenges, we invite you to read: Teambuilding Puzzles, by Jim Cain, Mike Anderson, Chris Cavert and Tom Heck, 2005, FunDoing Publications (www.fundoing.com). Visit the Teamwork & Teamplay website for more information about this book.

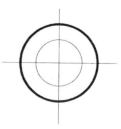

31. Zoom!

Here are three variations of the group activity "warp speed" where participants attempt to "move" something around the circle, as quickly as possible. Begin with a full-sized Raccoon Circle, with all participants holding onto the webbing. In this first version, the knot in the webbing becomes the object that is passed around the circle, and timed with a stopwatch. The challenge or goal is to see if the group can creatively problem solve a technique for reducing the amount of time required for the knot to traverse one revolution of the circle. Version 2 involves one person in the group clapping, and passing this clap around the circle, with each participant clapping once. Version 3 eliminates the tactile passing of the knot or clap, and replaces them with each person saying Zoom, for a verbal version of this activity.

32. Raccoon Circle Bracelets

Using a full length Raccoon Circle, or even a half-length segment of webbing, create a pair of webbing bracelets or 'handcuffs' by tying loops in the end of each piece of webbing. Now place your hands into these handcuffs, and with a partner, connect your handcuffs to theirs, as shown here. The challenge is become disconnected from your partner, without removing your hands from the handcuffs or untying the knots. The classic solution to this challenge involves passing your handcuffs through the wrist loop of your partner. For corporate groups, tell them that the challenge is for 'everyone' to successfully become detached from their partner, then process to see how many completed the task, and still tried to help others. For some audiences, calling these 'handcuffs' may not be appropriate. For times like these, 'rope bracelets' or 'buddy bands' seems to work fine.

One additional variation is to bond everyone in the group together in one large circle (so that your arms are initially interlocked with those standing next to you). This is possible, and an interesting way of making the solution for the whole group, rather than only those that happen to figure it out.

33. United We Stand

Here is a creative problem solving challenge that requires some skill, balance, and having group members choose their own level of commitment and challenge to the group. The goal is for the entire group to stand side-by-side, and cross the line in unison, taking a single step together (not a jump!), without anyone touching the line in the process. Two participants (or facilitators) are chosen to hold the ends of the untied Raccoon Circle at a challenging slope, ranging from ground level, to about 3 feet (1 meter) high.

34. All Aboard

Place a single Raccoon Circle on the floor, and like the wooden platforms typically used for this activity, ask all participants in a group to stand inside the circle, long enough to sing one verse of "Row, row, row your boat." Begin with a full length Raccoon Circle (15 feet—4.6 meters), tied with a water knot as the first size circle. Then have several other lengths of webbing ready to additionally challenge the group (or you can simply tie other full length Raccoon Circles with water knots that have progressively longer tails—which will create smaller and smaller circles).

A great 'leadership' model of this activity was created by Clare Marie Hannon. She discusses some of the leadership traits and practices proposed by Kouzes and Posner in their book, "The Leadership Challenge." For example, the largest All Aboard platform or Raccoon Circle could have all five of the practices suggested by Kouzes and Posner (inspiring a shared vision, modeling the way, etc.). Smaller and smaller platforms or Raccoon Circles would hold fewer of these talents or practices. The group is quick to realize that with fewer skills (i.e. smaller Raccoon Circles), getting the group to successfully finish the task, becomes harder and harder. The more leadership skills they possess (the larger the All Aboard platforms or Raccoon Circles), the easier the completion of the task becomes.

All Aboard typically results in participants standing in fairly close proximity. For a 'horizontal' variation, see the next activity.

34a. This Tent is Too Small!

Here is an activity that brings the group into close proximity. Think of this activity as a version of All Aboard, but this time with all participants laying down on the job! Begin with a super-sized Raccoon Circle (say one with three pieces of 15 foot long webbing tied together). The goal is for the entire group to find a comfortable resting place, laying down inside the Super Raccoon Circle. Stories of everyone in the same tent, or perched on a narrow ledge high on a mountain, or perhaps sleeping overnight in the nest of a prehistoric pterodactyl can be used. Light snoring when they are all comfortable and in place is a way of telling when the group has completed the task. After finding this comfort zone, ask everyone to turn over (which typically happens during a night's sleep at least 4 times). Next you can ask some folks to change places, without disturbing the other sleepers.

Finally, you might consider a game of "Ha!" while the group is this close together. You can even conduct a processing and debriefing session in this formation.

35. Trust Lift

As part of a complete trust sequence, the trust lift can be a very profound ending activity, without the need for a trust fall, trust dive, or some other higher adventure trust event. The trust lift, also known as 'birdlofting' or 'reaching for the sky,' involves the members of a group carefully and safely lifting a member of their team. While this can be done with hands only, some participants prefer the Raccoon Circle approach, because it does not involve contact with all parts of the participants body. While the explanation below describes the use of a Raccoon Circle for the Trust Lift, additional facilitator intervention is necessary for a safe and successful trust sequence. Be careful, and use appropriate spotting techniques.

Begin by creating a double hourglass shape with a Raccoon Circle (see below):

This shape forms the "cradle" or "litter" that will be used to lift the person. It also provides comfortable handholds, and a comfortable and supportive cradle for the person being lifted. Begin by having a participant lie down, face up, along this webbing 'cradle.' Three lifters are stationed on each side of the person (at approximately the shoulders, waist and knees). An additional spotter is located at the head, and is responsible for the head, neck and shoulder region of the person being lifted (the most critical spotting location for most participants). Another additional spotter is located at the feet of the person being lifted.

The head spotter, now invites the other lifters to join them, and lift the person to waist height in one smooth move. The head spotter is in a perfect position to observe each of the lifters, and to remind them keep their backs straight, and lift properly. This same head spotter is also in position to verbally reassure the person being lifted, "no problems, we have you, you are doing fine."

If the participant and lifters are comfortable, the participant can be lifted up to shoulder level. When returned to waist level, the cradle can be gently rocked back and forth for a very relaxing experience.

36. Shape Up!

Using a Raccoon Circle, with all members of the group holding on, form the following letters, numbers and shapes as quickly as possible. Three dimensional shapes are also possible, such as cubes, trees, pyramids, igloos, planes, and other simple 3-D shapes.

A, B, C ... X, Y, Z
1, 2, 3 ... ?, @, &

For a campfire skit (or a performance art piece) let different groups with appropriate color Raccoon Circles create the different shapes or objects in the story (such as green trees, a yellow sun, people, animals and other objects of various colors). Or, combine forces to have several groups each make a portion of a larger object (such as the wheels, engine, smoke, coal car and caboose of a small train).

37. Insanity (All the Gold in the World)

For this activity, you'll need a total of 5 Raccoon Circles of different colors, and about 100-150 tennis balls. Place one Raccoon Circle at the center, filled with tennis balls. Now space the four remaining Raccoon Circles around the perimeter of this first circle, about 20 feet (6 meters) away.

Begin by dividing the group into four approximately equal size sub-groups, and place one sub-group in each of the four external Raccoon Circles. The challenge of this activity is to get ALL the tennis balls into your Raccoon Circle. Any creative and safe solution is allowed. Once sub-groups have been placed in their four areas, allow them 2 minutes to plan their strategy—however, the following rules MUST BE FOLLOWED:
1. Balls can only be carried in hands (not inside clothing, or using other external containers).
2. Balls must be transported one at a time.
3. Anyone can take balls from any Raccoon Circle at any time.
4. No throwing of balls, they must be transported and "placed" not dropped, into each hoop.
5. No group can "block" another team from removing their tennis balls.
6. No sitting in the hoop, covering tennis balls.
7. You WIN when ALL the balls are in your Raccoon Circle.

This activity should have minimal discussion and be quickly introduced. The object is to encourage a flurry of activity quickly. This is a high-energy activity. Debriefing topics include: "Who was 'the team?' ", "How did you find a win-win solution?", "what strategies did your team employ?" Thanks to Sam Sikes and Michelle Cummings for this lively activity.

38. Cross the Line

This activity requires a single untied Raccoon Circle, stretched into a straight line. With half of the group on one side of the line and standing about 6 feet (2 meters) behind the line, and the other half of the team on the other side, the scene is set for a moment of conflict (of "us" vs. "them"). Make no mistake, this Raccoon Circle activity is a bit higher level than most, but it is excellent for setting the stage to talk about conflict, negotiation and win/win, win/lose, and lose/lose scenarios.

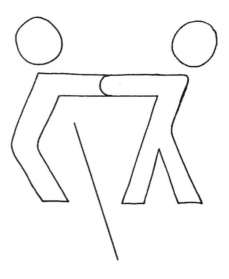

Tom Heck calls this activity, "Their Ain't No Flies On Me!", and begins this activity by having one side say, "There ain't no flies on me, there ain't no flies on me, there might be flies on you (point to folks on the other side), but there ain't no flies on me!", and then boldly take a step towards the line (with just the right amount of attitude). The other side now replies, "there ain't no flies on me, there ain't no flies on me, there might be flies on you, but there ain't no flies on me!", and takes a step towards the line. The first side now repeats, and moves to the line, followed by the second side repeating their lines, and stepping face to face with the other side.

Now the facilitator says, "you have 3 seconds to get the person across the line from you onto your side of the line!"

Typically, this phrasing results in a rather quick tug of war between partners, and usually a physical solution (for one person at least) to the challenge. Leaving open a major opportunity to discuss conflict, challenge, competition, collaboration, attitude, negotiation, win/lose, lose/lose and win/win scenarios, and how to resolve differences between people.

39. A Circular Story

Using a piece of paper, or an index card, and some large pens or markers, have each participant write down a single word. Place a Raccoon Circle on the ground, and have each person stand around the outside of the circle, with their backs towards the center, holding their card at shoulder height. The facilitator begins 'the story' by saying, "once upon a time . . .," and walking around the outside of the circle, looking at the cards as they pass by. The goal is to tell a story, incorporating several of the words written on the cards, as they walk around the circle. Each time a word from one of the cards is used, that person steps out of the circle, and follows the facilitator around. At the end of their short story, the facilitator says, "The End!" and quickly finds a place to stand with their back to the circle. The remaining 'followers' also try to quickly find a place, and the remaining person, with no place to stand in the circle, becomes the new storyteller.

In addition to printed words on cards, this activity can also use photographs from magazines, hand drawn pictures, computer clip art, new vocabulary words, elements of stories from newspapers, corporate 'power' words or real objects.

40. Pieces of a Mystery

Here is a great idea for short pieces of tubular webbing about 12 inches (30 cm) long. Create a mystery story, and write a portion of the story on each piece of webbing. The words can contain part of the story or even clues about whodunit. When group members arrive, give each of them a piece of the story, and ask them to assemble the story in order or to solve the mystery.

You can simplify the assembly of the story by using not only the context of the words, but also colored dots or symbols at the beginning and end of each piece of webbing. Permanent markers come in a variety of colors, and you can draw a dot on each adjoining piece of the story. You can also create another story on the flip side of each piece, by using a different color marker or even a different language.

Here is an example of one story, in 14 parts. Each line can be printed on a different strip of webbing.

It was cold in the room when Karen entered the office.

As she looked at the big clock on the wall, she saw that it read 7am.

Karen noticed that the back door was unlocked and open.

Snow was coming in through the door, and was already 6 inches deep in the room.

Just then, a big friendly-looking dog came bounding through the snow, into the room.

It the dog's mouth was a leather pouch, which contained a set of keys.

"These are John's keys," said Karen, "but who's dog is this?"

Just then, there was a crash in the alley behind the office.

Hearing the sound, the dog ran back outside, dropping the keys on the floor.

Karen entered the alley, just in time to see John, sprawled in the snow.

Next to John, were several dozen doughnuts, covering the landscape, and also covered with snow.

"I didn't have enough hands to open the door AND carry all these boxes," said John.

The dog looked up, his face covered with the remains of a large jelly doughnut and powdered sugar.

Karen laughed. John laughed. The dog howled and went back to eating jelly doughnuts and snow.

40a. More Pieces of a Mystery

Here is another mystery that can be presented in pieces, written on segments of tubular webbing. This is a variation of an activity shared by Allison Phaneuf.

This can be a particularly enlightening activity to be used when exploring differences in personality and works styles, according to Bob Faw of Organizational Growth Consulting. Myers-Briggs (MBTI), DiSC, True Colors and other useful tools typically rank or organize participants into various categories of behavior, style or personality. You might be surprised to know that each of these various groups can solve this puzzle, but often using very different techniques.

To perform this activity, write the following information on separate pieces of webbing (or paper), and give one complete set to each group attempting to solve the puzzle. Divide the clues evenly between the members of the group. Each person may read the information on their webbing out loud to the other members of the group, but no one else may look at this information.

The Corporate Research Tour

Each research group visits the same four universities but in a different order.

The first place the Alpha group visited was the University of Tokyo, Japan.

The University of Moscow, Russia was the third university the Alpha group visited.

In what order did the Beta group visit the universities?

The group that bought cell phones started their tour in Princeton, New Jersey.

Not all of the information provided will help to solve this mystery.

The Omega group visited Princeton before Japan.

The Beta group bought computer software in Moscow.

The Beta group visited the University of Paris after Princeton.

The Alpha group bought translation guidebooks in Moscow.

Each research group visited their favorite university last.

Research, Inc. took four research groups from four international corporations on a university research tour.

Of the different research groups, the Delta group liked Japan best.

The Delta group bought cell phones on their tour.

While many groups will attempt to find which universities each research group visited, only the order of the Beta group was asked for. But if you've made it this far, you probably would appreciate the complete set of answers, so here they are.

Alpha Group	Beta Group	Delta Group	Omega Group
Japan	Moscow	Princeton	Paris
Paris	Japan	Moscow	Princeton
Moscow	Princeton	Paris	Japan
Princeton	Paris	Japan	Moscow

41. Houses and Utilities

Here is a Raccoon Circle version of a classic 19th century puzzle. The challenge in this problem solving activity, using nine untied Raccoon Circles, is to create utility connections between each of the three houses and the three utilities (electricity, water and natural gas) with none of the utility lines (Raccoon Circles) crossing any other. For those that like stories for such activities, imagine that the three houses must pass a zoning inspection when the utility lines have been successfully connected.

You can use bricks, wooden blocks, books, pieces of paper or any other small rectangular objects to identify the three houses and the three utilities, as shown here:

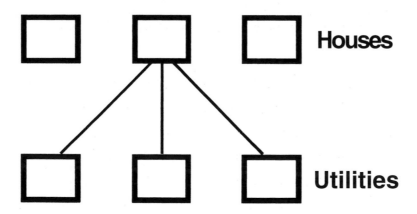

One possible solution, although not the only one, especially for a creative group that is willing to 'bend the rules' a bit, is shown below. This solution requires some creativity to keep the utility lines from crossing. In this case, one of the lines must either pass through one of the houses or one of the utilities, thus connecting all the other houses and utilities without crossing any utility lines.

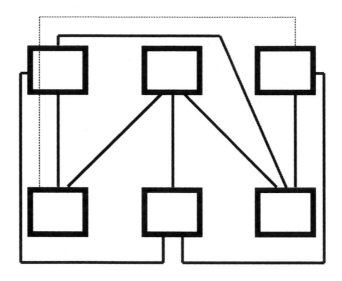

42. Pigs & Pens

The Pigs   **The Pens**

This puzzle requires four Raccoon Circles (for the four pens) and nine objects (for the pigs). Plastic bleach bottles can be decorated for the nine pigs, or perhaps nine plastic piggy banks, or even nine tennis balls. The challenge is to place an odd number of pigs in each pen. Odd numbers include 1,3,5,7 and 9 for this puzzle. Even numbers include 0,2,4,6 or 8. Begin this activity with the pigs and pens separated and scattered about the playing area. This is an example of a puzzle with multiple correct solutions. Two styles of solutions are shown below. Type One includes those solutions without the pens crossing each other. Type Two solutions require the pens to cross each other. Gook Luck—Oink!

Type One Solutions   **Type Two Solutions**

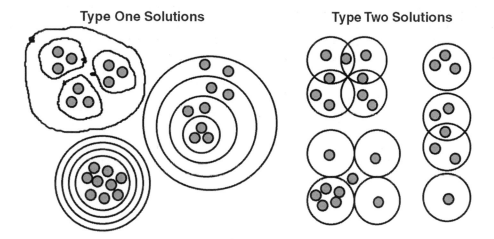

43. Cross Every Line

Here is another lesson in topology. Using duct tape or some other wide tape, paint, sidewalk chalk, plastic table cloth or tarp with this pattern or even a wooden frame, construct the five block shape shown here. The overall dimensions of this shape should be approximately 2 feet (0.6 meters) tall by 4 feet (1.2 meters) wide, with 2 inch (5 cm) wide lines. The puzzle or challenge here is by using one or two full length untied Raccoon Circle, to cross every line segment in the shape one time. One unsuccessful attempt is shown at the right. Notice that this attempt misses the vertical line in the lower center, and the horizontal line just above and to the right. One possible solution is shown below.

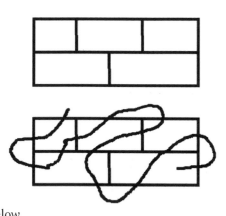

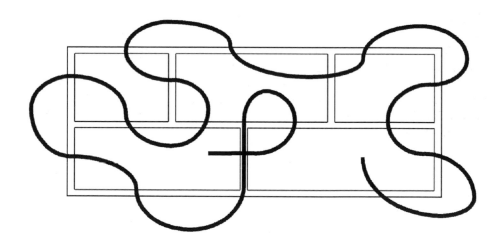

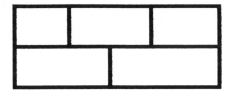

You can also perform the above challenge as a pencil & paper activity for your next group. For an even harder challenge, see if any of the members of the group can draw this shape using only three continuous lines, without retracing any line in the process.

44. A Secret Raccoon Circle Message

While high speed internet email, cell phones and fax machines have become common tools of communication, there was a time when sending a message to another person was not quite so easy, especially if you wanted to keep that message private. One technique was to write the message on a ribbon of parchment or cloth that had been wrapped around a tube or cylinder or even the branch from a tree. When unwound, the ribbon contained only letters, but no coherent message. Only when the ribbon was again wrapped around a cylinder of the same diameter did the message become clear.

To make your own puzzle, you'll need a Raccoon Circle and one of several tubes or cylinders (such as a short segment of plastic tubing, a foam pool 'noodle,' a baseball bat or the handle from a broom or garden tool). It is a good idea to have several tubes or cylinders of various sizes for the group to select from. Using one of the cylinders, wind a Raccoon Circle along the length. Then, using a permanent marker, write a single capital letter on each turn of the winding, to form your message, as shown in the illustration. The message might be where to begin the next activity, or some information on finding resources, or instructions to solving yet another puzzle, etc. Then unwind the Raccoon Circle.

As a group puzzle or creative problem solving activity, you can place the Raccoon Circle and several objects in the middle of the group, and ask them to decode the message. Encourage the group to try various approaches, including analyzing the information on the Raccoon Circle, and perhaps anything written on the cylinders and other objects (such as 'not this one' written in a foreign language), trial and error solutions, combining tools, etc.

45. Grand March

One of the most unique ways of visually meeting all the other participants at a gathering or conference in a very short amount of time is also one of the most fun. The 'Grand March' has been a popular form of dancing in a variety of cultures. Follow the Leader is another version of this same activity, but typically without music. This activity usually begins by creating a circle of all participants, having them hold hands, and then a leader begins to pull this long line of followers around the room to the beat of some music, creating spirals, twists and turns. As an energizer, the music can be loud with a definitive beat, such as a college marching band song. For a more contemplative atmosphere, quieter music can be chosen.

In environments where holding hands is not practical or could violate local customs, using one very long Raccoon Circle works well. Tubular webbing typically comes in 300 foot (92 meter) long lengths, and this is sufficient for at least a hundred adult participants. For more participants, knot several pieces of webbing together to make an even longer Raccoon Circle.

46. Knot By Myself

This old parlor trick has two rather unique solutions, one true and one involving 'slight of hand.' The challenge or trick here is to pick up an untied Raccoon Circle, and then tie an overhand knot in the webbing, without letting go of the webbing. While it is possible to perform this trick with a full length Raccoon Circle, it is a bit easier with a 6 foot (2 meter) long piece of webbing.

First of all, if you happen to pick up the webbing as shown in the illustration to the left, it is pretty unlikely that you'll be able to tie an overhand knot without letting go of the webbing. The secret for technique number one is to first cross your arms and then pick up the webbing. Then, by simply uncrossing your arms, you'll tie an overhand knot.

Technique number two requires a bit more work, and some practice to make this slight of hand version look authentic. I first learned this version from Sam Sikes. Begin by holding the webbing as shown, with about 4 inches (10 cm) of webbing over the top of each hand. The illustrations shown below are pictures of what your hands should look like as you execute this trick. This, however, is not an easy trick to visually explain here. If you would like a more complete explanation, look up Sam Sikes or Jim Cain at their next conference appearance.

After grasping the Raccoon Circle, loop the left hand over the right hand to form a "window" with the webbing. Next pass the left hand through this window, behind the part of the webbing marked "A" and then back out of the window. Now move the left and right hands away from each other.

If you pull the left and right hands apart now, no knot will appear. The secret move is to take the left hand and switch the position where it is holding the segment of the webbing marked B to the segment marked C. This is accomplished by dropping the center of the webbing down and moving the contact point with the left hand from the end of the webbing to about 1 foot (30 cm) inward (i.e. from point B to point C). The result is an overhand knot.

46a. Throwing Knots

Another method for creating knots with flair is called 'Throwing Knots.' This solo activity can fill the time you spend waiting for the bus, or waiting for the rest of the hikers to catch up with the leaders, or waiting for the teambuilding program to start . . .

The challenge here is to learn how to "throw" various knots into a straight piece of webbing. An entire Raccoon Circle is fine, but this activity also works well with only about 6 feet (2 meters) of webbing or rope.

A simple knot to begin with is a standard overhand knot. Begin by holding the webbing in both hands, as shown above. Move both hands together to create a twist in the webbing, and finally throw one end of the webbing through this twisted loop, to form an overhand knot.

For a second knot, although not the simplest, try the Figure 8. Holding the webbing or rope in both hands, so that it droops in the middle, and forms the letter "U." Next, create a twist in the webbing, by twirling. Finally, throw one end of the webbing through the opening in the lower portion of the twirled Raccoon Circle. The result should be a Thrown Figure 8. This knot requires one more twisted loop than the overhand knot. With a bit of practice, you should be able to "throw" a successful knot every time.

46b. Flipping Knots

A final, slightly more complicated technique is to hold only one end of the webbing, and tie an overhand knot simply by flipping the bottom end of the webbing upward and having it form the knot. This one will keep you busy for minutes if not hours.

47. Steal the Bacon

Here is a familiar playground game that works well with a Raccoon Circle. Wind the entire Raccoon Circle up into a tight ball or 'hank' (like you might wind up an electrical cord or long section of rope). Now place this below a person standing in the center of the group, guarding "the bacon." Other group members attempt to touch or steal the bacon, without being touched or tagged by the guard. The guard is not allowed to sit or stand on the bacon. If someone trying to steal the bacon is tagged by the guard they remain frozen until everyone is frozen (the guard wins), or someone else steals the bacon. Even though this is only a game, some interesting problem solving strategies, collaboration and teamwork evolve during play. The more tightly wrapped the Raccoon Circle, the tougher the challenge. The longer 'the bacon' the easier it is to steal without being tagged.

48. Ships & Sharks

This is an adaptation of an activity that is typically performed with hula hoops. It is a fun way to move groups across a field, as it requires large open space. Everyone in the group must hold on to the Raccoon Circle and run—until the facilitator cries out "Sharks!" They must then lay the web loop on the ground and stand inside of it. When the command of "Ships" is given, all must grab the circle and run. If there are two or more groups, a command can be given to "Change Ships," and everyone must scramble to another circle. This activity can be made more complex by limiting the number of people from one group that can board another ship.

This activity can also be played at any time during the program day, so make sure that your groups are ready to go with a moment's notice!

48a. Shark Attack

Here is an adaptation of Moving Towards Extinction (Number 5 in this section) and Ships & Sharks (above) from Rocky Top Ranch in Keller, Texas.

The first game we often play just for fun is a version of Lilly Pads and Islands. The Raccoon Circles are the Islands. After a few rounds of play, we end up with all the players safely ensconced on a few Islands. We have them applaud themselves for their efforts keeping each other safe and sharing the islands. We then ask for volunteers. We pick as many volunteers as we have Raccoon Circles (this usually goes to the "Fastest Hands in the West). The volunteers are now named lifeguards for the day. If at anytime they hear "Shark Attack" the lifeguard's job is to whip out their Raccoon Circle, place it on the ground and get all the players safely aboard. We really play up the importance of keeping the group safe. We use Shark Attack to energize them during the day. It's also a great way to gather kids back together after lunch or breaks.

49. Raccoon Circle Bowling

This activity has at least three names so far, and you are welcome to use the one that works best for your audience. Raccoon Circle Bowling, Horizontal Archery and Catchin' Flies all have made the list. First, you'll need a large archery target, or several concentric chalk circles that have been drawn on a playground surface, with the largest circle about 3 feet (1 meter) in diameter. Next pass out one untied Raccoon Circle per person. It helps if the Raccoon Circles are all a different color. Let the participants wind these Raccoon Circles up into spirals (bowling balls). With typical bowling style, participants roll their Raccoon Circles towards the target (unwinding as they go). The final zone or location reached by the end of the Raccoon Circle tells the score. A bullseye (a bowling 'strike') is worth 10 points. If the webbing does not reach the target, it is a 'gutter ball' and scores no points.

A group of elementary school children mentioned that a red Raccoon Circle looks a bit like the tongue of a frog stretching out to catch a fly, and so the name Catchin' Flies. Within the target area, you can place some empty film canisters, or tennis balls (these are the 'flies'). Points are scored (and frogs are fed) every time one of the unwinding Raccoon Circles moves one of these objects. Or, the closest webbing tip to the object, wins. Perhaps instead of playing for 'flies,' it can be the closest tip to the object wins the candy, or some other prize.

50. Where's the Knot

This simple observation game places one person in the center of the Raccoon Circle, while the remaining members of the group hold the Raccoon Circle. The object is to pass the Raccoon Circle clockwise or counterclockwise around the group, hiding the location of the knot. The outer group is allowed to slide their hands along the Raccoon Circle and of course vocally distract the person in the center. When the person in the center correctly guesses the person presently holding the knot, they change places with that person, and the game begins again. It helps to tie a water knot with very short 'tails' for this activity.

51. Grand Prix Racing

Now that you have turned the Raccoon Circle into a complete circle or loop using a water knot, you are ready for the ultimate in sport racing. Thanks to Tom Heck for not only the idea for this activity, but also the enthusiasm to lead it effectively. This activity will boost the enthusiasm of your audience, and provide some moderate competition in the process.

Begin by spreading several Raccoon Circles around the available space, in close proximity to each other. Ask participants to join one of the 'racing teams,' picking their favorite color in the process. This activity works best with approximately 5 to 7 participants per Raccoon Circle. Have participants hold the Raccoon Circle with both hands in front of them.

"Ladies and Gentlemen! It is summertime, and that means one thing in this part of the world—Grand Prix Racing! Now I know that you are such die-hard race fans that just the thought of a race makes your heart beat faster. So this race comes in three parts. First, when I say that "we're going to have a race," your response is a primal grunt. Next I'll say, "start your engines!" and I want to hear your best racecar sounds (audience practices making race car revving engine, shifting gears and braking sounds). Finally, with so many cars on the track today, it will be difficult to see just which group finishes their race first, so we'll need a sign indicating when your group is finished. That sign is to raise your hands (and the Raccoon Circle) above your heads and yell "Yesssssssss!""

Logistically, Grand Prix involves having the group transfer the knot around the group as quickly as possible, using only their hands. This activity can even be performed for a seated audience. To begin, you'll need a "start / finish" line, which can be the person that was born the farthest distance away from the present location. The race begins at this location, and ends when the knot is passed around the circle, and returns to this same location (Yesssssssss!)

Typically in Raccoon Circle Grand Prix racing, there are three qualifying rounds or races. The first race is a single lap race to the right, with the knot traveling once around the inside of the circle to the right (counterclockwise). The second race is a multi-lap race (two or three laps) to the left (clockwise) around the circle. And the final race of the series is a 'winner take all' championship race, with one lap to the right (counterclockwise) followed by one lap to the left (clockwise).

Incidentally, after this activity, the group will not only be energized, but perhaps in a slightly competitive mood. From a sequencing standpoint, you can either continue this atmosphere (with more competitive challenges—such as into a summer camp competition) or introduce a bit of counterpoint, by following this activity with one that requires the group working together in a collaborative manner.

A second variation of this activity comes from Tim Borton. Tim suggests that rather than a typical oval or circular racetrack, use the Raccoon Circle to construct a Figure-8 racetrack. When you begin the race, "On your mark, get set, go!" some groups will not immediately understand which way to move their hands in order to move the knot clockwise around the group. This is yet another simple but effective problem solving opportunity. Thanks Tim.

One final variation, and one of our favorites, is the pit stop. For the final long race of the season, spin the webbing two laps to the left, then everyone lets go, places the Raccoon Circle on the ground, spins around 360 degrees on their own, picks up the Raccoon Circle, and finishes by racing two laps back to the right. The energy in your group will be very high by this point.

52. Pencil Pushers

Don't be fooled, this simple activity is extremely physically challenging. Stretch an untied Raccoon Circle into a line. This is the starting point. The challenge now is for teams of three to four participants to push a new, unsharpened pencil beyond the line and across the floor, making contact with only their hands on the floor. This challenge typically results in the group forming some type of human bridge, with the first person's feet just behind the line and other team members climbing over them as they extend the bridge. The winners are those that push the pencil the furthest distance and still are able to return behind the line, without touching the floor in front of the line with anything but their hands.

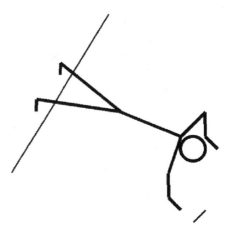

53. Raccoon Jousting

Here is a fun activity for two participants that requires balance, skill and a certain amount of understanding and anticipation of the other player's moves. It is also an excellent introduction into non-contact forms of martial arts where anticipating your opponents moves are paramount. Use two Raccoon Circles that have been tied together with a single water knot in the middle, to form a 30 foot (9 meters) long line. Use small carpet pads, paper plates or additional Raccoon Circles to form two 15 inch (38 cm) diameter circles (these are called platforms), 10 feet (3 meters) apart.

Two contenders (participants) now stand on their platforms holding only the very ends of the long Raccoon Circle. The object is to make the other person either let go of the Raccoon Circle, or to step off their platform by pulling, yanking and controlling the Raccoon Circle.

You can modify the positions in this activity for three people, by using three raccoon circles in a Y formation. You can also accommodate four players by arranging four Raccoon Circles in a square or cross formation. You can even turn this into an activity for the entire group by using one very large circle made by tying several Raccoon Circles together. After experiencing how it feels to be pulled off balance, introduce the group to the concept of the yurt circle, and see if everyone can balance without pulling anyone off their platform.

54. Mousetrap

Here is an activity borrowed from the world of parachute games. Begin by tying four or five Raccoon Circles together to form one large circle. Next invite participants to connect up around the outside of the circle, with some space between each person. Invite the group count off by fives (1,2,3,4,5,1,2,3,4,5,etc.) and remember their number. The game begins with everyone raising the large Raccoon Circle above their heads. The facilitator calls out a number (Number 3!) and everyone with that number is asked to change places, by running into the center and then finding an open position along the outside of the Raccoon Circle. At any time in the process, the facilitator can call out "SNAP!" and the remaining members on the outside of the circle quickly lower the circle, possibly trapping a few participants on the inside of the circle. When the next number is called, the 'trapped' folks join the new folks in trying to find a place, before the next SNAP!

Be sure that participants change places with 'bumpers up.' That means that everyone changes places with both hands up, to guard against bumping into another person while changing places. Another method of slowing down the speed of this activity is to ask participants to walk 'heel–toe' when changing places.

55. Tossing the Pizza

This activity definitely fits into the "harder than it looks" category. Begin with a group of 5-8 participants holding onto a knotted Raccoon Circle, hands upward, elbows straight, with no slack in the circle. The challenge is for the group to toss this Raccoon Circle pizza into the air, at least to the height of their heads, and then for everyone in the group to catch the circle as it drops back down, <u>without anyone moving their feet.</u> After a few unsuccessful attempts, encourage the group to plan their task, brainstorm new ideas and try them. A good pizza flipping team can toss their Raccoon Circle pizza in the air three times without anyone in the group dropping it or moving their feet.

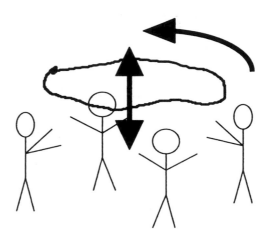

For a higher level of challenge, the ultimate pizza chefs can spin their pizza dough in the air. For the Raccoon Circle pizza, this means tossing the pizza into the air and having the knot come back down at least one person to the right or left of where it was when it was launched. A little 'spin action' can actually improve the team's performance. This simple problem solving activity is a fun way to begin the 'working as a team' portion of your program.

56. Passing Clouds

Here is a creative activity to follow Tossing the Pizza. As a team, toss a Raccoon Circle into the air and allow it to land on the ground. Then view the Raccoon Circle from various angles and sides, and creatively imagine what different shapes or objects can be found. This activity is similar to looking at those big, white puffy clouds and finding various shapes and images there.

57. Rock Around the Clock

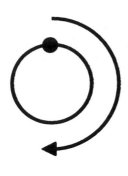

This activity begins with a group of participants standing around the perimeter of a Raccoon Circle that has been placed on the ground. While facing inward, each participant's feet should be in contact with the person's feet on each side of them. The person standing near the knot is asked to rotate clockwise around the circle to the opposite side (i.e. from the 12 o'clock position to the 6 o'clock position), moving everyone else in the process, with everyone keeping their feet in contact at all times.

Keeping other parts in contact is optional, but is a good problem solving idea (such as holding hands, shoulder-to-shoulder, etc.). This is one of those 'easy to explain, difficult to perform' challenges. If the group is having a difficult time, ask them to have a seat on the floor, then place their feet in contact with each neighbor and think of other strategies. It is amazing how many groups will try 'scootching' around the circle while seated as a new technique (and one they never thought of before). This is a great opportunity to discuss looking at a problem from a different point of view.

A good debriefing question includes: Why didn't the group consider this solution earlier? It is also interesting to process the group's own quality control analysis (i.e. did they call out their own mistakes, or try to hide them?)

58. The World Wide Web Challenge

This is a highly physical, challenge activity. Consider this a Raccoon Circle version of the "Living Ladder" initiative found on page 117 of the book, Teamwork & Teamplay. You'll need a large group of participants for this activity (at least 30 or more).

Begin by forming interconnected Raccoon Circles (shown at the top of the next page), with at least six participants holding on to each circle. A 'mountain climber' is chosen to traverse the interconnected circles, without touching the ground.

Beginning climbers can make contact with both Raccoon Circles and also the holders. For a higher level challenge (a 5.10 climb), climbers can make contact only with the Raccoon Circles. Use an additional spotter at the beginning and end of the climb. The 'holes' in the center of each Raccoon Circle are crevasses. Watch out!

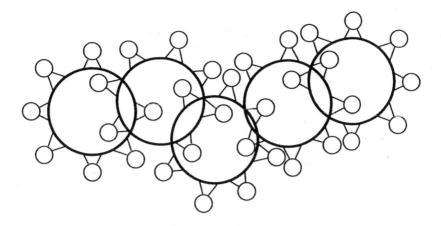

59. The Clothes Line

Here is an activity that works with three Raccoon Circles, but even better with a piece of 1/8 inch diameter shock or bungie cord. You'll also need a pet stake anchor (available in most pet stores, or discount stores) and a wooden spring clothespin. Begin by tying the bungie cord (or three Raccoon Circles) around a small tree at a height of about 3 feet (1 meter) above the ground. Be sure to use a tree with no exposed roots or uneven ground near the base of the tree. Next stretch out the bungie cord or Raccoon Circles and place the pet stake anchor in the ground at a distance of about 30 feet (9 meters) from the tree.

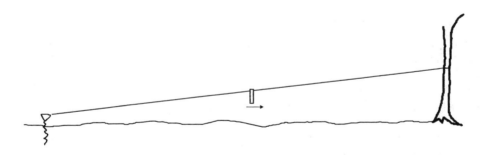

The challenge of this activity is to have the entire group cross over the line, without touching it, one at a time, with the assistance of the other members of the team. The first person over can cross at any point they choose, but each person after them can only cross the line to the right of this position. Each time a person crosses the line, the clothespin is moved to the right, limiting the remaining space available for the rest of the team. Encourage the team to plan in advance and perhaps to have a backup plan just in case something happens.

This is also a good activity to demonstrate that each member of the team doesn't necessarily have to cross at the same place, but that each participant's effort adds to the overall success of the team (and that even a mistake at the easiest lower portion of the line can have an impact on the overall success of the project).

Anyone touching the line while crossing is allowed to try again, however, the clothespin is still moved from their first attempt. Thanks to Patrick Caton for this challenge, and the next one as well.

60. The Electric Box

Here is a great variation of the traditional spider web or Window of Opportunity activity, and one that requires a bit more planning and strategy. The Electric Box is simply a raccoon circle opening through with the entire team must pass. The unusual feature of this Electric Box however, is that it starts as a vertical rectangle and ends up as a horizontal rectangle. For each person passing through the Electric Box, the box changes shape. This is a great 'Who Moved My Cheese' activity, and definitely one that requires planning to navigate the changing environment of the Electric Box.

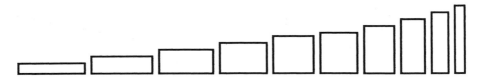

Who Moved My Cheese? by Spencer Johnson is a very intelligent story about adapting to change. It works well with corporate and youth audiences and has many teachable moments.

Who Moved My Cheese?, 1999, Spencer Johnson, Penguin Putnam, New York ISBN 0-399-14446-3

61. That's My Hat

Here is a simple activity for those participants that enjoy a physical challenge or need to burn off some energy. Three challengers are asked to hold onto a Raccoon Circle with one hand. The circle is placed at the center of a triangle of hats. At the word GO! each challenger attempts to pull the circle in the direction of their hat, so that they can grab it. This activity is best performed outside on a flat grassy surface.

Plenty of folks are using this activity with their groups. Here is another example and an interesting variation.

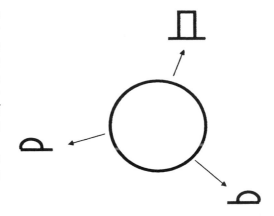

Dear Dr. Cain,

A while back you helped me learn how to integrate the Raccoon Circle into our programming at our therapy center. Since then, Raccoon Circles have become a staple tool in our life skills work with our clients.

Here's an activity that I found on your website. We play it a bit differently, but have found it a wonderful way to introduce passive, assertive and aggressive behaviors. I also love to play this when I have a group that talks about working together as a team yet can't quite get it together to demonstrate teamwork.

We start by asking the group to pick up the webbing and place it in a circle on the ground. We then invite them to step over to a large bucket of stuffed animals that has some different and interesting soft, toss-able objects in it. They are invited to select one item. The selection process can be framed as choosing something that represents: you, something you need, something you bring to the group, or just something that caught your eye.

Each person takes their item and returns to the Raccoon Circle. Standing with their heels just touching the webbing they are instructed to take three giant steps away from the circle and to place their item on the ground. Sometimes just watching how this part is completed by each participant is extremely enlightening – like the littlest player taking truly HUGE steps). Then we ask the group to return to the Raccoon Circle and connect up.

The following instructions are then announced to the group:

> *"When I say go, your challenge is to retrieve your object as quickly as possible. Once I say "go" you may not talk and at least one hand MUST remain on the Raccoon Circle at all times." Then quickly say "ready, set, go!"*

Chaos typically ensues with the strongest, largest or heaviest client eventually getting their item – to the detriment of the rest of the group. I stop them and let them discuss what has just happened. Dr. Cain, this has been an amazing activity, the clients just process themselves. Even with our youngest kids (aged 10) they are able to recognize their own and other's behaviors. We have talked about playground bullies, letting other people push you around, being a victim, older and younger siblings or parents—who can say "stop"? etc. The activity is incredibly rich. Depending on the set up, we may also discuss which item they selected and why.

I usually ask them what they would do differently if they could play again, and repeat this activity one more time. So far, most groups have demonstrated collaborative behavior on the second round. Then we discuss how different this round was, how it made them feel, which way they like better and why, and then how they can use this at school or at home.

We can often link this experience to horse behavior (one of our principal therapies) and to the relationship between the clients and their horses. To effectively lead a horse you must be assertive, not aggressive or passive. Sometimes we give each group member homework to practice assertive behavior or to notice times when they are passive, aggressive or assertive.

Jennifer Steinmetz

One step further! If you like the challenge of That's My Hat, here is a unique adaptation shared at the CCI/Canada conference in Kananaskis, Alberta in 2004. The creative folks at an all boys camp connected four carabiners to a Raccoon Circle and attached four deflated inner tubes (harnesses). This heavy-duty four-way tug-of-war  contraption uses a Raccoon Circle in a very kinesthetic way. The goal of this activity is for the four competitors connected to each try to be the first to reach their target (a tennis ball placed just out of reach).

62. The Flip Side

This is one of the simplest group problem solving activities for the Raccoon Circle, but it leaves the door open for some serious discussion about team consensus and group problem solving. Begin by drawing a large letter A on one end of the webbing (on the side with no black thread stripe). Next, place another symbol on the far end of the webbing, on the same side (such as the number 1). Then twist the webbing, and drop it on the ground. The task for the group is to decide whether the letter A is on the same side as the number 1, or not.

Note: some tubular climbing webbing is manufactured with a black thread on one side (similar to the dashed white line down the middle of most roads). You can elect to tell the participants about this information, or allow them to discover it for themselves. As in many problem solving activities, 'discovering' useful information is part of the process. As a second, higher level version of this activity, try using a piece of tubular climbing webbing that does not have a black thread.

63. Wind Up Challenge

There is a classic cartoon movie that has a great scene in which the two main character dogs are sharing a bowl of spaghetti. At one point, both dogs begin slurping on the end of a long strand of spaghetti, only to find that they are in fact eating the same strand of pasta, and ultimately end up in one of the classic cartoon kissing scenes in motion picture history. The Wind Up Challenge has a lot less contact than this now classic scene, but is every bit as fun.

This activity originated with two participants simultaneously performing W.A.M.F. (Wrapped Around My Finger – See 'Recent Additions' at the end of this book) when time was running out. You can include talking, or simply make this a kinesthetic challenge activity.

Begin by making a clearly visible line at the midpoint of an untied Raccoon Circle (on both sides of the webbing). Next, hand one end of the webbing to each person and instruct them that on the count of three, they are to begin winding the webbing around their index finger as quickly as they can, and to keep on winding the webbing until they have reached the center point. First one to reach the center line wins, but only if there is no twisting of the webbing between them and the other challenger. A twisted piece of webbing disqualifies both challengers. So now we have a bit of problem solving along with the kinesthetic challenge. Get to the center first without creating a twist in the webbing.

64. Both Sides of the Story

Here is an activity for the storytellers in your group. Take a light colored Raccoon Circle and clearly print a variety of words (nouns work best) along both sides, using a permanent marker. Knot the Raccoon Circle, have your group connect up, and then begin the story telling process with each person using the word nearest their position. For contrast, you can place words of opposite meaning on opposite sides of the webbing (happy / sad, winter / summer, etc.) Another technique is to have one person begin a story, again using the word nearest them, for one sentence. The person next to them continues the story, using their word, for the second sentence, and so on.

65. The Elevator

Here is a variation of the powerful Inside-Out Raccoon Circle Activity. The challenge is for a group of 8 to 10 people, standing inside a Raccoon Circle, to pass the circle upward over their heads, without touching each other in the process. For this activity, it is OK to use your arms, hands, or whatever body part is most useful (head, feet, etc.) but participants cannot touch each other while lifting the raccoon circle over their heads. This is an activity that sounds easier than it is, especially if the circle is crowded. It is also a great chance to have the group self-analyze their efforts, and call out any mistakes they make. There are no penalties for mistakes, just invite the group to try again.

As an additional challenge, you can begin with any group size, by tying the webbing into a circle around their waists, while they stand closely together. Then ask them to perform the elevator challenge. If you perform this activity with multiple groups at the same time, have each group share their best ideas for completing the task successfully, and then see if all groups can complete the task within a reasonable time limit (15 seconds or less).

For even more variation, see if your team can make the elevator ascend without anyone in the group touching any one else, while standing on one foot. Then see if they do it with both feet, without ever bending over.

66. Chasing the Serpent

This activity originates as a French children's game. One player stands at the center of a group of participants, holding one end of an untied Raccoon Circle (the tail of the snake), while wiggling the entire Raccoon Circle around. The other participants attempt to protect the other members of their group by standing on the head of the snake (the other end of the Raccoon Circle which has a flat knot). If a member of the group attempts to capture the snake, but does not, and the snake touches them, they need to seek first aid (which requires them to sit down outside the play area of the snake, with their feet raised above their head for 30 seconds). If the snake is captured, that person is chosen to handle the snake for the next round.

67. Crossing the River

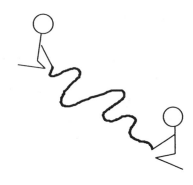

Here is a kinesthetically challenging game that requires some coordination, jumping and reaction skills. Two volunteers grasp the end of a standard untied Raccoon Circle, at ground level. They both begin to wiggle the webbing back and forth, creating some high frequency 'waves.' Other group members line up, and then try to walk, jump or leap over the waves, without touching them or being touched by them. In the first round, the waves can be small, but they can increase in magnitude with each passing round. For safety, keep the waves horizontal to the ground, so that all parts of the Raccoon Circle remain in contact with the floor. Avoid vertical waves in this challenge, especially indoors.

68. Casting Nets Upon the Waters

Here is a traditional game with some new equipment. With a knotted Raccoon Circle as a net, and a collection of partially filled and capped soda bottles as fish, the object is to throw the Raccoon Circle over as many bottles (fish) as possible. For each fish completely captured, one point is awarded. The fisherman with the most points after 5 throws gets to feed their village for the day. If you would like to bring in some environmental awareness into this activity, include a few special soda bottles, which represent non-game fish, endangered species or some other aquatic life caught in the net. This creates an opportunity to discuss the need for collecting food and still being environmentally responsible.

69. Singing in Circles

With several groups holding onto Raccoon Circles, have each group be responsible for one portion of a singing round, such as 'Row, row, row your boat.' You can also try songs with motions, such as, 'The Grand Old Duke of York.' Every time the group says the word 'up' or 'down,' have the entire group holding the Raccoon Circle, while pulling outward on the circle, stand up or down. For another variation, try singing 'My Bonnie Lies Over the Ocean,' and every time a word with the letter 'B' is sung, either stand or sit down. If you have more than one group, each group can move opposite the one nearest them (i.e. Group 1 goes up, when Group 2 goes down).

70. Ball Transport

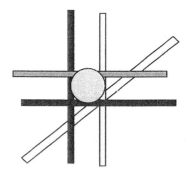

Here is an activity modified from the Bull Ring activity found in the book Teamwork & Teamplay. In this case, no ring is required. You'll need one untied Raccoon Circle for every two people, and a large ball (such as a soccer ball or volley ball (easier) or a softball, croquet ball or bocci ball (harder)). The goal is to transport the ball using only the straight Raccoon Circles. Each person can hold onto only one Raccoon Circle. You can impose additional challenges by requesting that no two Raccoon Circles can touch each other in more than one place, or that no knots can be tied in any piece of webbing. Passing through a doorway is a higher level challenge.

71. Worm Hole

Here is a simple activity in goal setting, challenge, cooperation, and group problem solving. Begin by having the group first decide on the size of circle they will form out of their Raccoon Circle. Big circles are easiest, smaller circles are more challenging. The objective or challenge here is for everyone in the group, working with a partner, to successfully pass through the Raccoon Circle "Worm Hole" without touching the webbing as they pass through.

Partners are required to be in contact with each other as they pass through the Worm Hole. Fellow team members can assist the pair going through the Worm Hole by holding the Raccoon Circle for them, BUT, once a person has held the Raccoon Circle and then let go completely, they cannot hold the Raccoon Circle again (this encourages different participants to take a leadership role during the activity. Should anyone make contact with the Raccoon Circle during their passage through the Worm Hole, one of the holders must let go once this pair has made it through.

For this activity, you can either tie different size circles from the same long piece of webbing, or you may choose to have several lengths of webbing for different size Worm Holes. Shock cord (bungie cord) is a suitable alternative material for this activity.

The chart shown here provides conversions between the length of webbing and the diameter of Raccoon Circle that can be created—allowing about 1 foot of the length for the knot and the "tails." You can find this activity, along with a more detailed set of instructions and possible variations in the book, Teamwork & Teamplay, Chapter 4, page 206.

Length of Webbing		Worm Hole Diameter	
Feet	(meters)	Feet	(meters)
15	4.6	4.5	1.4
12	3.7	3.5	1.1
8	2.4	2.2	0.7
6	1.8	1.6	0.5

72. A Circular Story

Here is an activity similar to "one word stories" in which a Raccoon Circle is used to determine who will continue the story. With all group members holding onto a Raccoon Circle, the story begins with the person presently nearest the knot. As they begin talking, the knot begins to be passed around the circle. When the person talking stops moving the Raccoon Circle, the person nearest the knot continues the story from that point and resumes moving the Raccoon Circle the opposite direction.

73. Moving Pictures

Tell a story with several groups of participants creating the various characters, scenery and events of the story using a Raccoon Circle. Each group can also be responsible for the sound effects of their character or object.

'Once upon a time, there was a little train (chuga, chuga, chug), that ran down by the seashore (wave sounds). The conductor on this train was very tall. His name was Walter (Hi y'all). He had a shiny pocket watch (tick tock) that he used to carry, just to make sure the train ran on time . . .'

74. Foot Knots

Invite a team of 3-5 participants to create specific knots, such as a bowline, overhand or square knot, using only their feet. You can further challenge the group to perform this task with their shoes and socks on. You may want to begin this activity with each person learning to tie a new knot using a short piece of rope, by themselves.

75. Musical Activities

During activities, try using some of the following music for motivation, inspiration and to reinforce the circles theme of the Raccoon Circle:

Song Title	Artist	Album Title
Circle of Life	Walt Disney	Lion King Soundtrack
All my Life's a Circle	Harry Chapin	Greatest Stories Live
Circle of Friends	Paul Winter Consort	Double Album
Circle Dream	10000 Maniacs	Our Time In Eden
Twisted Circle	9 Days	Twisted Circle
Full Circle	Aerosmith	Nine Lives
Circle	Barbara Streisand	Higher Ground
Full Circle	Collective Soul	Disciplined Breakdown
Perfect Circle	R.E.M	Murmur
Circle	Sarah McLachlan	Fumbling Towards Ecstasy
Circle	Big Head Todd & The Monsters	Sister Sweetly
May The Circle Remain Unbroken	13th Floor Elevators	Bull Of The Woods

Other musical ideas include using a Raccoon Circle for making a limbo pole, and then having participants limbo under the stretched Raccoon Circle as it is slowly lowered to the ground.

Finally, you can use two full length Raccoon Circles as a Chinese Jump Rope, and bring music together with balance, rhythm and individual style.

76. The Raccoon Shuffle

The Raccoon Shuffle is a warm up activity that requires some balance, skill, timing and teamwork. Start with 6 to 8 participants standing in a circle, supporting the raccoon circle with one raised foot. On the count of three, all participants are to jump and kick the opposite foot forward, catching the Raccoon Circle before it hits the ground. If the raccoon circle touches the ground, no points for that attempt. Collect your best score for ten attempts. Participants may notice that with no contact or connection between the members of the team, this is a difficult activity indeed. With connection, team balance and timing improves, along with the success rate for the Raccoon Shuffle.

77. The Chain Gang

Here is a 'harder than it looks' challenge for moving a group from one location to another, while using that time for teamwork.

Begin with the entire team standing in a line, one person about 6 feet (2 meters) behind the next. Starting with the leading participant, place a continuous piece of webbing (or several Raccoon Circles tied together) on the right shoulder of each person. The goal of the group is to see how far they can walk, without allowing the webbing to touch the ground or slide off of their shoulders, or to be touched with their arms or hands. As they walk, the webbing typically sways, slides and (eventually) will fall off. After the first failure, invite the team to brainstorm ideas for improvement (such as standing on opposite sides of the rope). For safety reasons, only place the rope upon participants' shoulders, NEVER around their necks or attached to their clothing.

←——————————— Walk this direction

78. The Moving Blob

Here is another way to creatively get your group 'from here to there.' Begin with a knotted Raccoon Circle lying on the ground. Invite a group to stand inside, and without using any part of their arms or hands, raise the web circle to waist height. Next, challenge the group to move from this location to your next location, without letting the Raccoon Circle touch the ground.

Variations include allowing half of the participants on the inside of the Raccoon Circle and the other half on the outside (but all must be in contact). You can also challenge the group to all face towards the center of the circle, or all face outwards.

Thanks to Shawn Moriarty of YMCA Camp Lakewood for this fun activity.

79. The High Five

Here is a tribute to folks at High 5 Adventures in Brattleboro, Vermont. First, carefully tie a Raccoon Circle between two trees, poles or corridor walls, about 10 ft (3 meters) off the ground.

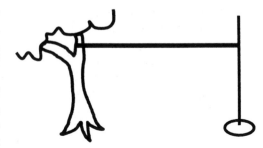

The High Five Challenge begins with half of the group on each side of the Raccoon Circle. The goal is to work as a team to make sure every person on one side has the opportunity to meet and greet one person from the other side, above the level of the Raccoon Circle. This greeting can be in the form of a handshake, a high five slap, nose to nose contact, or any other common and accepted local greeting or custom. Given the height of the line, this will require a bit of teamwork, lifting, spotting and creative problem solving. Be careful, and good luck.

80. Rescue Scenario

This next idea is not so much an activity, but a scenario for teambuilding activities in general. Thanks to Dave Knobbe and Deb Schuey for creating this excellent teambuilding scenario.

Teambuilding 911 begins with a team ready to face several upcoming challenges. In addition to the actual teambuilding activities, the team also has a Raccoon Circle that can be used as a tool throughout this scenario. For example, the Raccoon Circle can be used as a stretcher or rescue litter to carry a member of the team that may have been (temporarily) incapacitated. Or perhaps the actual teambuilding activity is to rescue a member of the team and transport them to safety.

The rescue litter is used just as the trust lift (activity #35 in this section) was used. If you like this style of thematic teambuilding, check out the rescue litter found in The Great Puzzle Quest of the book, *Teambuilding Puzzles,* by Mike Anderson, Jim Cain, Chris Cavert and Tom Heck. Visit www.teamworkandteamplay.com for more information about this book.

81. Classic Knot Theory

A Trefoil Knot

Shown below are a few configurations of rope 'doodles' made from a single Raccoon Circle. Each of the doodles shown are either a stable knot configuration (such as the trefoil knot) or can be reduced to an 'unknot' (that is, a simple rope circle). See if your team can reach consensus on which are knots and which are unknots. This can be done as a mental (hands off) challenge or by allowing the group to kinesthetically manipulate each rope doodle into a simple rope circle.

An Unknot

The Knot Book: An Elementary Introduction to the Mathematical Theory of Knots, 1994, Colin Adams, W. H. Freeman, New York, NY USA ISBN 0-7167-2393-X A simple introduction to the rather complicated mathematical theory of knots.

82. Blind Square

Blind Square fits into the category of challenges that are very simple to explain, but can be extremely difficult or even frustrating to actually accomplish.

In a safe environment (large open carpeted room with no obstacles, or perhaps a flat grassy outdoor space) blindfold the entire group (or ask each person to close their eyes) and allow them to search as a group and find a nearby collection of five, seven or nine segments of Raccoon Circles tied together into one long 'rope.' The reason for using an odd number of Raccoon Circles will become evident during the activity. If exactly four or eight Raccoon Circles are used, the four corners of the square are easy to find using the water knots as a guide. Odd numbers of Raccoon Circles (and water knots) makes this task a bit more difficult – which is important in the storming stage of group development.

After finding this 'rope,' instruct the group that their goal, while still blindfolded, is to create a perfect square using the entire rope. You might continue and remind the group that a square geometrically consists of a closed shape with four equal length sides, and four 90 degree corners. Participants are allowed to slide along the length of the rope, but cannot let go, change sides, or move around another participant.

This simple to explain but extremely difficult and time consuming to complete activity works best with a group of about a 10-15 participants. You can choose to invite one person to 'observe' the group, but not assist them in the completion of their task, and then to share their observations when the group has finished. The conflict typically experienced by groups in this activity will soon be very obvious. Communication breakdowns, leadership abilities, directions, power issues and resource constraints all contribute to team member frustration and often make what appears to be a simple task infinitely more difficult. If establishing realistic scheduling goals is appropriate for this project team, then ask them to estimate a 'time till completion' for creating this rope square. If establishing quality standards, or work performance standards is realistic, then ask them to establish (while blindfolded), the performance criteria on how they will measure the outcome of this rope square project. If team members are likely to encounter limitations in technology, wrong or misleading information, or confusion during their project work, consider tying one end of the rope

permanently to a tree, fence, car or other non-moving object. Be sure to conduct this activity in a large open space that contains no obstacles. As an alternative to blindfolds, you can ask participants to simply close their eyes (but even adults have a difficult time with this during the time required to complete this activity).

After the group has reached the end (notice, I didn't say 'completed' the activity), here are a few ideas to discuss: Was the time estimate reasonable given the task? What was most of the time spent doing? What was the 'breakthrough' point in this activity? Were all members of the group equally engaged in the activity? Did some members of the group have more 'power' than others? If the group was asked to create another shape blindfolded, do you think you could be more efficient? Quicker? Accurate? This stage of group development is called the Storming stage. What types of team behaviors did you notice during this activity that tells you the group was storming? What skills do you have now that you can use in the workplace when tasks become frustrating or difficult?

83. Unblind Square

While the previous activity is accomplished with the entire team blindfolded, this activity, called the Unblind Square, is challenging even with eyes open. It is also an interesting activity for exploring leadership and teamwork. Ask all members of the group to take hold of a long rope and stand in a circle. Ask the person standing nearest the ends of the rope to tie them together with a knot.

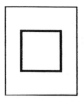

Begin by showing a single person the first illustration below. Instruct them to lead the group (without letting go) in creating this shape with the rope. After the group is finished, show another person the second illustration and ask them to lead the group this time. For the third illustration, show the entire group the picture, and invite them to create the shape. Finish with a final round, using the fourth or fifth illustration. The star is easier if the rope is untied first. For the fifth illustration, untying the knot is essential.

For a higher level of challenge, it is possible to create each of these shapes without crossing any lines. Debriefing topics include: What styles of leadership were displayed during this activity? How effective was the teamwork displayed during this activity? Would you say that this activity was carried out more like a military operation, a concert orchestra rehearsal, a little league practice, or the mosh pit at a Grateful Dead concert? Who untied the knot?

83a. String Figures

Mike Spiller shared his love of string figures and incorporated Raccoon Circles too. You can use string figures to reinforce key concepts in a presentation, pictures as part of a story or play, or symbols as part of a discussion or reviewing session. Here is how Mike uses this activity:

Jim, I just wanted you to know that I do quite a few things with Raccoon Circles. One of my favorite activities is making string figures. I find that both children and adults are fascinated by string figures. I use the Raccoon Circle just like a large loop of string. I first teach everyone how to make a star with their own small loop of string. Then we used a regular Raccoon Circle to make a larger one with the whole group. The kids said it was cool. After making the larger star, we sat down as a group and each of the kids talked about what a star meant to them. They mentioned things like stars in the galaxy, movie stars, and gold stars on homework assignments. I took a photo of the group and gave each child a copy to remind them that it takes a lot of help to become a star. When we work together, we all achieve more. I thought you might like to see the results of our efforts.

Mike Spiller

For more information about string figures, read:

String Figures & How to Make Them, 1962, Caroline Jayne, Dover Publications ISBN 0-4862-0152-X

Fascinating String Figures, 1999, International String Figures Assoc., Dover, ISBN 0-4864-0400-5

Cats Cradle: A Book of String Figures, 1993, Klutz, ISBN 1-8782-5753-6

Fun With String, 1985, Joseph Leeming, Dover Publications ISBN 0-4862-3063-5

You can also contact:

The International String Figure Association, P.O.Box 5134, Pasadena, California 91117 USA Phone/Fax (626) 398-1057 Email: webweavers@isfa.org Website: www.isfa.org

Mike Spiller L.T.D.F. (License to Deliver Fun), Physicians of Phun & Games of the World Website: www.physiciansofphun.com

84. The Coiled Raccoon Circle

Here is an interesting variation of the Human Knot activity. Start by loosely coiling several Raccoon Circles that have been knotted together on the ground, as shown in the illustration. Team members are asked to grasp one location along the webbing and to keep hold of this location throughout the activity. When all members have connected, the challenge for the team is to untangle this mess and eventually stand in a circle with every member facing inwards.

In addition to simply coiling and dropping the webbing, you can add several knots, weave several Raccoon Circles together or connect different pieces of webbing with rock climbing hardware. The Raccoon Circle illustrated here is untied at each end. You can create a higher level of challenge for the team if you tie the ends of webbing together first (creating a large circle) and then coiling this on the ground.

Invite the group to analyze this challenge and set a goal or estimate of a completion time before grasping the webbing. Discussions related to estimating and goal setting are appropriate here. You can also discuss how some team members had easy assignments, compared to other members that encountered difficulties in their portion of the webbing.

Encourage the group to untangle the rope slowly at first to avoid placing additional and unwanted knots into the rope.

Thanks to Mike Spiller for sharing this activity. Mike is an exceptional games resource.

85. Trust Walk

You can use one or several Raccoon Circles as a resource for connecting a group during a trust walk. To maintain spacing between participants, tie an overhand knot for each person along the webbing to identify their position. Alternating participants on both sides of the Raccoon Circle will maximize the number of group members attached to each Raccoon Circle.

Group members are encouraged to keep their eyes closed during this activity. Sighted facilitators should be placed at the beginning and end of the rope.

Be sure to avoid steep inclines, staircases and other places that pose any concerns for safety.

86. Alphabet Soup / Key Punch

In addition to three Raccoon Circles, you'll need a wide marking pen and about thirty large index cards (5x7 or 6x8 work better than 3x5).

Begin by drawing the numbers 1-30, or letters of the alphabet (26 in total) on index cards with a wide dark marker. Place these index cards in a random order, face up within a large circle made from two Raccoon Circles that have been knotted together. Teams begin a short distance away (10-20 feet (3-6 meters)) from this location behind an unknotted Raccoon Circle starting line.

The challenge of this activity is for each team to touch each of the cards in numerical or alphabetical order, one at a time, with the following restrictions:

1. Only one participant at a time can be within the perimeter of the circle.

2. The cards must be touched in order.

A 5 second penalty is assigned to any error committed during the completion of this activity. For example, if one person is inside the circle, and another person points toward the next card, and reaches over the Raccoon Circle line, they are 'in' the circle too, and a penalty is assigned every time this happens. If on the way to touch number 8 a person inadvertently touches number 21, another error has occurred, and another penalty is assigned. Total scores for each round are the combination of the actual time elapsed added to the number of penalties times five seconds each. So a team completing the task in 60 seconds with 4 penalties would have a total score of 80 seconds.

Before beginning each round, invite each team to establish a time and error goal. When finished, compare the estimate to the actual performance.

Small segments of light colored tubular webbing can be substituted for the index cards in this activity if desired. Draw either numbers or letters on these segments with a dark permanent marker.

87. Turn Table

Here is a high-energy activity that explores adapting to change, working together, and helping each other achieve success. This activity works best with at least three groups of five to eight participants holding knotted Raccoon Circles. Explain and demonstrate some of the following commands:

Circle Right	Holding the Raccoon Circle, the entire group walks to the right.
Circle Left	Holding the Raccoon Circle, the entire group walks to the left.
Spin	Standing still, the entire group uses their hands to spin the Raccoon Circle knot to the right.
Inside	Stand on the inside of the Raccoon Circle.
Outside	Stand on the outside of the Raccoon Circle.
Flip It	Flip the Raccoon Circle over (like a giant pancake).
Change	Every person individually goes to a new Raccoon Circle.
Switch	Every group goes as a group to a new Raccoon Circle.
Rotate	Everyone does a personal 360 degree rotation without dropping the Raccoon Circle.

After introducing this activity to the group, the facilitator begins to prompt the entire group with increasingly complicated commands, such as:

Right–Inside–Left/Rotate–Outside/FlipIt/Left–Rotate/Right/Change . . .

First perfect as many of these commands as possible. Group members can even create their own new commands. For a higher level of challenge, tell the group that every command actually means the opposite. For example right means left. Change actually means Switch. Outside means Inside.

As a debriefing discussion, ask group members if any of them happened to make an error while assisting their team in this task. How did it feel to know that other team members were there to help?

88. Challenging Knots

As a competitive event, see how fast a person can untie or unweave a Raccoon Circle knotted ball. The photograph here shows two possibilities. Design your own version.

As a variation, allow a whole team to work together to unweave a Raccoon Circle ball, without using their hands!

You can also use these knotted balls for group juggling, debriefing tools or even dog toys! If you want to make your Gordian Knot Ball last even longer without unraveling, you can knot, melt, stitch, hot glue or grommet the webbing together.

89. Human Tic Tac Toe

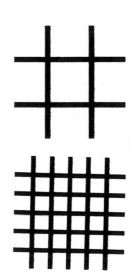

You can create a simple version of human-sized Tic Tac Toe by placing four unknotted Raccoon Circles on the ground as shown and using people as X's and O's. You can designate teams by hats, T-shirt color, shoe styles, crossing your arms above your head in the shape of an X or an O, or any other fun and imaginative technique you have available. This size works well for groups of about ten people.

For larger size groups, consider an extended Tic Tac Toe space, with a 4x4 or 5x5 grid, made with unknotted Raccoon Circles. You can play that any three-in-a-row wins the game, or you can play until all spaces are filled and the team with the most three-in-a-row combinations wins.

90. Shipwreck

Thanks to Chuck Lester of the New London County 4-H Camp for sharing this interesting communication and problem solving activity. You'll need one Raccoon Circle for every four people in your group.

Begin by tying all of the Raccoon Circles together into a large circle, using water knots. Gather your group together and explain the following information:

Your group has been shipwrecked on a small, uninhabited island. The wreck has left your group without sight or speech, but somewhere in the immediate area there is a long rope (the large Raccoon Circle). The universal symbol for 'help, we need assistance' is a perfect equilateral triangle. If your group can find the rope and create this shape, rescue is much more likely.

Chuck mentions, that in order to bring out the communication aspects of this challenge, he begins the activity with everyone blind (eyes closed or blindfolded) and mute (no verbal speech). A short time later, he allows speech but not sight, and then reverses and allows sight but not speech.

A significant portion of 'communication' is non-verbal. A good processing question is how much information was conveyed by sight rather than hearing or speaking?

91. Raccoon Tail Tag

This energizer requires shorter segments of tubular webbing (Raccoon Tails) about 18 inches (45 cm) long. Define a clear boundary for this activity. Each participant places one or more unknotted Raccoon Tails in their back pocket, so that approximately 9 inches (23 cm) are sticking out. These Raccoon Tails should not be tied or knotted to clothing.

At the beginning of the activity, everyone is 'It.' The object is to steal the Raccoon Tail from other group members while trying to keep your own. You cannot touch your own tail during the round. Those group members losing their Raccoon Tail move to the outside of the boundary and yell, "*I need a new Raccoon Tail!*" This is also a great opportunity to catch your breath. Anyone still playing the game that has an extra tail can pass it to those on the outside, which brings them back into the game.

Encourage participants to play carefully during this activity. Limit movement to fast walking (no running).

You can use this size of mini Raccoon Circle to make a personal bracelet after the energizer is complete. You can also use these short webbing segments for voting 'worms' and other activities. Thanks to Michelle Cummings for sharing this energetic Raccoon Circle activity.

92. Quotes in Order

Here is an activity that you can make from those left-over short pieces of webbing. Begin with your favorite quotation, or find one on the internet by searching key words, like 'quotations.' For example, you can search for specific topics, themes and key words at www.quotationspage.com.

Divide this quotation into small one or two word phrases and write these words in large block letters on the short segments of webbing. It is easier to read words that have been written in dark marker on light colored webbing. If you write two words per webbing segment, it will be easier to reconstruct the quotation, compared to a string of single words.

Next, present each member of the group with one of the webbing segments and instruct them to place the complete quotation in the proper order.

We suggest that you give each person a piece of webbing and require that they keep this particular piece throughout the activity. Why? Well, something interesting happens if you do not! Groups that begin to pass the phrases around often end up with all of the webbing strips on the ground, with only one or two people actively engaged in solving the puzzle. By requiring that each person keeps their own webbing, you increase the engagement of all team members.

This is also an effective and interesting technique for a group to learn new information, part of a mission statement, an international message or a motivational thought for the day.

Here are a few of our favorite quotations to get you started. It is a good idea to have quotes of various lengths, for the various number of participants you'll have in future groups.

"The person that grabs the cat by the tail learns
about 44 percent faster than the one just watching."
Mark Twain

"Never doubt that a small group of thoughtful, committed citizens
can change the world. Indeed, it is the only thing that ever has.
Margaret Meade

"Do not follow where the path may lead.
Go instead where there is no path and leave a trail."
Muriel Strode

"Problems worthy of attack,
prove their worth by fighting back!"
Piet Hein

If you like puzzle challenges like this one, you can find over 100 different team challenges in the book, Teambuilding Puzzles, by Jim Cain, Mike Anderson, Chris Cavert and Tom Heck, 2005, FUNdoing Publications (www.fundoing.com) ISBN 0-9746442-0-X. Over 300 pages of team challenges and puzzles that explore valuable life skills.

93. If You Need Help, Just Ask!

Here is an interesting challenge, with a unique solution, that is ideal for large groups (20-40 people). Begin by knotting six or more Raccoon Circles together, to make one very large webbing circle. With most of the group standing inside the circle, eight to ten remaining group members hold the circle about waist high (like a fence), from the outside of the circle. Those on the inside are asked to close their eyes. The rules for this challenge are then presented, as follows:

In this activity, the goal is to reach the outside of the circle.
You cannot go under the circle. You cannot go over the circle.
You cannot untie the knots. If you need help, just raise your hand.

While the challenge can seem a bit confusing and difficult, the solution is actually presented in the information above, if you need help, just raise your hand. All those raising their hands are assisted by one of the external members of the team to the outside of the circle. Sometimes it can be helpful to tell the remaining members of the group that one participant has made it out successfully.

It is ok, and in this case, appropriate, to ask for help.

94. Quality Circle Time (QCT)

In the U.K., nearly every elementary school has incorporated Quality Circle Time into their daily program. Some of the 'ground rules' for QCT are similar to adventure-based learning.

'Put downs' and negative comments are not allowed.
Everyone's contributions are listened to with respect.
The group themselves decide how the group will function.
Comments made in the circle, during circle time, stay in the circle.

For more information about Quality Circle Time, try an internet search at www.google.uk where you'll find dozens of inventive ideas, many of which can be performed around a Raccoon Circle as well.

95. Sticky Snake

Here is an engaging activity from Luke Kantor, LEAD Program Manager at Niagara County Community College.

Begin by loosely tying four overhand knots in a single untied Raccoon Circle and one figure eight knot with a long tongue (the snake's head).

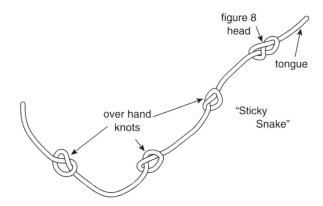

"While preparing for today's adventures outdoors, I found a very rare variety of snake on the path leading here. It is a bit different than normal snakes, and rather unusual for it to be out this time of day. Probably the only reason it is, is that it has managed to tie itself into some rather nasty knots. Probably something it ate recently. Anyway, the North American Sticky Snake needs our help. I'd like to see if we can help this snake out, by untying some of those nasty knots.

Before we begin however, I looked up some information about the snake on the internet, and here are some things you should know:

1. The North American Sticky Snake gets its name from a rather unique defense mechanism it has. Whenever it senses danger, the scales become extremely sticky, and anyone touching it would be permanently stuck there until the snake relaxed again.
2. The Sticky Snake doesn't actually bite like an ordinary snake, but rather transfers its venom through the saliva of its poisonous tongue. Anyone coming in contact with the tongue would be rendered speechless for this activity, and the one to follow too. It is *that*

serious! (This additional consequence has some real-life corollaries, and is often is discussed at length during the debriefing session).

3. Our goal will be to unknot the four overhand knots on the snake, but to leave the head untouched. Each participant will be asked to grab the snake at the same time with one hand, placing their other hand in their back pocket. From that time forward, no one can rearrange their hand position, so choose your contact point carefully!"

The facilitator can allow the group a few minutes to plan, or immediately begin the activity (and start again if necessary). One possible variation would be to invite the person nearest the tail of the snake to hold the snake with one hand, and a fixed object, such as a door, pole or tree, with the other (effectively making them an 'anchor'). Another variation would be to provide the group with a 'one use only' stickum remover, which would allow any one person to rearrange their hands, for comfort or to solve the problem. Whether the group uses this 'tool' or not during the activity is a valid debriefing point.

This activity is somewhat similar to Human Knots (#27 in this section).

96. Dancing Bear

Begin by tying two Raccoon Circles together in a long line, and then tying one of these people to a tree or pole. One player is chosen to be the bear. They must hold the free end of the Raccoon Circle with one hand at all times. The rest of the group strolls about near the 'honey tree,' occasionally trying to touch it.

With their free hand, the bear tries to tag other players. When tagged, that player joins hands with the bear and helps to tag other players.

97. Other Creative Ideas for Raccoon Circles

After holding a Raccoon Circle in your hands for a while, you quickly begin to think of other things that you could do with this simple webbing loop. Below are just a few ideas that we've had about other Raccoon Circle activities, ideas and things to make from webbing. If you invent some new activities, or creative things to make with webbing, and would like to share them with us, we would be glad to add them here in the future.

If you stitch the ends of the Raccoon Circle together instead of using a knot, you can made a plain loop, a loop with a twist (A Mobius Strip) or a loop with multiple twists.

You can make a Spider Web between two trees using a few Raccoon Circles.

On challenge courses with Spider Webs, you can pass an unknotted Raccoon Circle through every opening in the web (without touching it) instead of passing people through. You can then repeat the process and time the result. For a higher level of challenge, insist that not only can the Raccoon Circle not touch the web, but neither can participants touch the web or each other. For additional challenge, blindfold one or more participants during this activity. You can also use The CUBE, available from Adventure Hardware (www.adventurehardware.com) instead of a traditional Spider Web, and pass the Raccoon Circle though every possible path without repeating any. Thanks to Jordan Rimmer for these great ideas.

If you like the weaving technique for the spider web, here is an environmental awareness version created by Jim Cain. Instead of a Raccoon Circle or rope, use a garden hose completely filled with water. You can measure the amount of water in the hose before and after the activity as a quantitative measurement and compare this to evaporation, runoff or wastewater. Conservation of clean water is important in many communities around the world.

John Losey of Praxis Training in California suggests using a Raccoon Circle with the teambuilding activity Bull Ring (see Teamwork & Teamplay, page 79). Invite the entire group to pass through a knotted Raccoon Circle while holding the Bull Ring. This is an interesting challenge for the group and is perfect when a doorway is not available. Think of the Raccoon Circle as a magical doorway that just appeared out of nowhere!

You can explore a mathematical style of self-introduction and discovery by using two or more knotted Raccoon Circles to form life size Venn Diagrams and then inviting participants to stand in the region of their choice. For example, in the classic two-component Venn Diagram form shown here for types of ice cream, there are four possible locations to stand: chocolate [C], vanilla [V], both [C+V], neither [N] (standing outside the pattern).

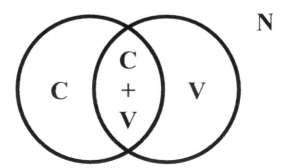

You can add more Raccoon Circles for even more choices, such as which main course to have at a banquet, or which summer camp activities to offer during free-time, or which location to hold the next corporate retreat.

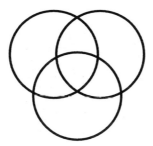 

For further reading on this subject, we recommend: *Cogwheels of the mind: the story of Venn diagrams,* by Anthony William Fairbank Edwards, 2004, Johns Hopkins University Press, Baltimore, MD ISBN 0-8018-7434-3.

It is possible to create a Raccoon Circle lariat or lasso. Use these for a Wild West program theme.

Fashion accessories, such as ties, belts, headbands, necklaces and bracelets made from webbing. So can Christmas tree ornaments, bookmarks and orienteering markers. Why not give a few Raccoon Circles to your next group and see what fashion accessories they can create? Or, give workshop participants a short piece of webbing to decorate as a bookmark for their adventure journal.

Use webbing (or surveyor's flagging tape) to create a labyrinth for quiet reflection. For more information about this subject, see the following books: *The Magic of Labyrinths—Following Your Path, Finding Your Center,* by Liz Simpson, London: Element. (ISBN 0-00-712047-8); *Exploring the Labyrinth: A Guide for Healing and Spiritual Growth,* by Melissa Gayle West, 2000, New York: Broadway Books (ISBN 0-7679-0356-0); and *Mazes and Labyrinths of the World,* by Janet Bord, New York: E. P. Dutton & Company (ISBN 0-525-47441-2).

"Try the Grand Prix racing activity found earlier in this section, using only your feet!"

You can also contact the Worldwide Labyrinth Project 1100 California Street, San Francisco, California 94108 Website: www.gracecathedral.org/veriditas

Send your ideas, activities, photographs and stories about Raccoon Circles and webbing to: jimcain@teamworkandteamplay.com and they could be included in future Internet and bound editions of *Raccoon Circle Activities*.

Exploring the Stages of Group Development with Raccoon Circle Activities

Forming, Storming, Norming, Performing and Transforming

Jim Cain

The stages of group development as presented here are based upon the research of Bruce W. Tuckman, professor of education at the Ohio State University. For more information about these stages, we invite you to read the following articles:

Tuckman, Bruce, 1965, "Developmental sequence of small groups," *Psychological Bulletin,* Number 63, pages 384–399. The classic original paper.

Tuckman, Bruce, & Jenson, Mary Ann, 1977, "Stages of small group development revisited," *Group and Organizational Studies,* Number 2, pages 419–427.

Tuckman, Bruce, 2001, Developmental Sequence in Small Groups, *Group Facilitation,* Number 3, Spring, pages 66–81. A look back, nearly 35 years after the original ground-breaking paper. Required reading for all group facilitators.

Cain, Jim, 2006, *Exploring the Stages of Group Development Using Adventure-Based Activities,* from the Teamwork & Teamplay website at: www.teamworkandteamplay.com.

Johnson, David W., and Johnson, Frank P. 1994, *Joining Together,* Allyn and Bacon, Boston, MA ISBN 0-205-15846-3 (See page 469).

Concepts

During any project involving more than a few people, a team is likely to pass through most if not all of the stages of group development, commonly referred to as forming, storming, norming, performing and finally, transforming. While entire graduate dissertations, college and management classes and seminars, and numerous journal articles have been written on this subject, this brief introductory article 'opens the door' to explaining and experiencing the stages of group development, and building some of the skills necessary to successfully navigate each stage. This introduction to the stages of group development is suitable for a staff training program. Additional resources and references are shown at the beginning of this article for those interested in a more detailed explanation of these stages, and techniques for exploring them with your team.

Directions

Consider the five stages of group development mentioned above. The following information details how a typical team might progress through these stages, and provides Raccoon Circle activities for exploring each stage of group development with the members of your team. Be sure to allow group discussion time after the completion of each activity. A manager or facilitator should also assist the group in understanding how each activity is significant in relation to the particular stage of group development that it explores.

The Forming Stage

This is the polite, opening, get acquainted, ice breaking stage of group development. This process begins at the moment new team members begin to assemble for the first time. The opening meeting, the general welcome comments from the manager, the facility orientation session and even the informal discussions after the initial gathering are all part of the forming stage. At this point, members of the group are just trying to identify who's who, and possibly where they fit into that plan. The true goal of the team may be unclear at this time. There is little communication initially. This stage includes forming an atmosphere of safety and acceptance, avoiding controversy, and should be filled with guidance and direction from the manager or facilitator.

Activities for the Forming Stage

Get acquainted and community building activities are used here to form the atmosphere of safety and acceptance. A few more activities are suggested in this stage because it is important to build a strong foundation if the rest of the stages are to be successfully navigated.

Believe It or Knot

Thanks to Mike Anderson for this excellent activity that is a simple variation of Two Truths and a Lie. With the entire group holding a Raccoon Circle (either seated or standing), the knot is used as a pointer to identify the person talking. Begin by passing the knot to the right around the group. Someone says "stop!" and when the knot stops the person nearest to the knot is invited to disclose some interesting fact about themselves, such as, "I have a twin sister!" It is now the discussion and responsibility of the rest of the participants to decide whether they believe that this information is true or false. Group members can ask the person speaking a total of three questions. After some discussion, the group gives their opinion of the validity or falseness of the disclosure, and then the person providing the comment tells the truth.

After a person has revealed the true nature of their comments (true or false), they say "left" or "right" and then "stop!" and a new person has the opportunity to disclose something to the group.

The level of disclosure to the group is often a measure of the closeness, unity and respect within the group. For example, a disclosure such as, "I have been with this company for 3 years," is a lower level of disclosure than "I need to be better at my job for this project to succeed." Depending on the group setting, and the purpose of this activity for your group, different levels of information or disclosure are appropriate. As the group becomes more unified, this activity can bring out greater disclosure between members of the project team ("I'm not sure if I have enough resources to complete my part of the project on time.")

Where Ya From? Where Ya Been?

Where Ya From? Where Ya Been? has become a great way for each member of a group to share 'their story.' One at a time, each member of the group (with the help of all other group members) create the outline of where they are originally from, or similarly someplace they have recently visited, using a knotted Raccoon Circle. After forming the geographic outline of that location, they then tell stories about this important place in their life.

W.A.M.F. (Wrapped Around My Finger)

W.A.M.F. stands for Wrapped Around My Finger, and pretty much explains this entire activity. Begin with an unknotted segment of webbing. One person in the group begins wrapping the webbing around their index finger, and while doing so, provides the group with some information about themselves (where they were born, family members, school experiences, childhood pets, dreams, goals, favorite foods, etc.) The goal is for this person to continue talking until the webbing is completely wrapped around their finger. When they reach the end, they allow the webbing to unwind and pass it along to the next person in the group.

This particular activity provides a bit more time for folks to talk about themselves, and also provides a kinesthetic activity coupled with a verbal activity for exploring multiple intelligence opportunities and whole brain learning possibilities. There is also a popular theory that for folks that may be a bit shy about speaking to even a small group in public, the action of wrapping the webbing around their finger occupies that portion of the brain where nervousness occurs. By wrapping and rapping at the same time, the speech center becomes less inhibited and the person talking is less stressed. It is also surprising what participants discuss during this wrapping and rapping session. The 15 foot length of the Raccoon Circle allows more than a minutes worth of communication, which means you'll learn quite a bit more about a person than just their name and where they are from.

You can find additional 'forming' stage activities in the icebreaker chapter of Section I of this book.

The Storming Stage

This second stage of group development introduces conflict and competition into the formerly safe and pleasant work environment. In many corporate settings, this stage typically is encountered around week two. Why week two? Because that is when most project team members have had the weekend to think about the resources and requirements of the job ahead. Suddenly those things which didn't seem to matter, begin to matter, and conflicts arise. There may be confusion over personal and team goals or responsibilities. Team members may lack the team skills to deal with conflict. Staff behavior ranges from silence to domination in this environment, and a project leader, manager or facilitator needs to effectively coach to successfully move through this stage.

Activities for the Storming Stage

While some project team members would rather avoid the conflict of this stage, it is important to build skills and show them how to cope and deal with the storming stage. The activities in this section, therefore, contain just a bit of stress (so that the door may be 'opened' to discuss what is really going on). The following activities are very challenging, and need to have a suitable amount of time after each one for discussion within the group.

Photo Finish

Thanks to Sam Sikes for this seemingly simple but yet complex activity. You can find this and other activities in his book, Executive Marbles (www.doingworks.com).

Photo Finish (or 'The Finish Line') uses one or more Raccoon Circles as a straight line. The task is for the members of a group to ALL cross the line at exactly the same time. You can additionally "stress" the group by minimizing the available space that they have to plan prior to crossing the finish line.

Tell the group that they have 15 minutes to make 5 attempts to cross the finish line at exactly the same time. This is a great opportunity to use a digital camera for instant feedback. Every time someone breaks the plane of the finish line, the facilitator yells, "Click!" even for the occasionally careless mistake.

This activity involves planning, communication, timing and occasionally the ability to deal with frustration.

Cross the Line

This activity requires a single straight line. With half of the group on one side of the line and standing about 6 feet (2 meters) behind the line, and the other half of the team on the other side, the scene is set for a moment of conflict (of "us" vs. "them"). Make no mistake, this activity is a bit higher level than most, but it is excellent for setting the stage to talk about conflict, negotiation and win/win, win/lose, and lose/lose scenarios.

Tom Heck calls this activity, "Their Ain't No Flies On Me!", and begins this activity by having one side say, "There ain't no flies on me, there ain't no flies on me, there might be flies on you (point to folks on the other side), but there ain't no flies on me!", and then boldly taking a step towards the line (with just the right amount of attitude). The other side now replies, "there ain't no flies on me, there ain't no flies on me, there might be flies on you (pointing at the other folks), but there ain't no flies on me!", and takes a step towards the line. The first side now repeats with twice the attitude, and moves to the line, followed by the second side repeating their lines, and stepping face to face with the other side.

The facilitator now says, "you have 3 seconds to get the person across the line from you onto your side of the line. GO!"

Typically, this phrasing results in a rather quick tug of war between partners, and usually a physical solution (for one person at least) to the challenge. This provides an excellent opportunity to open the door for discussion on conflict, challenges, attitude, negotiation, and how to resolve differences between people. For example, you can ask, "how many partner teams ended up in a win/lose scenario, where one member obtained what they wanted (getting their partner to their side), but the other member did not?" "What about a lose/lose scenario, where both members struggled, but neither one obtained their goal?" And finally, "were there any teams that achieved a win/win solution, where both partners changed sides?" "What is it about our corporate culture that so many members of our team end up in win/lose or lose/lose scenarios, rather than a win/win solution?" "How can we fix this situation?" The next time you are in a 'cross the line' situation, what is the first thing you will do to avoid a win/lose or lose/lose scenario?

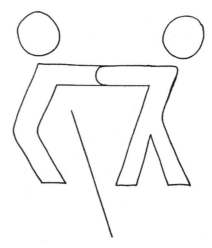

Blind Square

In a safe environment (large open carpeted room with no obstacles, or perhaps a flat grassy outdoor space) blindfold the entire group (or ask each person to close their eyes) and allow them to search as a group and find a nearby collection of five, seven or nine segments of Raccoon Circles tied together into one long 'rope.' The reason for using an odd number of Raccoon Circles will become evident during the activity. If exactly four or eight Raccoon Circles are used, the four corners of the square are easy to find using the water knots as a guide. Odd numbers of Raccoon Circles (and water knots) makes this task a bit more difficult—which is important in the storming stage of group development.

After finding this 'rope,' instruct the group that their goal, while still blindfolded, is to create a perfect square using the entire rope. You might continue and remind the group that a square geometrically consists of a closed shape with four equal length sides, and four 90 degree corners. Participants are allowed to slide along the length of the rope, but cannot let go, change sides, or move around another participant.

This simple to explain but extremely difficult and time consuming to complete activity works best with a group of about a 10-15 participants. You can choose to invite one person to 'observe' the group, but not assist them in the completion of their task, and then to share their observations when the group has finished. The storming stage of this activity will be very obvious. Communication breakdowns, leadership abilities, directions, power issues and resource constraints all contribute to team member frustration and often make what appears to be a simple task infinitely more difficult. If establishing realistic scheduling goals is appropriate for this project team, then ask them to estimate a 'time till completion' for creating this rope square. If establishing quality standards, or work performance standards is realistic, then ask them to establish (while blindfolded), the performance criteria on how they will measure the outcome of this rope square project. If team members are likely to encounter limitations in technology, wrong or misleading information, or confusion during their project work, consider tying one end of the rope permanently to a tree, fence, car or other non-moving object.

After the group has reached the end (notice, I didn't say 'completed' the activity), here are a few ideas to discuss: Was the time estimate reasonable given the task? What was most of the time spent doing? What was the 'breakthrough' point in this activity? Were all members of the group equally engaged in the activity? Did some members of the group have more 'power' than others? If the group was asked to create another shape blindfolded, do you think you could be more efficient? Quicker? Accurate? This stage of group development is called the Storming stage. What types of team behaviors did you notice during this activity that tells you the group was storming? What skills do you have now that you can use in the workplace when tasks become frustrating or difficult?

The Norming Stage

This third stage of group development is typically a welcome breath of fresh air after the storming stage. Although the team is not yet at the high performing stage, some of the bugs are beginning to be worked out within the group and good things are beginning to happen. Team members gain confidence in their personal and team goals and responsibilities. This stage of group development includes cohesion, sharing and trust building, creativity and skill acquisition. The manager or facilitator demonstrates support during this stage.

Activities for the Norming Stage

Sharing, trust building and skill building activities are used in the Norming stage.

Inside Out

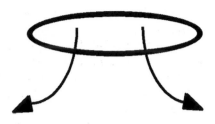

This is a great initial problem solving activity. Begin with a Raccoon Circle (15 foot long rope, tied into a circle) on the floor. Have the entire group step inside the circle. The task now is for the entire group to go from the inside of the circle to the outside, by going underneath the Raccoon Circle, without anyone in the group using their arms, shoulders, or hands.

What is important in this activity, is to stress the group problem solving process. In order for other members of the group to assist in the completion of the task, they need to know the plan, and what their part is in the solution.

To this end, encourage the group to "plan their work" and then "work their plan." This means that prior to ANY action, the group will need to plan their approach to solving this problem, and making sure that everyone in the group knows their part of the plan.

After completing the task, debriefing questions include asking the group if they had a plan, and did they change the plan during the completion of the activity, and if so, why? As a second part to this activity, you can also ask the group to go Outside In, again without using their hands, arms or shoulders . . . and see if they "plan their work" before "working their plan."

Finally, Inside Out can be used to explore ethical behavior in the workplace. At a time when corporate responsibility and financial accounting irregularities both make the business headlines, ethical behavior is certainly important. Once the group has returned into the circle, ask if they 'followed the rules.' Most will likely nod their heads yes. Then ask if anyone used their arms, shoulders or hands to complete the task. For example, to crawl on their hands and knees (see picture). Or to assist another member of their group, by holding them up. Suddenly some folks will realize that they interpreted the rules to mean, "not to touch the Raccoon Circle with our arms, shoulders or hands." This is an excellent opportunity to discuss the publics perception of this groups ability to follow rules, corporate guidelines, policies, civil ordinances or federate mandates.

Not Knots

In this activity, which can be accomplished with only a single piece of webbing (in a straight line, without a water knot), a "doodle" is constructed (see example below) and the group is given the choice of whether this doodle will create a KNOT or NOT A KNOT, when the ends of the webbing are pulled.

The object here is to provide the group with some tools to use when they cannot easily form a consensus. Typically, upon analysis, about half of the group thinks the doodle will form a knot, and the other half a straight line. If this is the case, ask participants to partner with another person that has a different viewpoint (i.e. one partner from the KNOT side, and one partner from the NOT A KNOT side). By learning how to listen to a person with a different viewpoint, group members learn how to cooperate. After this discussion, ask participants to choose sides, with the KNOT decision folks on one side of the knot doodle, and the NOT A KNOT folks on the other side.

At this point, it is likely that there will still not be a complete consensus within the group. Prior to slowly pulling the ends of the knot doodle, let the members of the group know that you will pull the knot doodle slowly, and that they can change sides at any time during the unraveling of the knot doodle (this illustrates the ability to make an initial decision, but still be flexible as more information becomes available). This is also a good time to discuss 'risk taking' on the job, and what the risk is of choosing what might be the wrong side.

Which Side of the Road are You On?

For corporate audiences, The Bus can be transformed into a corporate vehicle for making decisions. Which Side of the Road Are You On? invites participants to actively make decisions. The decisions to be made have been chosen specifically to meet the needs of the group. In this case, the more job related, the better.

Which Side of the Road are You On? requires a central gathering place and two boundary lines made from unknotted Raccoon Circles. Participants begin 'standing in the middle of the road.' As the first company truck comes barreling down the road, loaded with information for your project, team members must decide which side of the road they should be on. Some of the following decisions are fairly easy and the information content doesn't have severe consequences. Others may make or break the entire project. After choosing sides, give project team members a minute to see who is on the same side of the road with them, and to discuss why they chose this particular side.

PC		Macintosh
Loud		Quiet
Running	the	Walking
Fixed Salary	middle	Salary + Incentives
Fixed Schedule	of the	Flex Time
Group Decisions	road	Individual Contributor
Problem Solver		Problem Maker
Zero Travel Days per Year		Travel Far and Wide

The object here is to team members to make a fixed choice. Either / Or. Obviously team members can be on 'different sides of the road,' on some issues. These issues bear additional discussion. Be careful to choose topics appropriately for the audience that you are serving. This activity can be used with even large project teams, provided the folks in the middle of the road can hear when the truck is coming!

This activity also provides the opportunity for a bit of group discussion throughout the process. For example, were some folks left 'in the middle of the road' and only saved by another person pulling them to safety as the information truck came speeding towards them? Or did they become 'corporate roadkill?' Did some folks change their minds during a particular decision, and then change sides? Is there always a right and wrong side of the road, or more appropriately, two possible choices, both of which have merit? Does the entire project team need to be on the same side of a particular issue for the team to move forward successfully? How would you go about trying to get everyone on the team on the same side of the road for a key project decision?

In the book *Good to Great*, Jim Collins talks about 'getting the right people on the bus and the wrong people off the bus,' and then 'getting the right people into the right seats.' This activity can be used to explore where some members of your project team choose to be on specific team or management issues, but you might want to wait for the 'storming' stage of group development to bring this up, rather then here in the safe environment of the 'forming' stage. Thanks to Tom Heck for sharing this activity.

Good to Great—Why Some Companies Make the Leap . . . and Others Don't, 2001, Jim Collins, Harper Collins, New York, NY USA ISBN 0-06-662099-6

Jump!

Here is a forced choice activity that provides plenty of action. Locate three knotted Raccoon Circles on the ground. Designate one circle 'A,' another circle 'B' and the third circle 'C.'

Next, ask the group a series of questions and ask them to quickly move to the location that best represents their choice of answer. Once each group has gathered, ask them to discuss their choice of answer and why they personally chose it. For example, which of the following technologies is the best for communicating critical issues with the rest of the team: A) email, B) voicemail, C) in person.

You can find a wide variety of useful questions in the following books:

The Book of Questions, 1987, Gregory Stock, Workman Publishing, New York, NY USA ISBN 0-89480-320-4

The Book of Questions: Business, Politics and Ethics, 1991, Gregory Stock, Workman Publishing, New York, NY USA ISBN 0-56305-034-X

If . . . (Questions for the Game of Life), 1995, Evelyn McFarlance & James Saywell, Villard Books, New York, NY USA ISBN 0-679-44535-8

Think Twice—An Entertaining Collection of Choices, 1998, Bret Nicholaus and Paul Lowrie, Ballantine Books, New York, NY USA ISBN 0-345-41759-3

The Conversation Pie—Creative Questions to Tickle the Mind, 1996, Bret Nicholaus and Paul Lowrie, Ballantine Books, New York, NY USA ISBN 0-345-40711-3

The Performing Stage

The fourth stage of group development provides a feeling of unity, group identity, interdependence and independence. It is the most highly productive stage. Leadership from the manager or facilitator comes in the form of delegation. The team has all the skills, resources and talent needed to take full responsibility and to complete the task.

Activities for the Performing Stage

Continuous improvement, celebration of success and empowerment are found in this stage.

Grand Prix Racing

Turn the Raccoon Circle into a complete circle or loop using a water knot, and you are ready for the ultimate in sport racing. Thanks to Tom Heck for not only the idea for this activity, but also the enthusiasm to lead it effectively. This activity will boost the enthusiasm of your audience, and provide some moderate competition in the process.

Begin by spreading several Raccoon Circles around the available space, in close proximity to each other. Ask participants to join one of the "racing teams", picking their favorite color team in the process. Approximately five to eight participants per Raccoon Circle. Have participants hold the Raccoon Circle with both hands in front of them.

"Ladies and Gentlemen! It is summertime, and that means one thing in this part of the world— Grand Prix Racing ! Now I know that you are such die-hard race fans that just the thought of a race makes your heart beat faster. So this race comes in three parts. First, when I say that "we're going to have a race", your response is loud, "Yahoo!!!!!" Next I'll say, start your engines! and I want to hear your best race car sounds (audience practices making race car revving engine, shifting gears and braking sounds).

Finally, with so many cars on the track today, it will be difficult to see just which group finishes their race first, so we'll need a sign indicating when your group is finished. That sign is to raise your hands (and the Raccoon Circle) above your heads and yell "Yessssssssss!"

Logistically, Grand Prix involves having the group transfer the knot around the group as quickly as possible, using only their hands. This activity can even be performed for a seated audience. To begin, you'll need a "start / finish" line, which can be the person that was born the farthest distance away from the present location. The race begins at this location, and ends when the knot is passed around the circle, and returns to this same location (Yesssssss!)

Typically in Raccoon Circle Grand Prix racing, there are three qualifying rounds or races. The first race is a single lap race to the right, with the knot traveling once around the inside of the circle to the right (counterclockwise). The second race is a multi-lap race (two or three laps) to the left (clockwise) around the circle. And the final race of the series, is a "winner take all" championship race, with one lap to the right (counterclockwise) followed by one lap to the left (clockwise).

Incidentally, after this activity, the group will not only be energized, but perhaps in a slightly competitive mood. From a sequencing standpoint, you can either continue this atmosphere (with more competitive challenges—such as a volleyball game, or corporate olympics) or introduce a bit of counterpoint, by following this activity with one that requires the group working together in a collaborative manner.

The Electric Box

Here is a great variation of the traditional spider web, or Window of Opportunity activity, and one that requires a bit more planning and strategy. The Electric Box is simply a raccoon circle opening through which the entire team must pass. The unusual feature of this Electric Box however, is that it starts as a vertical rectangle and ends up as a horizontal rectangle. For each person passing through the Electric Box, the box changes shape. This is a great 'Who Moved My Cheese' activity, and definitely one that requires planning to navigate the changing environment of the Electric Box.

Who Moved My Cheese?, 1998, Spencer Johnson, Penguin Putnam, New York, NY USA ISBN 0-399-14446-3

The Transforming Stage

The final stage of group development is the other bookend to the initial forming stage. The transforming stage allows the group to regroup, thank the participants and move on at the completion of the project or task. This stage is marked by recognition by the facilitator and a conclusion followed by disengagement of the team members.

Activities for the Transforming Stage

Allow for the completion and conclusion of the group process. Feelings of celebration and affirmation are suitable. Different team members may experience this final stage at different rates. Don't rush for closure. For some team members, this project may have been the highlight of their career to date. The first two activities, A Circle of Kindness and A Circle of Connection incorporate appropriate contact between team members, and for many teams (nurses, primary care givers, teachers and other 'hands-on' professionals) this style is fine. The final activity, The Learning Rope, has no contact between team members, is largely verbal, and may be used in settings where less contact is desired.

A Circle of Kindness

With half of the group standing in a circle holding the Raccoon Circle, the other half stands just behind them (one person in the outer circle behind a person in the inner circle). The inside circle closes their eyes, and the outer circle has the opportunity to express a positive comment to their inside circle partner. For tactile audiences (in other words, where appropriate), the outer circle can place their hands on the shoulders of their inner circle partners, and whisper into their ears. Typical comments might include, "it was great meeting you, thanks for joining our group this week, I am looking forward to working with you, thanks for your help with the problem solving activity—I couldn't have done it without you!" This activity however is NOT a two-way conversation—the only response from the inner circle is "thank you." This avoids breaking the mood with laughter, giggling or any other fun but disruptive conversation.

When finished, outside circle participants move one person to their right, until they have encountered all the inside circle participants. Then the inner and outer circles trade places and the process is repeated.

A Circle of Connection

A special thanks to Dick Hammond for sharing this wonderful activity. A leader begins by introducing themselves and sharing some of their contributions, such as, "I was responsible for the software on this project. I worked at least a dozen evenings past 5 PM to get the job done. I traveled more in the last six months than I have in the past six years." At some point, one of these revelations is sure to be shared by at least one other member of the group. When this happens, the first person to link elbows with the previous person introduces themselves and begins to share some of their contributions to the group. The activity continues until all members of the group have 'linked together.' The final task is for the last person to continue sharing until the first person can link with them. At this point, there is an opportunity to say, "well, I think this project certainly brought us all a bit closer together. Thank you everyone. Goodbye."

You can find this and other teambuilding activities without props in the book: The Empty Bag—Non-Stop, No-Prop Adventure-Based Activities for Community Building, 2003, Chris Cavert and Dick Hammond, FUNdoing Publications ISBN 0-9746442-1-8.

The Learning Rope

Thanks to Chris Cavert for this innovative technique for remembering the teachable moments encountered during a program or project.

Throughout the project, each time a new skill or learning experience is encountered, the group places a single knot onto the learning rope. Before a new knot is added, the group reviews all previous knots to insure that the learning is not lost. At the end of the project, untie each knot as the group identifies and reflects on each of the things they have learned working together. As an alternative, instead of untying each knot, the manager or facilitator can cut the learning rope and present each member of the team with one of the knots as a reminder of their contribution to the team.

This concludes our discussion of the stages of group development and the use of Raccoon Circles to explore these stages with a team.

For additional Raccoon Circle activities for the forming stage, see the icebreakers, introductions and get-acquainted activities chapter of Section I of this book.

For activities that explore the skill building (norming & performing) stages, see the team challenges, active learning, adventure-based activities and games chapter of Section I.

For discussion and group bonding activities useful throughout the stages of group development, and especially in the transforming stage, see the processing, debriefing, reviewing, reflection and closing activities chapter in Section I.

Processing, Debriefing, Reviewing, Reflection and Closing Activities With Raccoon Circles

This section includes discussion, processing, debriefing, reviewing, reflection and closing activities using Raccoon Circles and is intended to help the facilitator bring a greater value to the program and a richer experience for each participant. The size of a Raccoon Circle is also ideal for bringing the participants closer together and allowing everyone to hear each other. Even if all participants are not actively talking during this part of the program, they remain "connected" to the group via the Raccoon Circle. Don't be afraid of silence when connected to the Raccoon Circle, many times the Raccoon Circle speaks for itself!

Number	Activity Name	Type of Activity
1	Starting with the Circle	Demonstration of What Joining the Circle Means
2	Experiential Learning Models	Teaching, Learning and Visualizing Through Models
3	The Power Line	Discussion
4	Elevation (Voting)	Analysis, Visualization, Voicing Your Opinion
5	Let's Ask the Raccoon	Processing and Debriefing, Choice
6	A Circular Story	Discussion, Reflection, Sharing, Storytelling
7	It's Knot Our Problem, is it?	Discussion
8	The Circle Speaks for Itself	Debriefing, Sharing
9	The Labyrinth	Reflection, Inner Peace, Quietness
10	Reflection with Music	Reflection, Inspiration, Connection
11	Worms	Allowing each voice to be heard
12	Step Into the Circle	Creating a space to be heard
13	One Word	A fast debriefing technique
14	Knot Race	Taking your turn
15	Question Marks	Framed Reflection
16	Shuffle Left / Shuffle Right	A Kinesthetic Debriefing Technique
17	Lots of Knots	Combining Thinking & Doing
17a	Available Space	Reviewing with a Time Crunch
18	Plus / Delta	A Group Debriefing Technique
19	Wrapping & Rapping	Active Communication
20	The Learning Rope	Remembering the Debrief
21	Engagement	A Lesson for the Road
22	Reviewing Activities	Nine Techniques Shared by Roger Greenaway
23	A Circle of Connection	Bringing Us All Together
24	The Final Transmission	Closing Activity, Movement and Goodbyes
25	A Circle of Kindness	Kind Words and Expressions
26	Bits and Pieces	Processing and Debriefing
27	A Gathering of Raccoons	Movement, Connection and Closure

For additional debriefing activities for your teambuilding programs, read: A Teachable Moment—A Facilitator's Guide to Activities for Processing, Debriefing, Reviewing and Reflection, 2005, Jim Cain, Michelle Cummings and Jennifer Stanchfield, Kendall / Hunt Publishers, Dubuque, Iowa USA (Telephone 1-800-228-0810) ISBN 0-7575-1782-X.

Visit the following websites for additional processing, debriefing, reviewing and reflection ideas:

www.reviewing.co.uk	Roger Greenaway's reviewing website
www.training-wheels.com	Michelle Cumming's debriefing website
www.teamworkandteamplay.com	Jim Cain's teambuilding website
www.ateachablemoment.com	Combined website of the authors

1. Starting with the Circle

In addition to the many teambuilding and problem solving activities involving the Raccoon Circle, one of the most interesting uses is for the debriefing or reviewing process that typically follows a teambuilding or adventure-based learning activity. By its nature, the Raccoon Circle brings a group closer together. For teachers and camp counselors that are tired of saying over and over, "ok kids, let's get in a circle, a circle, c'mon, shoulder to shoulder, a circle please . . ." the Raccoon Circle provides an easier method, "ok everyone, grab on!" or as Tom Smith would say, "connect up!" The result is a close circular shape, with everyone attached, connected, visible to the rest of the group, and at a distance where conversation can easily occur without shouting.

There is a great method to demonstrate how each member of a group has an effect on every other member. With all participants holding the Raccoon Circle, the facilitator joins them and shakes the Raccoon Circle. Notice that not only the participants near the facilitator are "disturbed" by this motion, but that it is transferred to everyone in the circle-the same way that negative comments affect not only the folks that hear them, but eventually everyone in the group. Next have everyone in the group, including the facilitator, pull lightly on the Raccoon Circle, so that they are balanced and leaning slightly backwards. If the facilitator now decides to let go, another type of disruptive wave goes through the group, disturbing the balance and again, affecting every one of the participants in the group. So, being a part of the group, hanging in there so to speak, is both helpful and important to the success of the whole group.

2. Experiential Learning Models

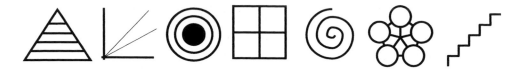

Within the field of experiential teaching, active learning, adventure-based education and corporate training, there are significant models that graphically illustrate key group concepts and Raccoon Circles can be used to create visual representations of these models. According to the now classic research of Edgar Dale of The Ohio State University, the greater the level of student involvement in the learning process, the greater the retention of the information presented. By using Raccoon Circles to create visual models for your participants, you increase their involvement with the material presented and their retention of this information.

A sampling of visual models is shown above. The three circle 'target' can be used to represent the comfort zone model. The spiral can be used to represent Tom Smith's version of 'the spiral journey' model. The pyramid can be used to illustrate Edgar Dale's 'cone of learning,' Abraham Maslow's hierarchy of human needs, or even the more recent 'Five Dysfunctions of a Team' model described by Patrick Lencioni. Other visuals, such as the four square window can be used for the Johari Window or the Situational Leadership model. The five circle illustration can demonstrate the five components of the experiential learning process or the five stages of group development. In each case, Raccoon Circles can be used to enhance the presentation of each of these models and to increase the retention of this information to your students and participants.

A Sampling of Valuable Models

Model Name	Subject Matter	Credited to
Cone of Learning	Retention of Information	Edgar Dale
Hierarchy of Human Needs	Human Needs & Motivation	Abraham Maslow
Team Dysfunctions	It all begins with trust	Patrick Lencioni
The Experiential Learning Process	How Learning Occurs	David Kolb, et. al.
The Stages of Group Development	How Groups Progress	Tuckman and Jensen
The Comfort Zone Model	Comfort, Growth & Panic	Reldan, Nadler, et. al.
The Spiral Journey	Alternative to Comfort Zone	Tom Smith
Between Boredom & Anxiety	Optimal Experience	Mihalyi Csikszentmihalyi
The Situational Leadership Curve	Direction vs. Readiness	Hersey and Blanchard
A Window of Opportunity	Disclosure & Feedback	Luft and Ingham
Bloom's Taxonomy	Levels of Cognitive Learning	Benjamin Bloom

References and Resources for these Models

Cone of Learning

Edgar Dale, a Professor of Education at The Ohio State University conducted research that illustrated an improvement in the retention of information with higher levels of learning involvement. This work was originally published as: *Audio Visual Methods for Teaching,* Edgar Dale, 1956, Holt, Rinehart and Winston, New York, NY USA. For institutions using primarily readings and lectures to present information to students, there is an opportunity to double or even triple the retention rate by using active learning to increase the level of student involvement in the learning process.

Hierarchy of Human Needs

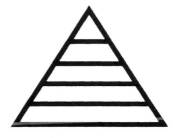

From the standpoint of Abraham Maslow's hierarchy of needs, there is a basic level of agreement that unless the most basic needs are met, it is difficult, and some say impossible, to achieve higher levels of fulfillment. In short, a trip up the hierarchy begins with basic physiological needs (such as sleep and shelter), next are safety needs (protection against danger), followed by social needs, ego needs and self-fulfillment needs.

Another way of using Maslow's concept of a hierarchy of needs is to consider that unless we are able to provide for and meet the social needs of our students, the possibility of them achieving self esteem and fulfillment is pretty unlikely. Again, because of the nature of adventure-based learning, teamwork, and group unification, students are more likely to satisfy their need for social fulfillment and progress onto higher levels of learning, and learning retention, when this third level need is met. An ideal learning environment then, would be one which provides for the basic physiological and safety needs, and provides a community building, team or social environment before attempting to achieve the higher level task of learning (fulfilling the ego and self-fulfillment levels).

Motivation and Personality, Second Edition, Abraham Maslow, 1970, Harper & Row, New York, NY USA.

Great Writings in Management & Organization Behavior, Louis E. Boone, Consulting Editor, 1984, Macmillan Publishing, NY, NY USA Library of Congress Catalog Card Number 78-771-60. The chapter related to Maslow's hierarchy is entitled 'The Human Side of the Enterprise,' by Douglas M. McGregor.

Team Dysfunction

In his best-selling publications, author Patrick Lencioni provides a simple and valuable model for helping corporate teams work better together. He provides not only information and assessment tools, but also hints for overcoming the five dysfunctions he reports as: the absence of trust, fear of conflict, lack of commitment, avoidance of accountability and inattention to results. Each of these dysfunctions he assigns to one of the layers of the pyramid visual model, beginning with trust at the bottom. We recommend not only the best selling book, but also the field guide for facilitators.

The Five Dysfunctions of a Team–A Leadership Fable, 2002, Patrick Lencioni, Jossey-Bass, San Francisco, CA USA ISBN 0-7879-6075-6

Overcoming the Five Dysfunctions of a Team–A Field Guide for Leaders, Managers and Facilitators, 2005, Patrick Lencioni, Jossey-Bass, San Francisco, CA USA ISBN 0-7879-7637-7

The Experiential Learning Process

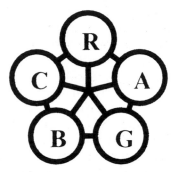

The experiential learning process discussed by such educators as Dewey, Piaget, Lewin and Kolb, and later embellished by many contributors discusses the cycle that initially begins with a concrete (C) experience (I am going to wait until payday to fill my car with gasoline). The result of this concrete experience (my car ran out of gas) provides the opportunity for some reflection (R) (that was a dumb thing to do). From this reflection comes the opportunity to analyze (A) the situation, the cause and effect relationships, and to abstract or generalize (G) this experience (even a small amount of gasoline would have kept me from having to walk for help in the rain). And finally, this generalization leads to developing new ideas and behaviors (B) for future (I'll make sure that I keep enough cash on hand to keep the car running).

A simplified model of the experiential learning cycle can be described in just three stages. The first stage, the Action Stage, involves some activity by the members of the group (we tried to complete the task we were given). The second stage, the Reaction or Reflection Stage, involves the group analyzing their previous actions, and the results or outcomes of these actions (we tried to complete the task individually, with limited success, but when we all worked together, it was easy). The third and final stage, the Application Stage, involves the group applying what they have learned from their actions and analysis, to new projects and situations (if we want future tasks to be easier to accomplish, we should try working together first).

By placing a Raccoon Circle on the ground, and having a participant physically move around the circle, the facilitator can explain the experiential learning process to the audience, in a very visual way. For clarity, you can provide knots at key locations around the circle to signify the various stages.

Experiential Learning–Experience as the Source of Learning and Development, 1984. David Kolb, Prentic Hall, Englewood Cliffs, New Jersey USA ISBN 0-13-295261-0.

Field Theory in Social Sciences, 1951, K. Lewin, Harper & Row, New York, NY USA

Experience and Education, 1938, John Dewey, Kappa Delta Pi, MacMillian Publishing, New York, NY USA

"I believe that the school is primarily a social institution. Education being a social process, the school is simply that form of community life in which all those agencies are concentrated that will be most effective in bringing the child to share in the inherited resources of the race, and to use his own powers for social ends."

John Dewey, My Pedagogic Creed
in John Dewey on Education—Selected Writings, page 430.
Edited by Reginald D. Archambault

"It is a commonplace that everyone talks about Dewey and no one reads him."

Reginald D. Archambault
John Dewey on Education—Selected Writings

The Stages of Group Development

A conceptual model of group development is presented by Bruce Tuckman. These stages idealize some of the rather complicated group behavior experienced within a group during their time together, but provides a simplified method for analyzing where the group is presently, how they are interacting, and even provides some ideas for successfully navigating through each stage of development.

As shown in our model, the five stages include: forming, storming, norming, performing and transforming (sometimes referred to as adjourning or reforming). In each stage, a facilitator must understand the needs of the group and how to assist them as they continue on their path together. For example, in the forming stage a facilitator provides guidance and direction to the group. The table below provides additional information and suggestions for facilitators.

To visually illustrate the stages of group development, place five Raccoon Circles of different colors on the ground or floor, along with a sign identifying the various stages. During your experiential activities, participants can discuss at what stage the group is in, and how to move forward in the process. Don't be surprised, very few groups move straight forward through the entire process. Sometimes, even after achieving the "performing" stage, it is possible for the group to slip back into the "storming" stage. This also occurs when team members change, new members arrive, or external situations alter the task or direction of the group.

Tuckman, Bruce, 1965, "Developmental sequence of small groups," *Psychological Bulletin,* Number 63, pages 384-399. The classic original paper.

Tuckman, Bruce. & Jenson, Mary Ann, 1977, "Stages of small group development revisited," *Group and Organizational Studies,* Number 2, pages 419–427.

Tuckman, Bruce, 2001, Developmental Sequence in Small Groups, *Group Facilitation,* Number 3, Spring, pages 66–81. A look back, nearly 35 years after the original ground-breaking paper. Required reading for all group facilitators.

For additional information on the stages of group development, see 'Exploring the Stages of Group Development with Raccoon Circle Activities' in Section I of this book

Comfort Zones

Using three unknotted Raccoon Circles (you'll see why later) of different colors, create a series of concentric circles, much like a target. The area within the innermost circle represent the comfort zone—that area where the individual feels perfectly fine about the situation at hand. "Need me to help you carry that chair to the kitchen? No problem! It is within my comfort zone."

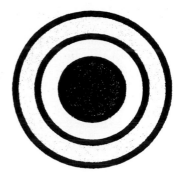

The area within the middle circle represents the growth zone— that space where I am trying something new, but I am not overly nervous or anxious about it. "So, the kitchen that you want the chair in is in your new house down the street. Ok, I am a bit short on time, but I'll help you do it. Not exactly within my comfort zone, definitely within my growth zone, but hey, what are friends for?"

The area within the third circle represents the danger or panic zone—the space where the challenge or experience is so physically or emotionally risky that I just can't go there. "You mean the kitchen in your new house 'down the street' is 1000 miles (1600 kilometers) down the street! No way! I'm not doing it!"

The area outside the third circle is sometimes referred to as the twilight zone—the space that most of us are not even aware of. The things in this space are so far off our radar that we don't even recognize them.

Now for most of us, we begin within the comfort zone, and increase the size of that zone as we experience new things in life, journeying into the growth zones (new experiences, college, meeting new people), and occasionally finding ourselves in the panic zone. But consider a model where the first time you see a challenge course, you are in the twilight zone. You have no previous experience with such a thing, and as a result, you have no fear or interest. "Oh, a challenge course? That's nice."

Next you enter the panic zone. "You mean we are going to climb all the way up there, and jump off?!?! NOT ME!" A little knowledge is a dangerous thing. At this point, you have learned just enough about the challenge course for your self preservation instincts to kick in.

As your journey continues, you find yourself moving into the growth zone, mostly due to the amount of information and learning you have experienced. "Oh, I see. We are going to be wearing safety gear, and those folks at the other end of the rope are specially trained. Oh, well, that makes a difference. I'm still a bit nervous, maybe I'll just watch for a few minutes, but I want to try."

Finally, after you have had the opportunity to climb, or zip, or help another partner high above the ground, you can say, "No problem, I've done that. Want to see me do it again, piece of cake." Welcome back to your comfort zone.

The goal then is to continuously make our comfort zone bigger and bigger. By using untied Raccoon Circles, it is possible to show the group how they can increase the size of their comfort zone as they gain confidence through new life experiences.

The Spiral Journey

Using a single unknotted Raccoon Circle create a spiral pattern. Tom Smith uses the spiral journey rather more often than the comfort zone model, because this version implies a journey or movement, rather than a static 'fenced in area.' Participants find themselves somewhere along the spiral, moving outward, towards new experiences and greater risk, moving inward towards greater security and comfort, or not moving but rather in a holding pattern, as they await the strength, the information, the courage or the self preservation instincts to begin moving in one direction or the other. In this case, it is not the location on the spiral that is important, but rather the direction that the person is moving.

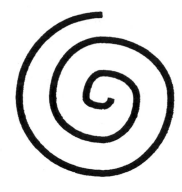

Between Anxiety and Boredom

There are two models which illustrate the concept of achieving the "sweet spot" in a learning or experiential activity. The concept of peak learning (also known as optimal alertness or arousal), and Mihaly Csikszentmihalyi's work on the concept of 'flow.' Both illustrate that somewhere between boredom and anxiety, a student achieves the optimal situation for learning or experiencing the moment.

Imagine that you are asked to learn how to print the block letters of the alphabet. For many of us, this simple task is so easy that we are bored by both the subject matter and the activity. Now imagine that you are asked to learn how to perform a rather complicated medical procedure and that you will actually be required to demonstrate this procedure later today on a live patient. For many of us, the seriousness of this request, and the potential risk involved creates some anxiety. The flow and optimal arousal models propose that only when a student is somewhere between these two extremes, are they in the position of peak learning. Someplace where the skills possessed by the student and the skills required by the task are well matched. Our goal then, is to design our experiential learning, active learning and adventure-based educational programs to challenge and excite students, without overcomplicating the issues. Only then will we achieve peak learning.

A good method for visually illustrating this point with Raccoon Circles is to create the XY axis of a graph, where the X-axis reflects the skill level held by the learner, and the Y-axis measures the skill level required by the task. The space between the two straight line segments identifies the optimal learning space, the flow region, and the peak learning opportunity. In this region, the skills possessed by the student, and the skills required by the task are perfectly matched. Travel above the top line, and the student's skills no longer match those required and anxiety results. Travel below the bottom line, and the student experiences no challenge and is bored.

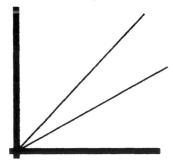

There is also a great opportunity here for discussing how within a group some members can be bored, some anxious, and some at optimal learning potential. Elementary classroom teachers know this well. For the high elements on a challenge course, asking participants to now stand where they feel they are (on the ground graph) gives the entire group a sense of the diversity of the group. Asking the group, "so how will we take care of each other to make sure we are all challenge and safe today," is a great way of understanding the diversity of the group, and helping them be aware of each other's needs and abilities.

Flow–The Psychology of Optimal Experience, 1990, Mihaly Csikszentmihalyi, Harper Perennial, New York, NY USA ISBN 0-06-016253-8

The Situational Leadership Curve

Based upon the writings of Hersey and Blanchard, Situational Leadership suggests that the proper leadership technique for any given situation is dependant upon the task and relationship needs of the team in that situation. This model progresses from the 'telling' and 'selling' stages to increasing levels of empowerment in the 'participating' and 'delegating' stages.

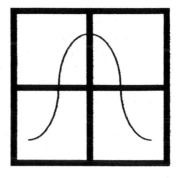

For more information on this model, read: *Management of Organizational Behavior: Utilizing Human Resources,* Fourth Edition, by P. Hersey and K. Blanchard, 1982, Prentice-Hall, Englewood Cliffs, NJ USA.

A Window of Opportunity

When group members share information about themselves, their dreams, fears, goals, they form "connections" with the other members of the group. When other members of the group identify with these same dreams, fears and goals, they build on these commonalities, and create an atmosphere of unity and an open arena for discussion and sharing. In more recent years, concepts such as 360 degree feedback (where an employee is evaluated not only by their supervision, but also by their peers and subordinates), have welcomed in the possibilities of open communication.

In order for the members of a group to "connect," they need to open the window of opportunity to discussion. An individual can do two things to increase the connection between themselves and members of the group. First, they can disclose more information about themselves, so that all members of the group know this information. Secondly, they can receive more feedback from the group members, so they understand how they are perceived by the group.

A simplified manner of visualizing this concept was created by Joseph Luft and Harry Ingham and is known as the Johari Window. This simple window shape can be made from six untied Raccoon Circles. The four individual window panes reflect four levels of connection between the members of the group. The first pane is the information that both the individual and the group knows (he has brown eyes). The second pane is the information that the individual knows, but the group does not know (the name of my favorite artist). The third pane is the information that the group knows, but the individual does not know (the wind has blown your hair into a tangled mess). The fourth and final pane is the information that neither the individual or the group knows (unconscious memories).

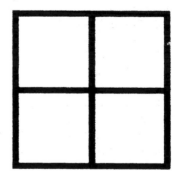

The goal for connection, is to make the first window pane as large as possible. To accomplish this, the individual needs to provide information to the group, and/or the group can provide information to the individual. In either case, the greater the exchange of information between members of the group and the individuals within the group, the greater the "connection" and the cohesive force that ultimately holds the group together.

For more information on the Johari Window, read: *Group processes: An introduction to group dynamics,* by Joseph Luft, 1970, Mayfield Publishing, Mountain View, California, USA.

The Johari Window: A model for soliciting and giving feedback, by P.G. Hanson, 1973, In The 1973 Annual Handbook for Group Facilitators, University Associates, San Diego, California, USA.

Bloom's Taxonomy

Bloom's taxonomy discusses various levels of learning and these can be illustrated using an unknotted Raccoon Circle in the shape of an ascending staircase. Next time you are pitching an adventure-based learning program, consider using this model to discuss which level the participants would like to achieve and the path or effort required to get there.

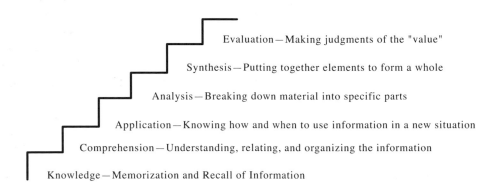

Levels in the Cognitive Domain—The Knowing Domain

Evaluation—Making judgments of the "value"

Synthesis—Putting together elements to form a whole

Analysis—Breaking down material into specific parts

Application—Knowing how and when to use information in a new situation

Comprehension—Understanding, relating, and organizing the information

Knowledge—Memorization and Recall of Information

Benjamin S. Bloom, *Taxonomy of Educational Objectives: The Classification of Educational Goals, Handbook I: Cognitive Domain,* 1956, David McKay Publishing, New York, NY USA

If you are interested in information from the affective domain, the feeling domain, read: D. R. Krathwohl, *Taxonomy of Educational Objectives, Handbook II: Affective Domain,* 1964, David McKay Publishing, New York, NY USA

3. The Power Line

What does an electrical power line or an extension cord do? It brings power from the source, to the location where it is needed. And that power can be used for a variety of useful purposes, such as lighting a sign, running a motor, powering a computer, creating light where there would be darkness, bringing warmth to cool environments and more. For this discussion activity, the Raccoon Circle is a type of extension cord and the members of the group can access that power simply by holding on. With the entire group attached to the Raccoon Circle, participants can discuss what "power" they would like to have and how they would use that power for the greater good.

4. Elevation

At some point, the facilitator may wish to ask the group a question so that they can decide where to take the group next. Using a single Raccoon Circle, and with everyone 'connected,' ask the group their views on the topic you wish to know more about. For example, "please lift your portion of the Raccoon Circle to the level of understanding you have related to the current challenge. Shoulder high—I have enough information to begin, stomach high—I'd like to discuss this more, knee high—could you explain again, from the beginning." This approach will give the facilitator a visual response to key questions they have. For large groups, you can replace a single Raccoon Circle with multiple Raccoon Circles connected together or a single long rope.

5. Let's Ask the Raccoon

Instead of using the knot on the Raccoon Circle as a pointer, here are three possibilities for creating other ways for the group to process the experience. First, using a permanent fine tip marker, write questions on the Raccoon Circle. Then when the group has 'connected up' ask someone to read one of the questions that their hand is touching. This approach allows different participants to take an active roll in the debriefing session, even if only by reading the question.

A second variation would be to number the questions on the Raccoon Circle, which could be written by one of those fancy lettering sewing machines! By rolling dice, participants identify which question they are going to discuss or answer.

A third approach is to create a grid on a large piece of cardboard or tarp. Nine large blocks should do. Write a processing question into each grid, using large, easy to read letters. Now pass out a few untied Raccoon Circles, and ask participants to roll these into spirals. When finished, they can 'bowl' these spirals towards the grid, holding onto one end, and watching as the other end rolls towards one of the questions. The person reads (and potentially answers) the question that is at the other end of their webbing.

6. A Circular Story

Here is an activity similar to "one word stories" in which a Raccoon Circle is used to determine who will continue the story. With all group members holding onto a Raccoon Circle, the story begins with the person presently nearest the knot. As they begin talking, the knot begins to be passed around the circle. When the person talking stops moving the Raccoon Circle, the person nearest the knot continues the story from that point, and resumes moving the Raccoon Circle the opposite direction.

7. It's Knot our Problem, is it?

The knots found in a piece of webbing can be helpful (the water knot helps to hold the Raccoon Circle together), or harmful (this Raccoon Circle is all twisted up and knotted!) Pre-knot a variety of short segments of webbing, and let the participants choose one that reflects the kinds of knots (problems or difficulties) they are presently dealing with in their lives, or some of the challenges, worries or fears that they are experiencing today. Discuss what needs to happen to remove the harmful knots (addiction, social problems, lack of resources, dysfunction), and keep the helpful ones (connection to family, friends, resources). Discuss what techniques are available to assist in removing the harmful knots (identify resources) and what needs to keep happening to reinforce and fully appreciate the helpful knots.

For the pre-knotted webbing collection, use a variety of webbing, narrow, wide, long, short, different colors, different styles of knots, some easy, some (well, I used a 10,000 pound hydraulic press to knot a few of them. I don't think those knots will be coming out any time soon!)

Just to show you how such activities can work, consider this true story:

". . . We had been working with a group of 13 & 14 year old girls. They were all struggling with issues (you know, the kind of stuff that breaks your heart). We had just completed a check-in with them. Clearly it had been a rough day for most of them and they had so much on their minds. We decided to use the activity "A Knot Between Us." We used the analogy of the Raccoon Circle as the road of life, where the knots signified the bumps in the road or the problems they were facing. We invited each girl to name their knot (problem) and then to work collectively to untie them. This was such an incredible experience!

When we processed after the initiative the girls candidly discussed their behaviors. They learned so much about themselves and working together. One girl really needed help, but found it hard to ask; one was thrilled that the girls helped her even when she didn't ask. Another girl noticed that she kind of sat back and let the other girls untie her knot (solve her problems), one girl noticed that sometimes well meaning friends try to help you out and actually make things worse.

This was truly the right initiative at the right time with the right group!

Jennifer Steinmetz
Rocky Top Therapy Center

8. The Circle Speaks for Itself

Here is an opportunity to use some of those short pieces of tubular webbing that you have been saving, but weren't quite sure how to use. Take the lighter colored pieces, and write a key word or phrase on each piece. Place these in the center of the group, and allow each person to choose one, and give it to the person that displayed that characteristic, talent or attribute during the activity.

Some youth organizations have specific goals and detailed descriptions of their key values. 4-H has the head, heart, hand and health model. The YMCA has their own version, with colors to match. So do many other groups. Why not write these specific words on a webbing segment, and help participants look for and appreciate when they see one of the key values being used? For corporate groups, take words from their mission statement, vision statement, core values or even from their website, annual report or investment portfolio.

9. The Labyrinth

A few years ago at the AEE Northeast Regional Conference, some wonderful folks created a labyrinth using flagging tape. Even though the entire labyrinth fit within an area roughly the size of a tennis court, it easily required a full 10 minutes of quiet reflection time to walk the entire path. What a peaceful experience.

On a recent trip to New York City, I even saw a labyrinth painted on the surface of a parking lot, near the farmer's market off Broadway. I'm not sure which is more unusual, a farmer's market in downtown Manhattan, or a labyrinth imposed in the midst of one of the biggest cities on the planet.

You can use a whole spool of webbing or multiple Raccoon Circles or surveyor's flagging tape to create a labyrinth for quiet reflection too. For more information about this subject, see the books: *The Magic of Labyrinths—Following Your Path, Finding Your Center,* by Liz Simpson, Element, Hammersmith, London, UK ISBN 0-00-712047-8. *Exploring the Labyrinth: A Guide for Healing and Spiritual Growth,* by Melissa Gayle West, 2000, Broadway Books, New York, NY ISBN 0-7679-0356-0. *Mazes and Labyrinths of the World,* by Janet Bord, E.P.Dutton & Company, New York, NY ISBN 0-525-47441-2.

You can also contact the Worldwide Labyrinth Project 1100 California Street San Francisco, California 94108 Website: www.gracecathedral.org/veriditas

10. Reflection with Music

During processing and debriefing activities, try playing some of the following music to reinforce the circles theme of the Raccoon Circle. There is a wide range of music styles here. So, please listen before you decide to play any of these for your audience. Make sure the song you choose, carries the lyrics, issues and values that you want to share.

The facilitator can play music in the background as the group discusses the last activity, or the music can be the focus, and a discussion can begin after the song, based on the lyrics, theme or style of music. Special thanks to Ann O'Flannigan for performing the song search and just being a really great person.

Song Title	Artist	Album Title
Circle of Life	Walt Disney	Lion King Soundtrack
All my Life's a Circle	Harry Chapin	Greatest Stories Live
Circle of Friends	Paul Winter Consort	Double Album
Circle Dream	10000 Maniacs	Our Time In Eden
Twisted Circle	9 Days	Twisted Circle
Full Circle	Aerosmith	Nine Lives
Circle	Barbara Streisand	Higher Ground
Full Circle	Collective Soul	Disciplined Breakdown
Perfect Circle	R.E.M	Murmur
Circle	Sarah McLachlan	Fumbling Towards Ecstasy
Circle	Big Head Todd & The Monsters	Sister Sweetly
May The Circle Remain Unbroken	13th Floor Elevators	Bull Of The Woods

11. Worms

Here is the perfect way to use all those short segments of tubular webbing you have lying around. 'Worms' are these short segments of colorful webbing, and they are used so that every person's vote can be registered during a reviewing session.

The processing, debriefing or reviewing that typically occurs at the completion of an adventure-based learning activity adds value. In some cases, it is not easy to hear everyone's comments, but the facilitator may still wish to poll the feelings of the entire group. In other cases, some participants may mimic the answers of others, when the facilitator would like to hear each person's individual voice. Here is a simple technique that allows everyone's opinion to be registered, even if their voices are not necessarily heard.

Begin by creating a dozen cards (made from 8 1/2" x 11" paper), filled with words, pictures or expressive faces. There should be a wide range of images or words to cover the wide range of responses that typically are expressed in a debriefing session. Place these pictures on the floor or ground.

Next create the 'worms' by cutting very short pieces of rope or webbing (about 3-4 inches long). Give each participant in your group one 'worm' and at the completion of an adventure-based learning activity ask them each to drop their worm on the picture that best represents their experience during the activity. Every participant should drop their worm at exactly the same time. Then begin the debriefing by discussing the pictures with the most worms, the next highest one, or even the ones with no worms. Thanks to Dave Knobbe for this brilliant debriefing technique.

Worms can also be used during the planning stages of a challenge activity, as a method of voting on various plans, techniques or options. Have a few cards that have words like YES, NO, Agree, Disagree, Plan A, Plan B, Plan C, or even Continue Planning, Start Working.

12. Step Into the Circle

At the completion of an activity, have the group gather around a large circle made from four or five Raccoon Circles that have been tied together, and placed on the ground. After proposing a question to the group, anyone wishing to answer is asked to step into the circle, so that each person might be heard. Reviewing continues until no one is left standing inside the circle.

13. One Word

While holding on to a Raccoon Circle as a group, invite each participant to summarize their experience in one word. For example, "tell us one word about how you think your team performed today. Or, think of one word that describes what you hope to accomplish when you return back to your class (or office, or home)."

14. Knot Race

Begin with the group holding a Raccoon Circle that has been knotted into a circle. The knot represents a racecar and the rest of the Raccoon Circle, the racetrack. Use this activity for debriefing by encouraging participants to move the car quickly around the circle, using just their hands. When someone yells 'stop!' the person nearest the knot has the opportunity to share their thoughts, comments or feelings. Individual participants can also say stop when the knot is directly in front of them—so that they can choose when they are ready to have their say.

14a. Group Processing—Pass the Knot (The Talking Knot)

Here is a debriefing method that is a variation of the activity 'Believe It Or Knot' where the knot tied in the Raccoon Circle acts as a pointer, and the facilitator or other participant instructs the group to move the knot to the right (counterclockwise) or to the left (clockwise), then stop, and the person nearest the knot or pointer has the opportunity to speak. This technique chooses the person, rather than allowing a participant to make their own choice when to speak.

As a variation, use the Raccoon Circle as a talking stick, by allowing participants to move the knot around the circle, and when a person is ready to speak, stopping the knot when it is in front of them. Or, one member of the team asks a question and then rotates and stops the knot and invites the person nearest to it to answer.

15. Question Marks

Place a variety of numbers, letters or symbols along the length of a light colored Raccoon Circle, using a permanent marker. Ask your group to connect up, and then pass the knot along to the left, using their hands. At the word stop, each member of the group is asked to describe their experience today, using a word that begins with that letter (or that has that letter within the word). Another variation is to ask the group to pass the circle along and then stop. One person from the group reads off the number or symbol nearest them, and then answers a corresponding question associated with that number or symbol. This technique allows you to make just one Question Mark Raccoon Circle, but continuously alter the questions used. Write these on index cards and keep them with your Raccoon Circles.

16. Shuffle Left & Shuffle Right

Here is a processing technique that allows for a bit of kinesthetic movement. If your group is active and doesn't like to sit still for any length of time, this activity is perfect. Begin by inviting the group to stand closely together around a Raccoon Circle that has been placed on the ground. Participants can hold hands, interlocking elbows with their neighbors or place their arms around each other. Begin by saying, "shuffle left" for a short distance until someone that has a comment to make says "STOP!" After they have their say, they remark "shuffle right" and the circle moves to the right until another person says stop and offers their commentary. Don't be afraid to let the circle move quite a distance—it may take a few moments for some participants to formulate their comments. If you like, you can suggest that anytime the circle completes one full revolution without any stops, processing will stop and the group will move on.

17. Lots of Knots

Begin by tying as many knots in an untied piece of rope as possible. Then, pass this knotted rope around the group. As each member of the group expresses some commentary about the day's events, they may untie a single knot for each comment. When all knots are removed, the processing is complete. This is a great technique for those groups that don't always have enough to talk about at the completion of a program. Waiting for someone to untie one of the last remaining knots can be a bit anxious, but don't worry, a voice will emerge from the group eventually.

17a. Available Space

Occasionally you may have insufficient time to complete a thorough reviewing session, but still want to hear a few comments from the group. In a variation of Lots of Knots, place a single untied Raccoon Circle in the center of the group, and loosely tie only the number of knots you have sufficient time to explore in discussion. If you have time for five participants to share, tie five knots. Then explain that although time is limited, there is time for some discussion. One person per knot can speak. Who would like to be heard at this time?

18. Plus / Delta

Plus | **Delta**

The Plus / Delta model, can be illustrated by passing an unknotted Raccoon Circle down the middle of the group and asking each team member to choose a side that reflects a topic they wish to discuss. For example, in the traditional Plus / Delta model, one side would be positive attributes demonstrated by the group during the program, the other side would reflect situations that would benefit from a change or modification of the groups behavior.

Other potential categories for the two sides include: Moving Forward/Standing Still, Needs Improvement/Works OK Now, World Class/No Class, etc.

19. Wrapping and Rapping

You can use the activity 'Wrapped Around My Finger' as a technique for encouraging longer debriefing discussions. Ask a question to the group and encourage participants to reach into the center of the group, grasp an unknotted Raccoon Circle and attempt to discuss this question for the length of time it takes to wrap the complete length of the Raccoon Circle around a single finger.

You'll find a get-acquainted version of this activity in the final section of this book.

20. The Learning Rope

Thanks to Chris Cavert for this innovative technique for remembering the teachable moments encountered during an adventure-based learning program.

Throughout the program, each time a teachable moment is encountered, the group places a single knot onto the learning rope (an ordinary unknotted Raccoon Circle). Before a new knot is added, the group reviews all previous knots to insure that the learning is not lost. At the end of the day, untie each knot as the group identifies and reflects on each teachable moment.

As an alternative, at the completion of the program, the facilitator can review each of the knots, and then cut them apart, giving one knot to each participant in the group. This process can also be used in corporate settings so that one person takes the responsibility to return to the workplace and take action on the lesson learned.

21. Engagement

A powerful corporate buzz word is 'engagement' and it refers to employees being fully committed to the task at hand. One corporate executive explained to me that, in his opinion, people could often be placed into various categories related to their level of engagement or buy-in to a corporate initiative. He suggested the four categories of: prisoner, tourist, student and leader.

A prisoner is present because they are forced to be there. Commitment is typically low. So is engagement. A Tourist is interested in looking around and may find something of value, but seldom has advanced expectations. A student comes prepared to learn something and has expectations for the day. A leader is not only ready to learn something, but is already looking for tools and techniques to take back and solve existing problems in the workplace.

The goal is to take each person in the group, and no matter what category they occupy at the beginning of the program, help them move up at least one level during the session.

As a physical representation, join several pieces of webbing together to form a long line. Ask the group to stand in a circle, and then wrap the webbing around the outside of this group. Note the amount of webbing required to 'tie the group together.' Ask them, "can we do the same thing with less rope?"

The answer (not surprisingly) is, "it depends." It depends on whether the participants in the group are prisoners, tourists, students or leaders. For a group of prisoners, you'll need quite a bit of webbing to insure that the members of the group stay together. The further up the ladder the group ascends, the less webbing is required. Why? Because it takes less webbing if people openly choose to be a part of the group. Less still if they don't mind being in close proximity with each other. Still less if the webbing is used to connect each member of the group, rather than binding them together. Still less if the members of the group do not struggle against the commitment to be part of the group.

We see that it takes less webbing if people choose to be there. Less still if they work together. Less still if they do not struggle against the commitment. Still less if they are willing to rub shoulders with their teammates, and even less if they are willing to really connect with each other to get the job done.

If groups are really creative, they can probably 'connect' the entire group with a very short amount of webbing. Once they realize this is possible, you have the perfect closing moment for your program. This would be a great time to present each member of the group with a short piece of webbing, just like the one that has connected them all together.

If you enjoy this style of corporate connection activity, be sure to read the book: The Value of Connection—In the Workplace, by Jim Cain and Kirk Weisler. See the Teamwork and Teamplay website for more information on this book, at: www.teamworkandteamplay.com

22. Reviewing Activities Shared by Roger Greenaway

Hello Jim. You are welcome to use the attached article that is also located at: http://reviewing.co.uk/articles/ropes.htm

I think (and hope!) I have already told you about this article, especially as it was inspired by your Raccoon Circle article published in Horizons magazine here in the UK. Old climbing ropes and brightly colored webbing make excellent reviewing tools. For some of the methods described here you can draw lines with pen and paper. But in most situations where you have enough space (indoors or outdoors) you and your learners will soon discover that ropes and webbing were made for reviewing!

All the best,
Roger Greenaway
www.reviewing.co.uk

The Goal Line

Place a piece of webbing in front of each participant, with three overhand knots along the length. Where the participants are standing now is the beginning of the day. The first knot represents some event in the first half of the session (morning), the middle knot is the midday break (lunch), the third knot is an event in the second half of the session (afternoon), and the other end of the webbing represents the conclusion of the program.

Now invite participants to verbally plan their experience, using this knotted webbing model. Where do they want to be at the end of the experience? Where do they want to be by the mid-point (lunchtime)? What 'events' need to happen to achieve their personal (or group) goals for the day?

Encourage participants to look at the distance traveled so far, in addition to the distance still left to go. What factors have helped you on your journey so far? Will any of these helping forces be useful later in your journey?

Spokes

This is a variation of The Goal Line and is perfect for reviewing progress towards group related goals. Each Raccoon Circle is placed on the ground to make the spokes of a large wheel. The outer end of each spoke represents the starting point and the center is the goal. This technique works especially well when the group establishes a goal that is shared by everyone in the group. For example, the spokes can all be 'listening' spokes. Each person then assesses the quality of their own listening during the activity (by moving to a location they choose along their spoke) and can also see where others are standing. Other spoke goals could be 'supporting others,' 'providing leadership,' or 'teamwork.'

It is useful to ask participants to individually decide their position for themselves before anyone moves (so as not to be influenced by the location of others in the group). Once everyone has chosen their position, you can ask if anyone feels that anyone else's self-assessment is inaccurate. Participants often invite others nearer to the center—which can be a form of positive feedback. You must decide whether to allow the moving of others away from the center—as this can be seen as a form of criticism. Encourage people to give specific reasons about why they would like to move others to a new position.

For the end of a program, workshop or course, reverse the polarity of the spokes so that the middle hub represents the starting point and the outer rim the future. Each person then walks into the future as they leave. Whenever someone turns back to look at their starting point, they are also looking back at the other members of the group.

The Horseshoe

In this activity, Roger creates a variation of The Meter, found in the teambuilding activities of this section, but with a few additional ideas for facilitators. This is a kinesthetic and visual way of exposing and discussing different points of view, opinions, preferences and predictions.

Begin by creating a horseshoe (U) shaped pattern on the ground with an unknotted Raccoon Circle. The U shape is helpful (compare to a straight line) for creating eye contact between members of the group.

Next inform the group what each end of the horseshoe represents. *"On this end, we performed pretty well on that last challenge, and on the other end, we were hopelessly lost on that activity."* Everyone chooses their own location on the horseshoe and then discusses with their two neighbors to see if they need to adjust their position. Once everyone is in position, encourage questions and discussion between team members.

If you place knots along the webbing horseshoe, you can include quantitative evaluation statements, such as: *"on a scale of one to five, how would you rate your teamwork on this last challenge?"*

Goldfish Bowl

Here is a reviewing process that focuses on both listening and talking. Begin by placing a Raccoon Circle on the ground. For large groups, you may need a circle made from two lengths of Raccoon Circles. Divide the group in half. One half sits inside the circle and is allowed to talk. The other half sits outside the circle and may only observe and listen. Those inside the inner circle review the previous activity or event. After a few minutes, each group changes place and the new inner group continues the reviewing process they have just been observing.

As an alternative, anyone in the inner circle can leave at any time, but the discussion does not continue until they have been replaced by someone from the outer circle.

As a final variation, begin this reviewing technique with everyone sitting inside the inner circle. When someone no longer has anything to say, they can move to the outer circle. They are also allowed to return to the inner circle any time they wish to speak. When the inner circle is empty, the reviewing process is complete.

Sketch Map

Here is a visual way to relive a journey or trek. This can be a personal journey or a group trek. Ask the members of your group to use several unknotted Raccoon Circles to trace the route of their journey. You can also supply index cards and markers so that the group can label key locations on the journey. Natural objects can also be used for this purpose. Participants are most likely internally processing the experience while creating this map. When the map is complete, it can be used as a visual aid for retelling the story or key moments of the journey.

Force Field

This technique uses a symbolic 'tug of war' to create a teachable moment about change. Using two Raccoon Circles that have been knotted together into one straight line, invite half of the group to hold the webbing on each end. Let one team represent change or moving towards the future and the other team to represent resistance to change or holding traditional values.

This activity is simply an active method for reviewing forces that are in opposition to each other. The key question to ask, how each force can be strengthened to help the team achieve their goals.

It is useful to have participants representing each side of the opposition so that they may seek solutions from that perspective. Dialog between the two teams is possible (and valuable).

It is not necessary to physically pull on the webbing with any force to set up this scenario.

Active Reviewing Cycle

Participants with different learning styles (or MBTI or DiSC classifications) process in different manners. While there are many reviewing techniques in this book that explore different styles, here is an activity that explores four styles at the same time.

Although you can perform this reviewing technique in four individually labeled Raccoon Circles, one very large circle is preferable. It gives the impression of 'parts of a whole' rather than 'we are different than those people over there.' Group participants within the large circle into one of the four stages of the learning cycle suggested by Roger Greenaway (Facts, Feeling, Findings and Futures). You can also create a space in the center for a 'catch all' category that is not covered by one of the other four areas.

Participants are now allowed to move to the reviewing area that most closely meets their needs. They can numerically evaluate their performance in the 'facts' group. They can process their own feelings from the experience in the 'feelings' group. They can discuss new insights, teachable moments and lessons learned in the 'findings' group and they can talk about how this information can be used in their future in the 'futures' group.

To create a sense of understanding for each of these groups, you can ask each location to write down some of their key insights, and then rotate groups to each of the four stages. When complete, ask the original group in each stage to read all the information recorded there.

Missing Person

Here is a discussion technique for helping group members assess their needs and what is important to them. Begin by creating the outline of a body with a Raccoon Circle. Explain that this represents a person who could join the group. As group members to think creatively about the kind of person they would like this to be. This person typically shares some of the characteristics already found in the group (sense of humor, enthusiasm, strength) and also some that are missing (leadership, specific skills). Bring depth to this character by giving them a name, assigning them a personality, interests, strengths and weaknesses.

Then pull the webbing away in a single movement and ask the group what they will do now that this person is no longer part of the group. The response is different for each group. Some groups like this person so much that you will find the Raccoon Circle person appearing throughout the program. Some groups remember this person's name and call for them when they need help. Some take it even further...

The Question Knot

Gather your group around a standard Raccoon Circle. The knot not only can be used to identify the person having their say, but in this case, identifies a person who has a question. As the knot moves around the circle, a participant with a question says 'stop' and states their question. Any group member is free to answer this question—or—the person asking the question can move the knot around the circle and stop it at the person they would like to answer the question.

About this Article   The information presented in this article by Roger Greenaway first appeared in Active Reviewing Tips, May 2002. It was also published in the Institute for Outdoor Learning's Horizons magazine, Number18, Summer 2002 to complement the Raccoon Circle article written by Jim Cain in the previous issue. Comments, questions, news, ideas and feedback are always welcome: write to roger@reviewing.co.uk. You can also be invited to join the discussion list 'Active Reviewing Exchange' and find others who share your interest in processing, debriefing, reviewing and reflection activities. Email Roger at the address above for more information.

23. A Circle of Connection

A special thanks to Dick Hammond for sharing this wonderful activity which can be used as both an icebreaker and a closing activity. It is helpful for a group to perform this activity on the outside of a knotted Raccoon Circle that has been placed on the ground (to keep the group in a circle). A leader begins by introducing themselves and sharing some information such as, "I enjoy crossword puzzles. I like to work in my garden. I enjoy old movies, and I like to travel." At some point, one of these recreations is sure to also be shared by at least one other member of the group. When this happens, this new person links elbows with the previous person, introduces themselves, and begins to share some of their interesting hobbies. The activity continues until all members of the group have 'linked together.' The final task is for the last person to continue sharing until the first person can link with them. At this point, there is an opportunity to say, ". . .and by the way. Those things which link us together, bring us a bit closer together as well!"

As a closing activity, group members can share their thoughts, comments and feelings about the program or goals for the future.

You can find this and other teambuilding activities without props in the book: The Empty Bag— Non-Stop, No-Prop Adventure-Based Activities for Community Building, 2003, Chris Cavert and Dick Hammond, FUNdoing Publications ISBN 0-9746442-1-8.

24. The Final Transmission

You can create a large "gear" system, by using a variety of colorful Raccoon Circles, and then asking various groups to "mesh" together, with participants turning like gears. This is an opportunity to say good-bye (or hello) to many of the other participants. If all circles turn in the same direction, participants from different circles can 'high five' each other as they pass. It can be inspirational and even more effective if music is used during this activity.

25. A Circle of Kindness

With half of the group standing in a circle holding a knotted Raccoon Circle, the other half stands just behind them (one person in the outer circle behind a person in the inner circle). The inside circle closes their eyes, and the outer circle has the opportunity to express a positive comment to their inside circle partner. For tactile audiences (in other words, where appropriate), the outer circle can place their hands on the shoulders of their inner circle partners, and whisper into their ears. Typical comments might include, "it was great meeting you, thanks for being in our group this weekend, I am looking forward to working with you, thanks for your help with the problem solving activity—I couldn't have done it without you!" This activity however is NOT a two-way conversation—the only response from the inner circle is "thank you." This avoids breaking the mood with laughter, giggling or any other fun but disruptive conversation.

When finished, outside circle participants move one person to their right, until they have encountered all the inside circle participants. Then the inner and outer circles trade places.

26. Bits and Pieces from Other Places

Several of the activities presented in the icebreaker and introductory activities section of this book are also suitable for debriefing and reviewing activities. For example:

Listening and Talking Circles—Create a physical space for those that would like to express themselves and those that choose to actively listen. When all participants are outside the Raccoon Circle (i.e. in the 'listening space'), including the facilitator, it is time to move on to the next activity.

Opening the Time Capsule—If the group created a time capsule by saving some items or information inside the tubular Raccoon Circle webbing, the closing ceremony can be a time to open the sealed ends of the Raccoon Circle, and read, share and discuss the contents.

Inside Out—One quick debriefing technique is to place the Raccoon Circle on the ground with the entire group standing inside. Offer participants the opportunity to comment on the results of an activity. Once they have concluded, or decided not to talk, they are welcome to step outside the circle. For groups that may over-process, or constantly return to previous arguments or discussions, this approach means that when you're done talking, you're done talking. When everyone is outside the circle, it is time to move on. Or, a person still standing inside the circle can choose to exchange places with another outside the circle, effectively giving them an opportunity to be heard again.

Zoom was introduced in the teambuilding activity section as a creativity and problem solving activity. For processing and debriefing, the zoom knot can be used for a one-word 'whip.' As the knot slowly passes around the circle, participants are asked to provide a one-word description of their experience, or just say 'pass.'

Untying Us All Together—If you began the day with the opening activity entitled Tie Us All Together, where each member of the group was given a short segment of webbing, and the group created their own Raccoon Circle out of these shorter pieces (by tying them together with multiple

water knots). Then you can conclude the day by untying this circle, and allowing members of the group to either keep their segment of the circle, trade it with others in the group, or perhaps give it away to another person in the group, along with some kind comments or personal reflection related to the experience.

Reviewing the Circle of Four (or, In the Loop Again)—If the group established some group goals and expectations during the opening session (which facilitators have written on large sheets of paper or cardboard), they can return to this same format, and review the results of each expectation or goal. There is something completing and familiar (and perhaps even circular) about using similar formations at the start and conclusion of a program.

The above activities can be used, but should not be 'over used' during any single program. It is best to have a variety of techniques ready, to best meet the needs of the group.

27. A Gathering of Raccoons

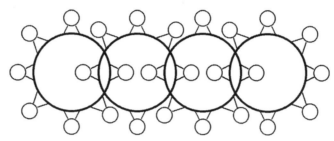

When there are two or more groups, this closing ceremony can be used, and involves overlapping the smaller Raccoon circles into a large community. This involves one person from each group moving into the circle of another group, but still staying connected to their own group's web loop.

If there are enough groups in this community, other geometric shapes are possible. When the whole community is connected, try working as a community by sitting down together. Then stand up. Repeating this pattern three times in a row. How about with sound effects (one sound for going down, a different sound when coming back up)? Or perhaps in a wave . . .

28. Personal Experience Graph

Using a single Raccoon Circle for the whole group, or individual Raccoon Circles for each member of the group, ask participants to create a line "graph" of their experience for this program. This could be a single line showing levels of enthusiasm, or knowledge gained, or personal energy versus time for various activities. Ask each participant to discuss the major characteristics of their graph (high points, low points, transitions).

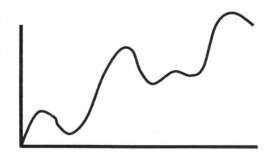

29. Listening and Talking Circles

Place a single Raccoon Circle on the floor at the center of the group. The "inside" of the Raccoon Circle is a place for talking, while the "outside" of the circle is a place for listening. Encourage everyone to share in the final discussion and reflection, and when the entire group is outside the circle, the experience is concluded.

30. A Part of the Whole

During the first workshop that I ever attended with Dr. Tom Smith, he mentioned that he often encouraged members of the group during debriefing sessions to write words of encouragement or significant phrases directly on the Raccoon Circle. He also encouraged them to write their own names. At the completion of their time together, he would cut the group's Raccoon Circle into small pieces, so that everyone in the group could take away some portion of the whole "spirit" of the group. Names and words will be most visible when you choose a dark color marker and a lighter color Raccoon Circle webbing (yellow, light gray, orange, etc.) If you would like to create water knot bracelets from these Raccoon Circles, be sure to cut into lengths of about 18-20 inches (45 to 51 cm). A typical 15 foot long Raccoon Circle will make 9 to 10 bracelets.

31. Keeper of the Sacred Circle

Rather than cutting the Raccoon Circle into pieces, especially if the group plans to be together again, the facilitator can ask the group for a volunteer to be the keeper of the sacred circle until the next time the group gathers.

32. The Tapestry

Here is a colorful variation of a closing activity often performed with a ball of string or yarn. Give each participant in the group an unknotted Raccoon Circle. Invite them to share something from their experience today. When they are done, they hold one end of their Raccoon Circle and pass the other end to another person in the group. When the entire group is finished, there will be a colorful tapestry woven by the group, showing the connection that the group has created with one another.

Thanks to Jordan Rimmer for sharing this colorful closing activity using Raccoon Circles, and also for Get the Picture, shown next.

33. Get The Picture

This activity works especially well with athletic teams. It is essential for such teams to clearly understand how they play best together. Think of this like a first year medical student being bombarded with anatomy classes. A successful doctor must know what a healthy body looks like, inside and out, to be able to see problems and know how best to cure them. It is very much the same for teams. They must get a picture of what playing at their best looks like, so that they can easily tell when the picture is not right.

You can illustrate this concept using a Raccoon Circle. Begin by asking your group to face away from you. Lay a Raccoon Circle randomly on the ground, in any shape or pattern. Invite the group to turn around and ask them what is wrong with the picture. Inevitably they do not know because they do knot know what a 'good' Raccoon Circle looks like.

Ask them to face away again, and change something about the Raccoon Circle. Then invite them again to turn around and study the Raccoon Circle carefully this time. This is what a Raccoon Circle is supposed to look like.

When the group faces away again, change something else. This time it is easy for the group to tell what is different, changed or wrong, because they know what a good Raccoon Circle is supposed to look like.

As facilitators, teachers, trainers, coaches, corporate managers and parents, we often have the tendency to look at what is wrong with the picture. This activity is excellent for helping groups see and understand what is good about what they do, and how to keep this picture firmly in their goals for the future.

34. The Timeline Technique

Staring with an unknotted Raccoon Circle, everyone in the group connects from either side of the webbing. The person standing at one end represents the beginning of the program while the person at the other end represents the completion. You can choose to identify each of the remaining members of the team (by activity or program components such as problem solving, brainstorming, teamwork, leadership, etc.) or to choose their topic of discussion themselves.

The goal is to tell the story of their efforts during the program, with each person adding their own interpretation to the whole picture, from start to finish.

35. The Passkey

The element of choice in adventure-based and active learning activities is essential. Here is a technique that not only gives the team you are facilitating real choices, but brings up opportunities for leadership, group discussions and decisions made as a whole.

With a full length unknotted Raccoon Circle (shorter lengths will also work) inform the group that during today's adventures they will have opportunities to make choices.

> *"The Raccoon Circle you are now holding is your 'passkey.' It works just like a security key. Any time your group decides (as a whole) that they would like to pass by a challenge or initiative, you can use one of the three knots I am now tying in the webbing. The passkey can also be used to gain additional resources, receive additional information or hints, and to recover a member of your team that may make an error during one of our challenges today. You can also use the passkey knots to ask a question, return sight to a blindfolded participant, speech to a muted member of your team or mobility to anyone in need."*

Tying two or three knots is a reasonable number to begin a program. Some groups hesitate to use these knots as a resource and complete the program without ever using them. This in itself is an interesting debriefing subject. Some groups may use their knots for trivial problems and may ask for more. As a variation, you can allow the group to tie additional knots (for more future choices) by performing essential tasks, such as elevating the enthusiasm of the group, achieving consensus on a task, singing a favorite song or collaborating with another group to solve a problem.

36. Additional Resources for Processing, Debriefing, Reviewing, Reflection and Closing Activities

In addition to the information provided in this section, we recommend the following resources:

A Teachable Moment—A Facilitator's Guide to Activities for Processing, Debriefing, Reviewing and Reflection, 2005, Jim Cain, Michelle Cummings and Jennifer Stanchfield, Kendall / Hunt, Dubuque, IA USA ISBN 0-7575-1782-X. More than 130 different ways to review with groups.

Reflective Learning: Theory and Practice, 2000, Deborah Sugerman, Kathryn Doherty, Daniel Garvey and Michael Gass, Kendall / Hunt Publishing, Dubuque, IA USA ISBN 0-7872-6561-6.

Hot Tips for Facilitators: Strategies to Make Life Easier for Anyone Who Leads, Guides, Teaches, or Trains Groups, 2003, Rob Abernathy and Mark Reardon, Zephyr Press, Tucson, AZ ISA ISBN 1-56976-150-7.

Processing the Experience: Strategies to Enhance and Generalize Learning, 1997, John L. Luckner and Reldan S. Nadler, Kendall / Hunt, Dubuque, IA USA ISBN 0-7872-1000-5. A classic.

Warm Ups & Wind Downs: 101 Activities for Moving and Motivating Groups, 1993, Sandra Hazouri and Miriam McLaughlin, Educational Media Corporation, Minneapolis, MN USA ISBN 0-932796-52-4. Icebreakers and closing activities.

www.training-wheels.com Michelle Cumming's website filled with reviewing tools and more.

www.reviewing.co.uk Roger Greenaway's website filled with dozens of reviewing tools.

37. Other Activities

Use the space below to list your own versions of reviewing and closing activities using Raccoon Circles.

Section II
The Ritual, Ceremony, Theory and Philosophy of Raccoon Circles

I n this section, you'll find several articles that explore the spiritual, philosophical and ceremonial qualities of circles in general, and the Raccoon Circle specifically. You'll also find some discussion of 'connectedness' and the future of adventure-based learning.

With each new printing of the Book of Raccoon Circles, you'll find the newest thoughts and writings from Tom Smith and Jim Cain in the final chapter of this book, entitled Recent Additions.

The First Raccoon
Circle Document

In his original pamphlet on the theory and practice of Raccoon Circles, Tom Smith laid out a significant foundation for the future. Because of the impact of that first overview of the philosophy, symbolism, and community building potential of the Raccoon Circle, it seems appropriate to reproduce it here, for historical purposes, and so much more.

Here then are the words from that little blue booklet. Except for a few new illustrations and computer generated artwork, all the words are just as they were in the very beginning. By the time this new edition of *The Book of Raccoon Circles* goes to press, that original pamphlet will be more than a decade old! We hope you enjoy this historic document.

Dr. Tom Smith
Raccoon Institute
January 1996

"You have noticed that everything an Indian does is in a circle, and that is because the Power of the World always works in circles, and everything tries to be round. In the old days, when we were strong and happy people, all our powers came to us from the sacred hoop of the nation. . . . The flowering tree was the living center of the hoop, and the circle of the four quarters nourished it. Everything the Power of the World does is in a circle. The sky is round like a ball, and so are the stars. The wind, in its great power, whirls. The sun comes forth and goes down in a circle. The moon does the same, and both are round. Even the seasons form a great circle in their changing, and always come back to where they were."

(Black Elk)

In the past few years, the theory and practice of experiential challenge/adventure education has had increasing popularity as an educational, training, and therapeutic alternative. (c.f., Schoel &

Prouty, 1988; Smith, et. al., 1992; Gass, 1993; Roland, et. al., 1995). The methodology has strong roots in outdoor adventure and the ropes/teams course sequences, but more and more leaders are recognizing the potential of procedures that follow challenge education theory but need not involve the outdoors or the ropes course. Leaders are concerned with activity sequences that can be offered in activity rooms, classrooms, gymnasiums, schoolyards and boardrooms. The diversity of programs are offered to enhance clients awareness and understanding of . . . .

> Self. . . .
>
> Others. . . .
>
> Environment. . . .
>
> The Other. . . .
>
> The Self-Other Interdependency. . . .
>
> The Self-Environment Interdependency. . . .
>
> The Self-Other Environment-Other ONENESS. . . .

Different programs, and different program sequences, can be designed to focus on these various goals, singularly or in combination. Challenge/adventure leaders have tended to set goals in terms of self (enhanced self-concept, locus of control, empowerment, risk-taking, etc.), others (trust, communication, cultural and gender awareness, etc.), and the self-other interdependency (teamwork, group problem solving, networking, etc.). They have not always given appropriate attention to goals associated with environmental consciousness and the spiritual quest of clients. (Smith, 1996). Those leaders with background in outdoor and environmental education have more often focused on goals related to the environment and the self-environment interdependency. Leaders who have focused on spirituality are infrequent, and yet many have found special value in the wisdom of the Native Americans, thus attending to that encompassing and holistic goal of enhancing clients awareness and understanding of the self-other-environment-Other-ONENESS.

Groups

The challenge/adventure sequence is typically offered as a small group experience. Even when the goals are stated in terms of individual gains, the activities are offered to a group. The power of groups has been noted by many authors. Johnson and Johnson (1987), have suggested a number of ways which the group influences the individual, including:

> Groups provide a more heterogeneous social setting in which interpersonal skills may be learned, mastered, and integrated into one's behavioral repertoire.
>
> Groups generate a sense of community, belonging, support, acceptance, and assistance.
>
> Groups influence the behavioral and attitudinal patterns of members.
>
> Groups may induce and then reduce powerful feelings.
>
> Groups require the use of a wide variety of interpersonal skills and competencies.
>
> Groups provide opportunities for participants to understand and help their peers. Helping others is an important opportunity for altruistic behavior that may be absent from daily life.
>
> Groups provide sources of comparison for the participants.

Groups provide a variety of sources of feedback. In a group setting, participants can test their behavior and seek feedback.

Groups provide constructive peer relationships needed for healthy social and cognitive growth.

Carl Rogers noted that the intensive group experience also gives rise to "a healing capacity in the group." As groups evolve, a number of the group members show natural and spontaneous interest and capacity for dealing with others in a very helpful, even therapeutic manner.

> *"This kind of ability shows up so commonly in groups that it has led me to feel that the ability to be healing or therapeutic is far more common in human life than we suppose. Often it needs only the permission granted—or freedom made possible—by the climate of a free-flowing group experience to become evident."*

(Rogers, 1970)

The history of the challenge/adventure methodology is filled with applications in counseling, therapy, and rehabilitation. The development of Project Adventure's "Adventure Based Counseling" has been summarized in their publication, Islands of Healing (Schoel, Prouty, and Radcliffe, 1988). One of the expanding applications of the challenge/adventure methodology has been in counseling centers and psychiatric hospitals. (Smith, 1996).

Obviously, distinctions can be made between various patterns of group. A therapy group may typically be focused on the clients behavioral problems or emotional distress, while the educational or recreational group has other goals. It might be said that the therapy group is concerned with the inner reasons or the "why" of behavior, and tends to focus on past behaviors; whereas the educational or recreational group is concerned with development of new social skills or the "how" of behavior, and focuses on the "here-and-now".

There are a number of ways to characterize the many forms of groupwork performed by challenge/ adventure leaders. There may be a continuum of application. Some groups are basically recreational or designed to teach recreational behaviors. Other groups have goals that can be classified as enrichment, as offered under education and training formats. Many contemporary leaders consider themselves as facilitators of personal growth, and in recent years there has been ever increasing utilization of the challenge/adventure format for counseling and psychotherapy.

Such classification should be tenuously applied because of the overlap of operational procedures whatever the intent of the program. Perhaps there is a continuum of "depth" for challenge/adventure groupwork, in that the deeper patterns require different leadership skills. Certainly, as one moves along such a continuum there is requirement for ever increasing attention to the processing aspects of the group, and the required skills become more complex.

Whatever the goals of the group, challenge education leaders would suggest that their methodology can enhance the necessary developmental stages of the group. The experience-based activities of the challenge/adventure sequence tend to connect people rather quickly. Issues of cohesiveness, trust, inclusion, and involvement are tackled quickly in a playful but meaningful manner. Most would suggest that there is a potency, a magic, that happens when the challenge group begins to share experiences, and many have observed a group together for only a few hours feeling joyously connected.

Challenge/adventure groups typically number 6-16 people, with the more desirable count being 10-12. They may be quite homogeneous (e.g., a group of 8th grade girls from a suburban Catholic school), or somewhat heterogeneous (e.g., the staff of a hospital or school, ranging in age from 20-60, coed, and multi-racial). Sometimes the group has had considerable contact before the challenge sequence (e.g., office teams, counseling groups, adventure clubs, etc.), and sometimes they have had limited pre-program interaction (e.g., new group at a treatment facility, college orientation group, professional training workshop, etc.).

The program offered may be quite short (e.g., 2-3 hours in the gym or at an outdoor center); a sequence of short sessions (e.g., 1-2 hours daily as part of a 90-day placement in a psychiatric hospital or reasonable intensive and long (e.g., the 2-3 week challenge/adventure camp or wilderness adventure, or the 9-10 month residential treatment center).

Many challenge/adventure groups are facilitated by a single leader, but co-leadership is often provided for the higher risk activities (i.e., high ropes, climbing, etc.), where closer supervision is required.

Designs for programs are as diverse as the composition of groups and the background training of leaders, but there are common denominators. Most challenge groups recognize and attend to concepts of goal-setting, warm-up, sequencing, processing, etc. Even more basically, one could symbolize the communality of all challenge/adventure groups in terms of the circle.

Circles

The circle is often suggested as a symbol of unity, community, and connectedness, and it forms the basis for many activities of the challenge/adventure program. Numerous challenge education activities begin with the instruction, "connect hands in a small circle." This circle of connection becomes a circle of influence for the individual, in a manner similar to that of other groups that are important in growth and development.

The family is often overviewed as the primary circle of influence on the person.

> *"Under normal circumstances the family is—both in time and by physiologic geometry— every person's first circle . . . It is in the family that the first steps are taken—steps that determine in large measure how the rest of life's journey will be walked."*
>
> (Nagler, 1982)

Individuals whose family circle is essentially positive are interested in bonding with other circles (small groups) as their life unfolds. It is the family which gives one the security that is necessary to expand what Albert Einstein called "the circle of compassion." Individuals whose early experiences were with a dysfunctional family circle, and thus are fearful of the very connectedness essence of the small group, need to learn how to connect to others in order to grow. As the 20th century closes, it appears that more and more people have not had good connections with family, or are disconnected from biologic family by the rush of society, and therefore need surrogate circles of connection. The challenge education group addresses that very basic human need to be connected to others, and for some it may even be a very first "family." In broadest definition, "family is any setting of close interpersonal relationships in which bonds of deep trust and mutual responsibility are formed. (op.cit.)

Many people recognize the need for belongingness and connectedness, and seek out meaningful small group circles.

> *"More and more people are coming together regularly to create rituals and ceremonial circles which promote individual growth as well as create close bonds between the participants. As these circles intersect and overlap they begin to create feelings of extended family and community.*
>
> *I have come to think of these circles as a kind of practice. There are "practice" in the Buddhist sense of a path, a mindful behavior which shows us who we are, that give us an opportunity to be authentic, to speak our truth as we know it in the moment as we learn to take full responsibility for ourselves and our actions."*
>
> (Cahill, 1994)

Circles are symbolic for humankind in many other ways. Many Native American peoples developed a comprehensive cosmological overview to life based on the Medicine Wheel. This overview provided them with a "map" for the journey of life. Native authors have reported on the practice and the philosophy of the Medicine Wheel (c.f., Storm, 1972; Sun Bear, et. al., 1980, 1991; McGaa, 1990).

Some challenge/adventure leaders have looked to the wisdom and the traditions of the Native Americans for ideas that would enhance program offerings.

> *"The Medicine Wheel is the very Way of Life of the people . . . The Medicine Wheel is the Total Universe . . . In many ways, this circle, the Medicine Wheel, can best be understood if*

you think of it as a mirror in which everything is reflected . . . and each person is a Mirror to every other person."

(Storm, 1972)

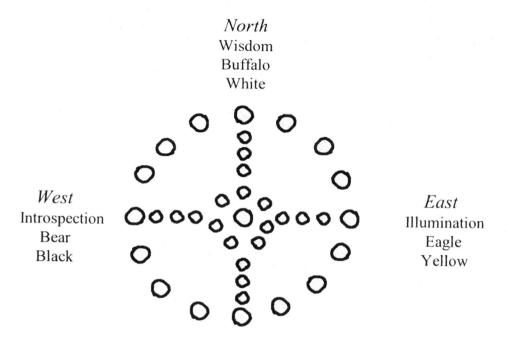

North
Wisdom
Buffalo
White

West
Introspection
Bear
Black

East
Illumination
Eagle
Yellow

South
Innocence
Mouse
Green

"If we want to have a better world, people must be in balance and harmony . . . The sacred Medicine Wheel can teach proper balance . . . By traveling around the wheel we bring life-giving changes into our own lives and into the world . . . As each of us learns how to live in a sacred manner, how to walk in a way harmonious with all the creation, we put our steps on the path of love and harmony. When enough people on the planet are walking on that path, then we will have a better world."

(Sun Bear, 1991)

In an earlier book about the personal growth journey, I noted:

"There is a wilderness beyond . . . there is a wilderness within . . . We go to the outside to learn about the inside, and we go to the inside to learn about the outside; and the inside is the outside, and the outside is the inside."

(Smith, 1990)

There is a Wilderness Beyond

You Are Here

Adventure Trails Lead You Here

The shortest distance between two points is not always a straight line....

There is a Wilderness Within

If we view life on a linear plane, then the wilderness beyond might seem in oppositional polarity to the wilderness within. This position might be reinforced by the apparent extremes of Eastern cultures, with exaggerated emphasis on the search for the "within" and self-mastery, and Western cultures, with focus on the "without" and technological mastery of the natural world. It is possible to view life as more spherical than linear, circles flowing from beginning to end and back to the beginnings again. It appears that the Native Americans tended to have this flowing, harmonious, cyclical cosmological overview to life and the universe.

The circle is also an important symbol in Eastern philosophy and religion, as in the form of the Mandala. A Mandala is a catalyst for the student of Buddhism. Through it one sees the various states of being. The word "mandala" actually means "circle" or "center," and the representations are not meant to be flat, but three dimensional.

"Mandalas are based on the squaring of a circle. Their basic motif is the premonition of a center to the personality, a kind of central point within the psyche, to which everything is related, by which everything is arranged, and which is itself a source of energy."

(Jung, 1964)

This graphic symbol of the universe, the Mandala circle, can also symbolize the small group circle. Each person is a connected part of the whole, and, at the same time is a whole themselves. As groups share experiences, personal reflection can lead to awareness of one's potential, power, and place in the unfolding universe.

Also from the East, from Taoism, is the circle of balance, yin/yang. Taoism is a philosophy, a spirituality, of inner tranquillity.

"The yin/yang symbol is the interlocking, melting together of the flow of movement within a circle. The similar—and yet at the same time contrasting—energies are moving together. The whole idea of a circle divided in this way is to show that within a unity there is a duality and polarity and contrast. The only way to find real balance without losing the centering feeling of the circle is to think of these contrasting energies moving together in unison, in harmony."

(Hang, 1973)

T'ai Chi Ch'uan is an exercise sequence based on Tao, which focuses on energy within the body (physical and mental) coming to balance and rhythmic flow. The yin/yang symbol is circular representing the required balance of body and spirit, movement and stillness, masculine and feminine, inside and outside.

In any case, the symbolic circles of the medicine wheel, the mandala, the yin/yang, and the interactional circles of family, group and community, have common denominators. They can help us find our place, our energy, our significance, our purpose, and our direction in the world. They can guide us to awareness of the cyclical flow of all that is, and of the desirability for balance in our lives.

The Raccoon Circle

There is, then, a rich body of philosophical base underlying the sequence of challenge education activities that are called "Raccoon Circles." Focusing on the symbolic significance of the circle, and recognizing the importance of ritual in groupwork, this sequence of small group activities holds promise for many challenge/adventure programs.

The basic Raccoon Circle is a 12-15 foot length of 1" tubular webbing (available in camping and sporting goods stores). This webbing is knotted into a loop of about 4 feet in diameter. The knotting of the loop can be an initial exposure to the ritual and symbology of the experiential sequence. While a simple overhand knot may be safe enough, there is a greater safety in tying the two ends together by a "water knot." This is a basic overhand knot tied in each end of the webbing, weaving the two knots together so that they pull against each other in impasse. The very process of carefully tying this knot, and explaining how it strengthens the loop can orient participants to the power of the circle.

Activities for the Raccoon Circle should be facilitated with appropriate attention to guidelines for challenge programs. Leaders must be attentive to the following:

> **Safety.** Some of the activities will require special safety instructions and attention to "spotting" procedures. Those who have not had appropriate training should not utilize the

higher risk activities. Ultimately, the leader is responsible for the safety of the group, and the activities should be used only when the group develops to readiness.

Health. Usually the rule that "you are your own best doctor" applies for activities in this sequence. People know of their own bad backs, knee injuries, pregnancy, etc., and should be encouraged to self-care. But again, it is the responsibility of the leader to be aware of clients' health problems and physical precautions or limitations.

Choice. From onset, everyone has the option of choosing to not participate. No one should be pressured to participate by anyone in the group. No one should "volunteer" anyone else to a particular task. While some groups request that those choosing to not participate give explanation, this is not necessary. The basic philosophy of "challenge by choice" is overviewed in Project Adventure's book, Islands of Healing (Schoel, Prouty & Radcliffe, 1988).

Sequencing. The concept of sequencing implies that all groups should begin with activities that are appropriate to psychological and physical readiness. More difficult and higher risk tasks should typically be offered only after the group evolves. However, there is no rigid sequence to follow. Good leaders become skillful at matching the activities to the developmental readiness of the group involved.

Processing. In order for awareness and learning to unfold in the challenge/adventure sequence, there must be attention to de-briefing. Activities which are worth doing are worth talking about. The power of experiential activities is their contribution to group dynamics and individual awareness which lead to personal growth and learning. Facilitators of challenge education activities must also facilitate the process of reflection for participants. While many who lead challenge/adventure programs have not had extensive training in leading group processing, there have been valuable suggestions provided in the past few years (c.f., Boud, et. al., 1988; Nadler & Luckner, 1992; Knapp, 1992; Gass, 1993).

The most standard procedure for facilitating the de-briefing phase of the experiential sequence is small group discussion—the processing circle. This method certainly fits the general mode of a sequence of activities with the Raccoon Circle. (Recently, an experienced leader informed that she has come to carry two different colored Raccoon Circles into the program sequence. The red circle is used for the activities, but when the blue circle is brought out the group knows that it is time to connect, sit back and participate in a session of reflection, sharing and processing of the experiences.)

However, there is also value in what have been called "alternative methods of processing (Smith, 1987; 1993). Individual reflection can be introduced by facilitating basic relaxation, centering, and also time for introspection or journaling. Break-outs to smaller groups (diads, triads, etc.) can also be valuable. Many people will share more in the smaller group, and it also provides opportunity for more people to discuss feelings and insights (One leader reported that he usually assigns participants to a "sharing group" of 3-4 for the whole sequence. He even created smaller web loops (2 ft. lengths) about which the sharing group is to connect, balance, and sit down for debriefing sessions.).

Suggestions for Special Activities with the Raccoon Circle

When facilitating a time-limited sequence of experiential activities with the Raccoon Circle, or using it periodically in a more elaborate challenge/adventure sequence, there are a number of special activities possible.

Color Coding. After the group has completed an activity and instructions are to connect to the circle for a de-briefing session, give them a different color webbing with previously assigned focus. For example: A red circle could mean that the group did very well on the task, and should enjoy the focus on reasons for success; A blue circle could mean that the group did not do well on the task, and should then struggle with analysis of their under-achievement; A yellow circle could signify a developing interpersonal conflict or group problems which require attention (and could be brought forth for the group at time of any crisis or any interactional breakdown).

Keeper of the Sacred Circle. When the group breaks for mealtime, or finishes a day's program with intention to come together again in a day, a week, or a month, have the group choose someone to be the "Keeper of the Sacred Circle." That person would have responsibility for taking care of the Raccoon circle until the group is together again.

Record Keeping. After each activity accomplished by the group, have them come to consensus about the best world of description for their performance (e.g., cooperative, active, dysfunction, competitive). They could then print that word on the webbing with magic marker, thus keeping record of the group as the sequence unfolds. Or, have each person write their choice of word(s) describing the group in general.

Power Strips. At termination of a program that has incorporated the Raccoon Circle, untie the web loop and cut the webbing into foot-long strips. Each person can take away a piece of the power, the "good medicine," that the group has generated. (Tie it to your belt, sew it to your jacket, keep it on your desk, tack it on your bulletin board, or just carry it in your pocket). Later, holding the strip, reflect back on the circle of experience, and personal power will be enhanced.

Activities

Circle of Trust

This is the beginning experience with the Raccoon Circle. Standing in a circle, all members of the group hold on to the web loop with both hands. By moving the feet slightly to the center of the circle and leaning back, a circle of trust (trust in the webbing, self-trust, trust-in-others) is formed. This is the basic connection to the Raccoon Circle and to the basic trust circle. Instructions can be to close eyes, come to center, breathe deeply, and sense the connection, the support, and the security of the circle.

The facilitator can focus the group's attention on comfort by pointing out the value of not twisting the webbing. The group can also be told that they can re-arrange people to attain the best balance. If it is observed that the group, or some members of the group, are not in a full trust lean, instructions to move feet a few more inches inward are appropriate.

When the group achieves balance and stillness, trust is apparent to everyone. Typically, this circle of trust brings the group to a state of connectedness and involvement that would usually not occur for some time in a group's development.

When the group is comfortable with the trust lean, have the participants open their eyes, look about at others in the circle, share names, memories of favorite places, or the animal they would most like to be. There can, of course, also be sharings of feelings and thoughts about trust, interdependency, cooperation, safety and/or belongingness.

Once the group has learned to connect in this basic circle of trust it can be re-established when appropriate through the challenge/adventure sequence. Leaders can take out the Raccoon Circle and instruct the group to "connect up." This can be a precursor of announcements, breaks, processing sessions, or decision making discussions.

If there are group members who choose to not "trust lean," or have difficulty with the task because of physical strength or disability, they can still be involved. Even though the trust lean is not possible for the wheel chaired, they can hold on to the web circle. I have seen persons with disability or obesity become the center of the circle, thus connected to the group and a part of the experience.

This trust circle can also be the basis for some appropriate warm-up and stretching before more physically demanding tasks. There can be instructions to breath deeply, do neck rolls and shoulder rolls, and isometrically stretch out arms and legs. Holding the trust lean, it is possible to do one leg extension stretch/lifts; and then reverse that process. Facilitators can guide the group to connect to the web loop with only one arm, leaning out and windmilling the other arm forward and backward; and then reverse that process.

Circle of Cooperation

When the group can hold the balance, instructions are for them to slowly, cooperative, rhythmically, lower themselves to a sitting position—keeping the plan of the circle parallel to the ground. Then, slowly, cooperatively, pull back up to a standing position. Let the group practice the down and up moves until they are comfortable with them. Again, if they wish to move people about to insure group parallel movement they may do so.

Next, instruct the group to make a three time sequential flow of the movements—down, up, down, up, down, up. It may be appropriate to tell the group, when standing, that they can relax the pressure of the Raccoon Circle and shake out hands and arms. In the early going, some people tend to make the task more physical than it need be, but with practice they will relax their operating tension.

Finally, the group is to create an appropriate sound for the down and the up movement. When they have agreed on sound effects, they can then enjoy their circle of cooperation in the three time sequence—with sound effects.

Willows and Waves

Starting from the standing balance, the group can shift the essential responsibility for supporting the group about the circle. This involves "giving up" or "surrendering" control sometimes, and "taking on" the responsibility for helping hold the group in balance at other times. This "wave" of support can be passes about the circle, first one direction and then the other, demonstrating the flowing balance that can be achieved.

In the early going, the Raccoon circle should not move from side to side more than a few inches, or people will be off-balanced. However, as the group becomes more proficient at shifting responsibility from person to person, they may be able to have the web loop move 10-12 inches without anybody losing balance.

Debriefing of this exercise can focus on the reality of one's involvement in a group—sometimes being dependent and "leaning on" others for support, and sometimes standing strong and being available for others to "lean on."

One variation of this activity is to focus solely on the cooperative task of synchronized creation of the "wave." This involves individuals sitting down and then pulling back up in a pattern that flows about the circle. This is a difficult activity, and requires that people opposite each other in the circle coordinate movement—when one is down the other must be up. Also, whenever one sits down, that takes the web loop down, and means that those nearby must be in synch.

Shake-Up

While my own utilization of the Raccoon Circle has usually been to create balance and harmony, a friend recently shared this lively version. It is similar to a standing game of wrestling, where one opponents tries to off-balance the other while staying in balance. Have the group start in the basic trust circle, and give instructions that each person is to shake and move the web loop and try to off-balance others in the group, without moving their own feet.

Those with more upper body strength or greater range of movement may be independently successful. Others will consciously or unconsciously begin to cooperate with neighbors and succeed in off-balancing those across the circle. This exercise gets people in touch with their competitive and aggressive tendencies, but the activity is designed to create conflict between that tendency and their supportive, care taking tendency.

After the group has had some time with the instruction to try and off-balance others, introduce a second instruction. While working to off-balance others, everyone is to take responsibility for helping the person to their right stay in balance. Participants will often respond quite differently. Some will tend to put more energy on the goal of off-balancing others, while others will put great effort into the goal of helping their neighbor stay in balance. When most of the people emphasize the care taking goal, the whole group will shake and tug the web loop—but no one will be off-balanced.

Pass-the-Loop

This is an adaptation of the standard challenge/adventure activity that is typically done with a hula hoop, or a bicycle tire inner tube. Knot the Raccoon Circle so there are two smaller loops (24"—30" diameter). Have the group stand in a circle with hands connected, and put one of the circles around

the arm of one person. (Just let the other loop dangle) The task is to pass the loop completely around the circle without disconnecting hands. People may not help each other much at first—but they will as the task proceeds.

After the group masters the task, have them give time estimate for performance. There will be overachievers and underachievers, but the group will usually decide on a compromise time estimate. The task can be made more difficult by knotting the web loop to create a smaller circle.

Figure-Eight-Pass

A more complex task, requiring greater cooperation and forcing closer involvement, is the figure-eight-pass. Make sure the knot is centered so the two loops are of equal size, and place both over one person's arm. Instruct the group that one of the loops is to be passed around the circle clockwise, while the other is passing along counterclockwise. At some point the loops will cross over each other, and then move on around the circle.

Crossover

The loop is halved and laid on the ground in the center of the group. An outer boundary can be set with 30-40 ft. of twine or any longer rope. The task requires an even number of participants, so any extra person becomes the time-keeper.

Instruct the group that the task is for everyone to change places with the person directly opposite them, and that as they do so they much touch one foot inside the centered small Raccoon Circle. This must be accomplished as fast as possible, and without the "errors" of touching the web circle or any other person. The group has three things to decide:

> The procedure the group will use to accomplish the task?
>
> The procedure for keeping track of errors?
>
> How fast they can do it?

After 10 minutes for practice, the group spokesperson will describe their methodology for the problem, describe the system for counting errors, and set the group goals—We can do it in ___ seconds with ___ errors.

This problem/activity offers many opportunities for processing. Who become spokesperson? How? How many different procedures were discussed and tried? How are they handling errors? Self-report? Peer-report? Observer? Was their time estimate accurate? Could they do it faster?

The O.K. Corral

This is a fun activity for moving the group from one place to another (e.g., outside to inside, lunch break). The task is for everyone in the group to get inside the Raccoon Circle (waist high) and figure out how to move safely. If the group is too large, a couple of people can become "wranglers," with responsibility for leading the corralled group around. If the group is small, knot the web loop so that the corral will be nicely crowded!

Once the group is inside the corral and figures out a pattern of movement, the facilitator may give instructions—"three steps forward," "turn right," "over here."

Ships and Sharks

This is another adaptation of an activity that is usually done with hula hoops. It is a fun way to move groups across a field, as it requires large open space. Everyone in the group must hold on to the Raccoon Circle and run—until the facilitator cries out "Sharks!" They must then lay the web loop on the ground and stand inside of it. When the command of "Ships" is given, all must grab the circle and run. If there are two or more groups, a command can be given to "Change Ships," and everyone must scramble to another circle. This activity can be made more complex by limiting the number of people from one group that can board another ship.

The Clock

Raccoon's Circle is twisted into a series of four small circles so that a web bed is formed for one member of the group to lie on. Four people each side should be sufficient. One person should take responsibility for cradling and supportive care of the head, and others can life/support the legs. The facilitator can instruct the group that they should gently lay the person onto the webbing, as the activity does not involve any "trust fall."

The task is for the group, attending to safety, to rotate clockwise so that the head of the reclined person points to the facilitator—12 o'clock. The facilitator then calls out times, and the group rotates the reclined person. Whenever it is 12 o'clock, a different person is placed in the web bed.

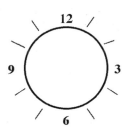

Whenever group activities begin to involve lifting and/or carrying, instructions on safety and comfort may be appropriate. Leaders should overview spotting readiness and the requirement for careful attention to the task. The group should be informed about making sure that people who have been lifted or carried are solidly back on their feet at the end of their experience; groups tend to hasten to lift the next person before the last person is completely back in balance.

Raccoon's Cradle

This is an activity for quiet, gentle, energizing, and healing interaction. It should be offered when the mood of the group is such that they can approach the activity with appropriate attitude. The experience can be powerful for the participants, and may best fit near the end of the activity sequence—or even be the closing exercise. Raccoon's Circle is twisted into a series of three or four small circles so that a web bed is formed. This should be referred to as the "cradle" throughout the exercise, and members of the group take turns being rocked by their peers. Four people on each side should be sufficient, and one person should take responsibility for cradling the head of the reclining person.

Throughout the exercise the facilitator should stress the gentleness, warmth, quiet, peaceful, healing capacity of the cradle. Instruct group to relax, breathe deeply, and focus on transferring positive energy to the person in the cradle. The person cradled should close eyes and enjoy!

Let the group decide on their cradling motion. Some will rock the person from head to toe, others from side to side, and still others in a circular motion. Each member of the group should be invited to have a 2-3 minute relaxing ride in the cradle.

Electric Fence

This is a variation of the standard teams course task, but accomplished with the Raccoon Circle. Stretch the web loop into rectangle about 1' x 4-5'. The corners can be tied off to trees or gymnasium poles, or can be held in place by two members of the group.

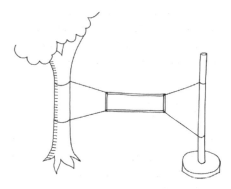

The task is to pass all members of the group between the top and bottom "electric fence" without touching. The problems of passing first and last person make the task quite difficult. Depending on group readiness, the task can be simplified by having half the group start on each side of the fence, and then alternately passing people through until everyone is opposite where they started.

Four Corners

A variation on electric fence and the teams course task called "porthole" involved doubling the Raccoon Circle, then squaring it, and having the group pass people through without touching it. If the square is not mounted, then the people holding it can be considered as "free-floating". The group can lift a person, hold them stationary, and those holding the square can pass it over the person's body while carefully avoiding any contact. This activity is similar to Jim Cain's "Wormhole."

Toss Up

This is a higher risk activity that begins with the Raccoon Circle being twisted into three or four smaller circles (as for "the Clock" and "Raccoon's Cradle"). The task is reminiscent of the "blanket toss", but it is much safer. The person lying on the web bed is raised up and down, and then tossed into the air. They will free fall back into the security of the group. Most groups will quickly learn how to perform a "1,2,3,up" maneuver, and they will have tendency to want to toss the person as high as possible. The facilitator may want to set a limit of "no more than a foot" or "no higher than your head."

Knot Around

When the group has connected to the Raccoon Circle in trust lean and then sat down, have them release pressure but keep both hands on the webbing. Note the position of the knot, and assign the task of passing that knot about the circle as fast as possible. Instructions may be that every person must touch the knot, or to allow larger movements of the knot. Precautions about avoiding rope burns would be appropriate. After the group practices, there can be goal setting of time to completion. The task can be varied by having everyone in the group use only one hand; or having them lay back, hold the web loop with their feet, and pass the knot. Consider this a Raccoon Circle version of Warp Speed.

A Gathering of Raccoons

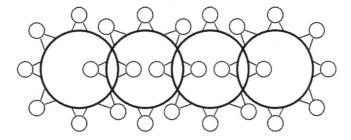

When there are two or more groups, there can be a closing ceremony that involves overlapping the smaller Raccoon circles into one community circle. This involves one person from each group moving into the circle of another group, but still staying connected to their own group's web loop.

If there are enough groups the ends of a connecting line can be connected to form a larger circle. When the whole community is connected, experience the experience! Can they work together to sit down? Stand up? Three times in synch? With sound effects? In a wave?

A Final Word

The appropriate way to learn about challenge/adventure activities is by experiencing them. Leaders should not use these Raccoon Circles unless they have had experience with them in a small group sequence. Also, remember that "creativity" and "adaptation" are the key words in using these activities. Know your groups, and know yourself!

> *"When the Raccoon looks out from inside, the circle of connectedness*
> *of all things in the universe becomes quite evident."*
>
> Tom Smith

Why Raccoon Circles?

Tom Smith

During the past decade, one of the most popular tools in an experiential educator's "bag-of-tricks" has been the 15 foot long nylon webbing strip known as a Raccoon Circle. The theory and practice of "Raccoon Circles" was circulated amongst challenge and adventure leaders for 5-6 years; then, *The Book on Raccoon Circles* (Cain and Smith, 2002), further popularized the methodology. Because of the broad interest in the power and potential of the many activities that can be facilitated with this simple prop, it seems appropriate to ask, "Why Raccoon Circles?" This paper answers that question by focusing on the rationale and the realities of the Raccoon Circle for working with small groups.

A majority of the programs facilitated by experiential education leaders involve small groups proceeding through a sequence of activities. The methodology for facilitating these groups has a variety of historic precedents. There are roots in adventure education, outdoor education, humanistic education, awareness education, somatic education, recreation education, and other fields of theory and practice. (Smith, et al., 1992).

> There are a number of ways to characterize the many forms of groupwork performed by challenge/adventure leaders. There may be a continuum of application. Some groups are basically recreational . . . other groups have goals that can be classified as enrichment . . . Many contemporary leaders consider themselves as facilitators of personal growth, and in recent years there has been an increasing utilization of the challenge/adventure format for counseling and psychotherapy.
>
> (Cain and Smith, 2002).

The goals of these groups vary depending on the program, the leader, the client population, and the location and duration of the sequence. A generalized statement about the goals of typical challenge/adventure programs would be that they are offered to enhance the personal growth and learning of the participants. So, why Raccoon Circles?

Symbolism

The circle is a symbol of connectedness, community and unity. A circle of connection becomes a circle of influence. Circles have been symbolic for humankind through all history, and experiential education leaders can open the doorway to many broad philosophies and practices by starting from a simple circle of connection with the Raccoon Circle. One example would be the philosophy and practices of Taoism. If one wants to approach the facilitation of holistic personal growth from the perspectives of Taoism, the Raccoon Circle can be related to the symbolic circle of yin/yang. Basic exercises that involve stillness, balance, energy flow, and harmonious group movement can readily be interpreted in terms of the wisdom of the Tao. Another example would be the cosmology and traditions of the Native American cultures. If one is interested in the wisdom of the Native Americans, the Raccoon Circle can be interpreted as a "Medicine Wheel," and that opens the door for introducing many other small group exercises adapted from traditions of the indigenous Americans. (Smith & Quinn, 2004).

Those who seek "sharing circles" of connection for personal growth and support in the quest for psychological and spiritual fulfillment can also find value in Raccoon Circle exercises. There are many books on small group processes that speak to the symbolism of the circle. In her book, *Calling The Circle* (1998), Christina Baldwin ties small group processes to the 12-step program, contemporary spirituality, and the search for mental health. In *The Circle of Simplicity* (1997), Cecile Andrews talks about "learning circles" to simplify life and find inner peace and balance. The real meaning of the words and theoretical perspectives about the value of small group circles that appear in books can be understood experientially with Raccoon Circles.

Whatever the symbolic interpretation of the circle, people can better understand the lessons if they are learned experientially, and the Raccoon Circle offers that. When one leans back in a circle of connection and trust, there is somatic learning in parallel to cognitive learning. Whatever the goals of the adventure group, or the operating philosophy of the facilitator, the Raccoon Circle can experientially exemplify the value of circles of connection.

Ritual

The enthusiastic acceptance of Raccoon Circle activities by group facilitators is partly related to the fact that these activities can bring some basic ritual into the challenge/adventure program. Even if the group leader does not emphasize ritual, groups will usually find ways to create and incorporate ritual into their evolving group process. With the Raccoon Circle, groups can create rituals for bringing the group together to begin a new activity, for celebration of their successes, for caring for the sacred web circle when it is not in use, and for "connect up and sit down" (perfect circle) readiness for debriefing sessions.

There can also be meaningful ritual for creation of the Raccoon Circle, emphasizing the transformation of a simple strip of webbing into a symbolic, and power packed circle which can guide, teach, and heal everyone in the group. A ritual of creation of the group's Raccoon Circle can be a significant experience in its own right, with lessons about earth connections and personal powers. *The Book on Raccoon Circles* (2002), and this book outline a creation ritual based on the notion of the ancient Greek Philosopher, Empedocles, that all of creation is made up of four elements—earth, air, fire and water.

The Raccoon Circle can also contribute to meaningful closing ceremonies for any experiential/adventure group. I have had groups cut their circle into carry-away strips for each participant, symbolizing personal discovery and the growth and learning of the whole program. At one outdoor education center, each group autographs their circle and then hangs it from the rafters of the lodge.

Simplicity

One of the obvious values of Raccoon Circle activities is that there is no need for numerous, complex and expensive props. Activities with the Raccoon Circle can address many of the standard goals of the challenge group—communication, cooperation, trust, inclusion, problem-solving, risk-taking, sharing, caring, nurturance and fun. Even if the experiential program involves more complex equipment—like a rope course; the ropes, carabiners and helmets of a climbing trip; the canoes, paddles and life jackets of a canoe journey—Raccoon Circles can still have significant value.

Raccoon Circle activities can be used to demonstrate basic experiential education concepts when a leader goes out to a school to provide information and orientation on a forthcoming program. They can be used in the lodge or campsite when the group first gathers. They can demonstrate the power and the joy of group connection before and after more complex activities. During basic activities with the Raccoon Circle, leaders can observe individuals and group dynamics and gather information that might be valuable when the activities get more complex.

A standard 15 foot length of tubular nylon webbing can typically be purchased for under seven dollars. Even if one is working with large gatherings, which would be sub-divided into groups of 10-12 participants, the total "equipment budget" for a Raccoon Circles program would be minimal. There is no doubt that the simplicity and the cost efficiency of Raccoon Circles is a factor for many who want to facilitate personal growth and learning through experiential education sequences.

Portability

Starting about twenty years ago, many experiential education facilitators recognized that they could create portable equipment which could be taken away from the ropes and teams course center. It was an extension of the earlier rational for building ropes and teams courses: "If you can't take the students to the mountains, take the mountains to the students." At the same time that many schools, hospitals, outdoor education centers, and corporate training centers were building ropes and teams courses, demand for experiential challenge/adventure programs became even greater. Many of those interested in having client groups experience some of the dynamics, teambuilding, problem-solving, and risk taking processes of the adventure program, began asking for equipment they could use in their gymnasiums, conference rooms, classrooms and schoolyards. There was a market for portables, and the professionals responded.

Challenge/adventure professionals began carrying all the equipment they would need for facilitating a meaningful ½ or full-day training in their backpack. When I began using Raccoon Circles, I found that I could reduce my need for props considerably. Professional colleagues used to chuckle when I told them that I could facilitate an all day workshop out of my fanny-pack—if I could include a web-loop. To my surprise, the repertoire of activities that could be done with the Raccoon Circle kept expanding, and by the turn of the century I needed nothing much beyond a few web loops and a stopwatch! One experienced facilitator shared with me his interpretation of Raccoon Circles as "a teams course in your pocket."

More recently, airlines have been limiting the weight of luggage a passenger can bring on an airplane. For facilitators acquainted with Raccoon Circles, it is possible to bring enough webbing for groups of a hundred or more participants, without exceeding the maximum weight allowance.

Acceleration

When I ask others to share the reasons for their enthusiasm about the theory and practice of Raccoon Circles, there is frequent citing of the rapidity of group development during the early interactions. Many years ago, I noticed that myself, and it was one of the reasons that I became excited about exploring the possibilities of the web circle. In groupwork, one wants the people to connect to each other and begin to feel the acceptance, trust, safety, and understanding of the group as quickly as possible. When a group can connect, relax, laugh together, and find those feelings of trust and safety, they are ready to respond positively to the opportunity that the small group process can provide for personal growth, learning, and healing. Oftentimes, groups will struggle together for considerable time before finding those feelings of community, belonging, support and compassion.

Raccoon Circles can accelerate the process of group building. The simple instruction, "connect up, take a deep breath, look around at others, and then lean back," is like leaving rubber on the pavement when a group starts forward. When the group can find the balance, support, and cooperation necessary to do a simple sit-down and stand-up with the circle of connection, the power of the circle is immediately experienced by both body and mind. So much seems to be happening for participants and for the group in those early activities that it is difficult to explain. I have even suggested that the unfolding dynamics may not need to be explained, for "the circle speaks for itself.

Continuity

One of the major challenges for the facilitator of small groups proceeding through a variety of activities is to guide participants to sense the inter-connectedness of those activities and their relationship to the overall goals of the program. Sometimes the activities presented are perceived as piecemeal, and the sequence is felt to be disjointed. At best, the participant may feel as if they are moving down a cafeteria line with no labels on the food just stacking items on their tray; and what we would like them to experience is a gourmet dining experience of personal discovery.

The Raccoon Circle can provide a needed thread of connection for various program activities. If the group circles up to ready for an initiative, to celebrate their success, and to create a debriefing circle, then aspects of the group process become contiguous. Like the Raccoon Circle itself, a program can have a beginning, a middle, and an end, and be knotted into a circle of wholeness.

At one outdoor center, where school groups visit 5-6 times a year, the staff had long attempted to relate all the activities and all the visits to their overall mission. They explored having classes discover an appropriate "beginning place," and start there every time they came to the center. That was somewhat effective, but lacked the experiential connection to the program and place that they wanted students to feel. Raccoon Circles met their needs. Now, when groups de-board the school bus they walk to their beginning place and "connect up." With a little briefing from the leaders, they quickly feel the sense of place and purpose. They are then ready for that days' activities, but they can also perceive the connection between that day at that place and the day some six weeks earlier.

Processing

Perhaps the best reason for introducing Raccoon Circles to experiential education groups is the contribution that simple instructions of "connect up, lean back, and sit down" can make to the briefings and debriefings. Some of the typical problems of small group discussions—e.g., splintering, where subgroups interact simultaneously; individuals moving physically away from the group and not participating; silence—can be addressed with a Raccoon Circle. When everyone in a group connects to the circle, leans back in basic trust, and sits down, they form a perfect, totally inclusive, circle. Leaders can instruct participants to relax their hold on the webbing and move to center to reduce the tension, but suggest that everyone should always keep at least one hand on the circle. This keeps everyone in their place for group discussion.

One debriefing procedure with the Raccoon Circle is called "the talking knot," which is an adaptation of the Native American tradition of "the talking stick." The procedure sets the rules for group discussion; whomever holds the knot (the stick, charm,, or sacred object) talks, and everyone else listens. The knot can be passed around the circle freely, with anyone who wants to contribute to the discussion grabbing it as it travels by; or it can be passed from person to person, stopping by everyone and requesting their input. One leader told me of varying the free moving procedure by grasping the webbing when the knot was in front of one of the group members who had not contributed, thus requesting some sharing.

The Raccoon Circle becomes a symbol of the groups sharing, caring, and listening. When everyone is closely connected in a processing circle, what Carl Rogers (1970) calls "a healing capacity in the group" has opportunity to unfold. In line with the concept of Gestalt psychology, that the whole is greater than the sum of the parts, it might be argued that the healing power of the whole group is greater than that of any one individual—especially when that whole group is connected in energy and spirit.

Celebration

Human beings have a deep-seated need for connection. (Flinders, 2002). In moments when this need for belonging is fulfilled, and the individual senses the energy and warmth of human connections, the blood flows with a joyous rapture. Like children enjoying the laughter and comradery of the "pig pile" or a game of musical chairs, all people can set aside inhibitions and playfully interact. Raccoon Circle activities are often as play with a purpose, and groups do tend to have fun. There is frequent laughter and joyful exchange as participants create movements, experience the goodness of the connections, and sense the developing connections with others. Such laughter and celebration of belonging does not diminish the impact of the experiences; in fact, it suggests that the group is relaxed and ready for more adventure experiences.

In the initial sequence of activities with Raccoon Circles, I have the group proceed through four steps. First, I have them connect up and do a basic trust lean, finding personal and group balance and stillness. Second, I have them experience and practice sitting down and standing up, keeping the plane of the circle parallel to the ground and in balance. Third, I have them create "an appropriate down-sound, and an appropriate up-sound" for their group. Finally, I have them do a sequence of "three

---

Raccoon Circles—Why Indeed!

Jim Cain

In the past decade, I've had the opportunity to travel to most of the fifty United States and ten or so foreign countries. On every one of those trips you could find several Raccoon Circles in my luggage. Without a doubt, Raccoon Circles are the most portable and versatile teambuilding tool on the planet. You can carry them onto an airplane (at least according to today's regulations!) Which means that even if the airlines lose your luggage, you can still carry on enough Raccoon Circles to easily fill an entire program. They are also easy to take into the back country without overloading your backpack. You can pack enough for even 100 people in a small day pack. River rafting guides and outfitters like the fact that they can get wet and still do the job. They can be used on the bus during school outings. They easily fit into bicycle storage bags for trekking programs. They are one of the only teambuilding props that you can use from the ice-breakers at the beginning of the program, to teambuilding challenges in the middle, to debriefing, reviewing and closing activities at the end. They come in dozens of colors, and some even have cool designs on them. They are probably available in your school or corporate colors. They are economical. You can buy enough for every one of your camp counselors without breaking the bank. You can change the size of a Raccoon Circle simply by tying several together, which means you'll always have the right size ready for your group. They provide a tactile experience that connects group members together. You can find dozens of metaphors related to circles–one is bound to be perfect for your group. They are one of the few teambuilding props where participants can sit or stand and both be connected (perfect for audiences where mobility impairments are present). Even left-over pieces of webbing are good for something! A single Raccoon Circle makes the perfect size gathering for people to feel connected without feeling crowded. There are new Raccoon Circle activities growing every day!

times down and up, with sound effects." There is always laughter and joyful interaction as they do their "Yee - Haw," "Oooh - Aaah," "Wild - Thing," or "Snap, Crackle - Pop" cheers. As the group creates a meaningful group cheer, which they then use for moments of celebration throughout an activity sequence, there is warmth, good group energy, and FUN. The very experience of connecting to others in a safe and trusting way gives rise to joy—and that is one of the values of the Raccoon Circle.

Summary

So, "WHY RACCOON CIRCLES?" My temptation is to argue that experiential educators who facilitate small groups with goals of personal growth and learning can count on the Raccoon Circle to enhance participants' awareness of self, others, environment, The Other, the self-other interdependency, the self-environment interdependency, and the self-other-environment-Other ONENESS. The power and potential of the circle of connection is unlimited.

I have come to recognize a number of reasons for the success and acceptance of Raccoon Circles. The associated activities have potential to incorporate meaningful ritual and symbol into the any program of challenge/adventure. A Raccoon Circle is a simple and portable prop which can be carried in pocket to introduce people to the methodologies of experiential education. For the small group, Raccoon Circles can accelerate the process of group building and provide some meaningful threads of connection between various activities. Using the Raccoon Circle can even provide some connection between outdoor growth and learning sessions that are separated in time. When groups are connected by a Raccoon Circle, they are perfectly arranged for a meaningful briefing or debriefing discussion. Finally, the Raccoon Circle offers people a chance to experience connectedness and belongingness, which gives rise to joyous celebration of the human species. Living that involves loving and laughing is good.

References

Andrews, C. (1997). *The Circle of Simplicity: Return to the Good Life.* New York: HarperCollins Books.

Baldwin, C. (1998). *Calling the Circle: The First and Future Culture.* New York: Bantam Books.

Cain, J. & Smith, T. (2002). *THE BOOK on Raccoon Circles.* Oklahoma City, Oklahoma: Learning Unlimited.

Flinders, C. L. (2002). *The Value of Belonging.* San Francisco, CA: HarperCollins Books.

Sidle, Clinton C. (2005). *The Leadership Wheel–Five Steps for Achieving Individual and Organizational Greatness.* New York: Palgrave Macmillan

Smith, T., Roland, C., Havens, M. & Hoyt, J. (1992). *The Theory and Practice of Challenge Education.* Dubuque, IA: Kendall/Hunt Publishing.

Smith, T. & Quinn, W. (2004). *The Challenge of Native American Traditions.* Lake Geneva, WI: Raccoon Institute.

Rogers, C. R. (1970). *On Encounter Groups.* New York: Harper.

Ritual and Ceremony of the Circle

Tom Smith

"There is something magical about any intense, tightly knit group of people working together and playing together, a feeling of being in the world while at the same time being apart from it, apart together. We believe that even those of us who have not experienced that magic hear its distant music, feel its ancient call. A transformative community is a nearly indispensable launching pad for transformation. Such a community can create the context and the confidence for a transforming journey."
(George Leonard and Michael Murphy, The Life We Are Given)

Challenge/adventure programs are usually offered as a small group experience. Even when goals are stated in terms of personal development, most of the activity sequence is offered to a small group. The power of groups to affect the individual members has been noted by many. Johnson and Johnson (1987) have pointed out a number of ways that a group may influence its members, including:

- Groups provide a setting in which interpersonal skills may be learned, mastered, and integrated.
- Groups can generate a sense of community, belonging, support, acceptance, and assistance.
- Groups influence the behavioral and the attitudinal patterns of members.
- Groups require the use of a wide variety of interpersonal skills and competencies.
- Groups provide constructive peer relations needed for healthy social and cognitive growth.
- Groups provide opportunities for people to understand and help their peers. Helping others provides an important opportunity for altruistic behavior that may be absent in daily life.
- Groups provide a variety of sources of feedback. In a group setting, participants can test their behavior and seek feedback.

Carl Rogers noted that intensive small group experience often gives rise to "a healing capacity in the group." As the small group experience evolves, a number of the group members show natural and spontaneous interest and capacity for dealing with others in a very helpful, even therapeutic manner.

"This kind of ability shows up so commonly in groups that it has led me to feel that the ability to be healing and therapeutic is far more common in human life than we suppose. Often it needs only the permission granted - or freedom made possible - by the climate of a free-flowing group experience to become evident."
(Rogers, 1970)

There are a number of ways to characterize the many forms of groupwork facilitated by experiential, challenge and adventure leaders. Some groups are basically recreational, while others are designed to teach outdoor skills. Many groups have goals for personal development of the members - leadership, self-esteem, values clarification, empowerment, etc. In recent years there has been focus on goals of improving social relationships and teamwork - communication, cooperation, trust, tolerance, etc. Whatever the goals of the group, challenge education leaders would suggest that the methodology can enhance the necessary developmental stages of the group. The experience-based activities of challenge/adventure programming tend to connect people quickly. Issues of cohesiveness, trust, inclusion, cooperation, and involvement are tackled in a playful and non-threatening way. When groups begin to share experiences of challenge and adventure, they typically bond quickly and meaningfully, and after a few hours they can become joyously connected. This has certainly been the case when facilitators have utilized the sequence of activities known as "Raccoon Circles." It is as if that circular loop of tubular nylon webbing has some very special power to connect people.

The circle itself, is one of the most frequently used symbols in human history. It has often been suggested as a symbol of unity, community, and connectedness, and it is incorporated into many meaningful cultural rituals. Even though numerous challenge education activities begin with the instruction, "connect hands in a circle," experiential educators seldom point up the significance of that circle. This circle of connection becomes a circle of influence for the people involved.

One of the values of developing a sequence of experiential activities with the Raccoon Circle is that there can be meaningful attention to ritual and symbol. I think it is time to give thought to the importance of, and the potentials for, rituals and ceremony in challenge and adventure experiential education groupwork.

The Importance of Ritual

In the past few decades, a number of sociologists, cultural anthropologists, historians, and critics of contemporary society have suggested that a contributing factor to many of our current psychological, social, and spiritual problems is the lack of significant ritual and ceremony in our society. (c.f., Eliade, 1958; LaFontaine, 1972; Clark & Hindley, 1975, Moore & Myerhoff, 1977; Turner, 1969, 1982). This thesis is not supported by all anthropologists, and there is certainly very limited empirical data on the issue. However, even after a controlled observational study led a research team to conclude that it was certainly possible for cultures to survive with relatively little attention to ritual, they still concluded that:

> *"We have no record of societies up to the present that have existed*
> *without ritual. Hence if they existed they did not survive!"*
> (Fried & Fried, 1980)

Ritual and ceremony has often played an important role in the transmission of cultural value orientations, behavioral expectancies, and identity awareness from one generation to the next. Rituals were often conducted by cultural leaders (the elders, the chiefs, the shamans, etc.) to steer people in positive directions for society, but sometimes evil-doers (witches, wizards, tricksters, etc.) used it to steer people along less desirable paths. Ritual has been important in cultivating, enhancing, or maintaining particular spiritual awareness and commitments, as offered through organized religion or other cultural teachers. In many ways, it has been the rituals and ceremonies of societies that have passed major cultural, philosophical, sociological, cosmological, and spiritual paradigms from one generation to the next.

In most primitive cultures, one of the significant rituals was the "rite of passage." This ritual helped individuals and societies define the transition from childhood to adult status and responsibility. Myerhoff has suggested that the rites of passage rituals served to "resolve social problems and perpetuate social order." (Myerhoff, 1982) Indeed, there is much wisdom in the rituals, ceremonies, and traditions of the so-called "primitive cultures," and many have suggested that we seek to re-discover that wisdom.

> *"Western man is lost in his search for happiness, and may begin to find his*
> *way again only if he is prepared to look to the world of the primitives."*
>
> (Clark & Hindley, 1975)

Ritual also binds people of a group or society together, giving them common vision for making sense out of the nonsense of experience. Carl Jung noted the importance of ritual and symbol in the development of what he called the "collective unconscious." Ritual is one way of dealing with the chaos of natural disaster, cultural conflicts, and the personal feelings of isolation, alienation and psychological impotence. Some have suggested that ritual helps people deal with thoughts and feelings about the loss of meaning in their lives. When darkness permeates an individual's awareness of existence and cosmological significance, ritual can be the light that shows the way. Ritualistic experiences can result in discovery, organization, reorganization, and affirmation of fundamental beliefs, values, and relationships. Ortner has argued that our society needs ritual and ceremony to guide people toward changes in consciousness and toward meaning in their life and their relationships.

> *"The re-shaping of consciousness or experience that takes place in ritual is by definition a*
> *reorganization of the relationship between the subject and what may for convenience be*
> *called reality. Ritual symbolism operates on both elements: reorganizing (representations*
> *of) reality, and at the same time reorganizing (representations of) self."*
>
> (Ortner, 1978)

The impact of ritual on individuals can be quite intense, and one prominent ritualologist , Victor Turner, has suggested that we might even consider them as "meta-experiences." (Turner, 1982). That description seems to parallel Maslow's concept of the "peak-experience." Certainly, when young Native Americans went through the sacred ritual of "Wiwanyag Wachipi (the Sun Dance Ceremony), which sometimes involved hanging themselves from lodge poles by skewered skin, they probably considered it as a "meta-experience."

In this time of recognition of the limitations and errors of many of the dominant cultural values of the 20th century—racism, environmental and gender chauvinism, hedonism, capitalism, etc.—many people are now seeking new visions, new values, and alternative paradigms for finding meaningful life. Challenge/adventure education facilitators can provide sequences of activities that provide people with opportunity to explore new paradigms for life and living.

There is, however, little significant theory and research on how ritual and ceremony results in the transmission, discovery, and affirmation of knowledge, values, and cosmological orientations. One of the problems of researching the nature and impact of ritual has been the difficulty of converting the "knowledge" of historians and ritualists into the realm of objectivity. There are parallels to the old arguments about medicine or psychotherapy being an "art" as opposed to a "science," and thus being difficult, if not impossible, to quantify for empirical study. Victor Turner has noted:

> *"A ritual specialist, who knows how to conduct a complex sequence of rites involving many*
> *symbolic objects, may have difficulty in explaining their meaning in words. He has*
> *operational knowledge akin to a carpenter's, who knows the feel of the wood, even though*
> *he is not a dendrologist, not a tree botanist."*
>
> (Turner, 1982)

It is also quite common for those who purportedly understand the meanings of various rituals and symbols to report that there is, and should be, great mystery involved. They talk of the learning's being of the heart, not the head—implying that interpretations and significances are difficult to cognitize. I have offered workshops which utilize the Raccoon Circle under the title, "The Circle Speaks For Itself." That may, in part, be a cop-out to the difficulty of putting the significance into words, but it does leave room for each participant to discover their own personal meanings from the activities.

In overviewing the sacred sweat lodge ceremony of the Sioux, Ed McGaa, Eagle Man, writes:

> *"While the sweat lodge itself is simple to describe it is beyond any mortal writers ability to adequately convey the ultimate culmination of the spiritual, mystical, and psychic expression of the Sweat Lodge Ceremony. The Sweat Lodge Ceremony is impossible to describe fully. You have to experience it to truly realize its fullness and depth."*
>
> (McGaa, 1990)

In spite of this lack of adequate theory and research, ritualists have advocated their importance. Anthropologist Myerhoff has made a suggestion that there should be development of rituals, ceremonies, and celebrations appropriate for our times. She calls for a new "applied anthropology," based on the study of ritual and ceremony, that would help contemporary educators and group leaders develop meaningful rituals. All that is required, she argues, are small groups in process, and "courage" on the part of the leaders of the group. (Myerhoff, 1978)

Through the latter decades of the 20th century, personal growth facilitators, group workers and counselors, and some experiential educators have begun to incorporate rituals into their practices. In the myriad of programs offered as part of the "Human Potential Movement" that began in the 1960's, workshops were formulated after rituals of Sufism, T'ai Chi Ch'uan, the ceremonies and celebrations of the !Kung of Nyae in the Kalahari, the procedures of the Tarot and the I Ching, and the "Medicine Wheel" and "Vision Quest" traditions of the Native Americans.

In the 1980's, many facilitators of special growth and learning groups realized the importance of ritual and ceremony. In what is now called the "Men's Movement," there has been exploration of rituals that involve chanting, drumming, dancing, special fire building celebrations, and the sweat lodge. These groups set goals for guiding men to explore identity, sexuality, spirituality, creativity, and personal power. One recent book about the movement is titled "Tending the Fire: The Ritual Men's Group." (Liebman, 1991) Many writers in the movement point up the significance of ritual, ceremony, and celebration. (c.f., Keen, 1991; Moore, Gillette, & King, 1991)

There has been a parallel "Women's Movement," which also places emphasis on ritual. One author describes her own growth journey in terms of the "Great Medicine Wheel Mandala." (Nadon, 1988) Like the men's groups, ritual is afforded by drumming, changing, dancing, and incense. There is also focus on mythology, folklore, and the creation of "spontaneous ritual," in order to guide women toward exploration of their feminine identity, their creative potential, and their spirituality. One proponent of that orientation suggests the importance of the ritual for finding "sacred space," where a woman can search, find, and become.

> *"Ritual can help us create boundaries. To create sacred space is an act of protection. Ritual can create a "liberating zone" of the spirit, can change an atmosphere, and make a space ours."*
>
> (Starhawk, 1987)

Matthew Fox, theologian and founding editor of the journal "Creation Spirituality," travels worldwide offering special workshops designed to guide participants toward an appropriate "earth-based spirituality." One of the regular features in that journal is about creating ritual, and Fox and his colleagues are advocates of searching other cultures, past and present, to discover significant ritual and ceremony for contemporary times. Most of the writings by those in this "Earth-Spirituality Movement," which recommends that people become Earth/Heaven sensitive and cultivate a meaningful "eco-consciousness," make frequent reference to the importance of ritual and ceremony for grounding oneself in a cultural/cosmological perspective. (c.f., Berry & Swimme, 1991; Hays, 1988; McGaa, 1992)

The "Challenge Education Movement," has roots back to the 1970's, drawing on the traditions of adventure education, outdoor education, risk recreation, New Games, awareness education, and a host of other sources. (Smith, et.al., 1992) Basically, the challenge/adventure model involves facilitating small groups of people through a sequence of innovative activities and experiences. The methodology has been utilized in a variety of educational, counseling, rehabilitation, leadership development, and corporate training programs. The challenge curriculum is flexible. Sometimes the programs focus on individual growth, learning, and empowerment. At other times the goals are more group related, concerning trust, communication, cooperation, group problem solving, and teamwork.

In this challenge/adventure education movement, there has been but limited attention to the powers and potentials of ritual. One of the early programs offered as an alternative therapeutic intervention for adjudicated youth, which involved a three month wagon train journey, was called "Vision Quest." Early reports of outdoor leadership programs, such as "Outward Bound" and the "National Outdoor Leadership School," included a solo journey patterned after the Native American "Vision Quest." Some of these programs also explored ceremonies with the "Sweat Lodge." Activities and exercises based on Native American practices have been advocated for adaptation to the personal growth or outdoor challenge/adventure programs. (Smith, 1978, 1980; Smith & Quinn, 1998)

It is apparent then, that although there is not yet adequate theory and research on the psychological, social, and spiritual impact of ritual and ceremony, many professionals sense their value. In her book, "Ritual Theory, Ritual Practice," Catherine Bell offers an analysis of group leaders attention to ritual. She suggests that the emphasis has most often been on highly specialized religious and cultural usage of ritual, and leaders have failed to recognize that there is also a long history of ritualistic practice on a day-to-day or week-to-week basis that is simply meaningful social activity. Rituals that are quite simple can still be important and influential for people. Bell's arguments support the exploration of traditional rituals, both complex and simple, for possible meaningfulness with contemporary educational groups. Even if the purpose of those groups is not some grandiose transmission of cultural values, or awakening of new humanistic, ecological, or spiritual consciousness, ritual may be meaningful. (Bell, 1992)

As we seek to build meaningful ritual into our programs, there are three words to keep in mind. The first is "SIMPLICITY." A little bit of attention at a few points in the program sequence can create significant ritualistic impact. We need to recognize that certain small and simple things that are repeated throughout a program can become ritual. The second word of importance is "ADAPTATION." It must be recognized that ritual which was appropriate for the Native American warrior, hunter, or coming of age youth, is usually not appropriate for challenge/adventure groups of our times. Both the underlying rational and the particular practices for various rituals and ceremonies will need to be modified to our program goals, and to the dynamics of the divergent groups with which we work. Besides, since many rituals and ceremonies of other cultures are related to sacred spiritual beliefs, it is inappropriate for anyone who is not spiritually connected to those cultures to offer them to contemporary groups. We can look to traditional ritual practices for ideas, but we must then develop our own ritual practices. The third key word is "CREATIVITY." Whether one is adapting ritual from other cultures, past or present, or simply seeking to build some meaningful ritual into a program or activity sequence, there must be a heavy dosage of creativity. Challenge education programming is offered in many different models, in many different places, for many different client populations. Our leaders have very diverse backgrounds academically and experientially. Program models that work one place with a particular client population, seldom work elsewhere with a different client population. Therefore, challenge/adventure leaders have usually had to be creative with the ideas they discover. This will certainly be the case in any attempt to build some significant ritual into a program or program sequence. Each leader, each program, will have to create ritual that is appropriate for their client population, and that fits into their program goals. Sometimes this may involve creative adaptation of historic ritual and ceremony, and other times programs and leaders may develop their own ritual and ceremonies of relevance. It is also significant when leaders guide the group toward creation of their own meaningful ritual. In any case, creativity will be important.

The Importance of the Circle

The Raccoon Circle is, indeed, a circle—a length of tubular nylon webbing knotted to form a loop. Most of the activities in a Raccoon Circle Sequence involve the group working with that circle of webbing. There is probably no symbol that is as universally understood as the circle. Vicki Noble, writing of the importance of women connecting hands to discover their spirit and their healing powers, has suggested, "the circle is an ancient form whose time has come again." (Noble, 1991) The significance of the circle was eloquently described by Black Elk:

> *"Everything the Power of the World does is done in a circle. The sky is round, and*
> *I have heard that the earth is round like a ball, and so are all the stars. The wind,*
> *in its greatest power, whirls. Birds make their nests in circles, for theirs is the*
> *same religion as ours. The sun comes forth and goes down again in a circle. The*
> *moon does the same, and both are round. Even the seasons form a great circle in*
> *their changing, and always come back to where they were. The life of a person is a*
> *circle from childhood to childhood, and so it is in everything where power moves."*
> (Neihardt & Black Elk, 1932, 1972)

Most challenge/adventure programs are offered to small groups, and these groups often become a circle of influence. A small group circle of connection has influence on people in manner similar to that of other "groups" that are important in the individual's growth and development. The family is often recognized as the primary circle of influence on a person.

> *"Under normal circumstances the family is, both in time and by physiologic geometry,*
> *every person's first circle. It is in the family that the first steps are taken. Steps that*
> *determine in large measure how the rest of life's journey will be walked."*
> (Nagler, 1982)

Individuals whose family circle is essentially positive are usually interested in bonding with other circles (small groups) as their life unfolds. It is the family, which gives one the security that is necessary to expand what Albert Einstein, called the "circle of compassion." Individuals whose early experiences were with a dysfunctional family circle may grow up fearful of the very connectedness that is the essence of the small group. They need to learn how to connect with others in a circle that can support their personal growth and development. As the 21st century unfolds, it appears that more and more people have been deprived of good connections with family in the developmental years, or are now disconnected from their biologic family by the rush of society. They need, and some of them seek, surrogate circles of connection.

> *"Community. Somewhere, there are people to whom we can speak with passion*
> *without having the words catch in our throats. Somewhere a circle of hands will*
> *open to receive us, eyes will light up as we enter, voices will celebrate with us*
> *whenever we come into our own power. Community means strength that joins*
> *our strength to do the work that needs to be done. Arms to hold us when we falter.*
> *A circle of healing. A circle of friends. A place where we can be free."*
>
> (Starhawk, 1989)

Challenge/adventure groups can address this very basic human need to be connected to others. For some of our clients, the circle of connection they find in a challenge/adventure sequence may be their very first "family," and for many it may be a very important addition to their life state. In emphasizing the importance of creating ritual for groups, Sedonia Cahill notes:

> *"More and more people are coming together regularly to create rituals and*
> *ceremonial circles which promote individual growth as well as create close bonds*
> *between participants. As these circles intersect and overlap they begin to create*
> *feelings of extended family and community."*
>
> (Cahill, 1994)

Circles are symbolic for humankind in many other ways, some of which relate to life's journey of personal growth and learning. Native Americans of the Great Plains developed a comprehensive cosmological overview to life based on the "Medicine Wheel." This overview provided them with a "map" for the journey of their life. Native authors have reported on the practice and the philosophy of the medicine wheel. (c.f., Storm, 1972; Sun Bear, et.al., 1980, 1991; McGaa, 1990) Many have suggested that it is time to look to the wisdom of Native American cultures to find harmony with others and with our Mother Earth. There has been considerable attention to the Medicine Wheel as symbolic of the circle of connection of all that is.

> *"The Medicine Wheel is the very Way of life of the people. The Medicine Wheel is the Total*
> *Universe. In many ways this circle, the Medicine Wheel, can best be understood if you*
> *think of it as a mirror in which everything is reflected, and*
> *each person is a mirror to every other person."*
>
> (Storm, 1972)

This symbol serves as a mirror for the universe, humankind, and all that is of the world. People should cultivate their consciousness to stand at the center and understand the wisdom of all directions, and all the viewpoints of the circle. Then one is truly in harmony with the universe and all that is.

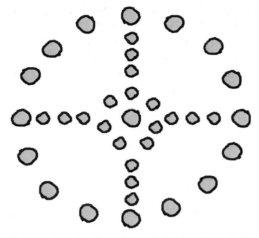

A Complete Medicine Wheel. With 36 symbols identifying the Creator at the center, Animal Spirits around the perimeter and the traits which bring balance and harmony.

"If you want to have a better world, people must be in balance and harmony. The sacred Medicine Wheel can teach proper balance. By traveling about the wheel we can bring life-giving changes into our own lives and into the world. As each of us learns how to live in a sacred manner, how to walk in harmony with all creation, we put our steps on the path of love and harmony. When enough people on the planet are walking on that path, then we will have a better world."

(Sun Bear, 1991)

My own personal and professional growth journey, which included study with and about Native American traditions, has led me to some understanding of the Medicine Wheel cosmology and the emphasis on the connection of all things. In an earlier book about the personal growth journey, I noted, "There is a wilderness beyond . . . and there is a wilderness within. . . . We go to the outside to learn about the inside, and we go to the inside to learn about the outside." (Smith, 1980, 1990, 2000) In those writings, I presented a diagram to overview the personal growth journey - and it forms a circle!

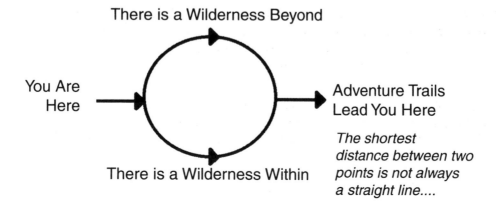

If we view life on a linear plane, then the wilderness beyond might seem to be in oppositional polarity to the wilderness within. This position might be reinforced by the contrasting extremes of the Eastern cultures, with exaggerated emphasis on the search for the "within" and self-mastery, and the Western cultures, with focus on the "without," and technological mastery of the natural world. However, it is possible to view life as more spherical than linear, circles flowing from beginning to end and back to beginnings again. It appears that many Native American cultures tended to this flowing, harmonious, balanced, cyclical cosmological view of life and the universe.

The circle is also an important symbol in Eastern philosophy and religion. In India, the raja-yoga prescribes balanced development. The "Mandala" is an important symbol in Buddhism. It is a catalyst for the student of Buddhism, symbolizing various states of enlightenment. The word "mandala" actually means "circle" or "center," although the representations are not meant to be flat, but three dimensional.

> *"Mandalas are based on the squaring of a circle. Their basic motif is the premonition of a center to the personality, a kind of central point within the psyche, to which everything is related, by which everything is arranged, and which is itself a source of energy."*
>
> (Jung, 1964)

A typical Mandala contains four circles symbolizing four levels of enlightenment, which the meditating person must gain before entering the illuminated place. The outer circle is the fire of wisdom. The next, the vajra circle, symbolized strength and fearlessness. The third circle is the "tombs," where one recognizes the eight states of consciousness, and the fourth circle is of the "lotus," the open state of devotion. The Lotus flower has been used as a symbol of teaching and learning, where one must have roots in the mud, but blossoms raising toward the light. The symbol of Buddha lives in the center, and is surrounded by eight deities - four male and four female. These figures facing the four corners of the earth and the eight directions form a lotus.

Also from the East is the circle of balance, yin/yang, based on Taoism. Taoism is a philosophy, a spirituality, guiding people to inner tranquillity as symbolized by the circle of yin/yang.

> *"The yin/yang symbol is the interlocking, melting together of the flow of movement within a circle. The similar, and yet at the same time obviously contrasting energies are moving together. The whole idea of a circle divided in this way is to show that*

*within a unity there is a duality and polarity and contrast. The only way to find
real balance without losing the centering feeling of the circle is to think of these
contrasting energies moving together in unison, in harmony, in interlocking."*

(Huang, 1973)

T'ai Chi Ch'uan is an exercise sequence based on Taoism, which focuses on energy within the body (physical and mental) coming to balance and rhythmic flow. The yin/yang symbol is circular, representing movement and stillness, masculine and feminine, inside and outside.

Also from Native American tradition is the symbolism of the turtle, often related to the people's stories about creation. The representations of the turtle are usually from above, so the shell forms a circle symbolizing the whole earth. When challenge education programs include goals for enhancing participant's awareness of earth connections, the symbolism of the turtle and the Raccoon Circle can be incorporated.

The circle of the medicine wheel, the yin/yang, the family, the mandala, the turtle, the small group circle, and the Raccoon Circle, have a common denominator. They can help us find our place, our energy, our significance, our purpose, and our direction in the world. There is then, a rich body of significance for the circle.

Raccoon Circles

Group leaders who facilitate small group experiences with the Raccoon Circle can find many ways to point up the symbolic meaning of the circle, and many ways to build significant ritual into their programs. As suggested earlier in this paper, a key word for the facilitator is "creativity." Attention to ritual and symbol requires attention to the groups being worked with, and the goals of the program sequences. I strongly suggest that leaders be creative in developing ritual appropriate to their personal and program philosophy and the goals of their client groups. So what I will present here are some ideas for contemplation, some examples that may stimulate the imagination of others.

A Symbolic Overview to the Challenge/Adventure Sequence

Frequently, as I give the group overview and orientation to the program ahead, I will take out a length of webbing and talk about it as a symbol of our goals. As I knot the webbing, I speak of the task for the group being to grow from being just a "line" of people to becoming a connected, sharing, caring, trusting, "circle" of cooperation. This, I explain, will enable the group to complete activities and solve problems throughout the day. Holding the webbing and tying it while talking to the group usually focuses everyone's attention as I give them pertinent information about health, safety, and their choices in the upcoming experience.

Then, as an initial group experience, I instruct the group to "connect up" to the web loops, and we then proceed to some of the basic activities with the Raccoon Circle. This also serves as an excellent psychological and physical warm-up.

A Ritual of Creation for the Raccoon Circle

When I want to incorporate a good deal of ritual and symbol into the program sequence, I guide the group through a sequence that is designed to bring "wisdom, energy, tolerance, love, and healing energy" to the circle. I have offered a ritual of creation to groups where we were making a single Raccoon Circle to use for the day, and to trainer groups where each participant was creating a personal Raccoon Circle to take away and use with their client populations. I have sometimes used words of overview to the Medicine Wheel, with emphasis on the potentials for our group to become a wheel of reflection and learning.

I have often offered a ritual of creation based on the energies of "Earth, Air, Fire, and Water," with reference to the ancient Greek philosophers who thought them to be the four basic elements of the universe. First, a length of webbing is placed on the ground with notation of the nurturing powers of our Mother Earth. The participants can press the webbing to the ground in silence, while they focus on the goodness of the earth, or it can be cooperatively picked up and rotated to the significant points of direction. There can be words of wisdom about the directions as noted in Medicine Wheel cosmology, about the significance of the four winds, or from the teachings of Buddhism's Mandala. Sometimes I simply read some lines about the joys of touching the goodness of the earth. An example is:

> *"The old people came literally to love the soil, and they sat or reclined on the ground*
> *with a feeling of being close to a mothering power. It was good for the skin to touch the*
> *Earth, and the old people liked to remove moccasins and walk with bare feet on the*
> *sacred Earth. Their Tipi's were built upon the Earth. The birds flew into the air and*
> *then came back to the Earth, and it was the final abiding place for all things that lived*
> *and grew. Soil was soothing, strengthening, cleansing, and healing."*
>
> (Luther Standing Bear)

Second, I have the group raise the webbing into the air, up to the sky, towards the sun. A stretching and breathing exercise that begins with pushing hands to the earth and then raising them to the sky, called "roots and wings" or "the Raccoon and the Eagle," can add much to the transition of focus from "earth" to "air." One leader told me that he had the participants do some of the group jump rope activities, while noting the importance of the webbing moving freely in space. When I am facilitating a group where everyone is creating their own Raccoon Circle, I have them swing the webbing strip

high above their head, and I have them blow air into the hollow ends of the webbing, with reference to insuring that their own personal power and wisdom is placed inside the webbing. The air is all about us. It is the sky, the clouds, and the winds of change.

> *"Now I see the secret of making the best persons. It is to grow*
> *in the open air, and to eat and sleep with the earth."*
> (Walt Whitman)

> *"Let's sit down here on the open prairie. Let's have no blankets to sit on,*
> *but feel the ground with our bodies, the earth, the yielding shrubs. Let's listen*
> *to the air. You can hear it, feel it, smell it, taste it."*
> (Lame Deer: Seeker of Visions)

Third, as there is discussion of the powers and potentials of fire, the end of the nylon web strips are burned to seal in the wisdoms and energies. This also has the pragmatic effect of keeping the ends from unraveling. If there has been a campfire, coals can be used for this burning. When inside, I use a special candle of significance, given to me by a dear friend. In recent years I have always lit the candle with sticks that were first burned in the "7th Fire." Contact Dan Creely at Northeastern Illinois University for information about the 7th Fire, he knows a great deal of the history associated with this sacred fire.

Remember that the Sun is a ball of fire, and there are many inspirational words about the powers and the energy of the sun. Many words of wisdom can be found about the significance of fire and the sun.

"Turn your face to the sun and your troubles will fall behind you."
(the Moari)

"Some day after mastering the winds, the waves, the tides and the gravity, we shall harness for God the energies of Love. And then, for the second time in the history of the world, man will have discovered Fire."
(Teilhard de Chardin)

Fourth, the webbing is tied into a loop with a water-knot, as there is discussion about strength, safety, and the security of the circle. The knot can be dipped in symbolic waters from a nearby lake, river, or well; or a few drops of that chosen water can be ceremoniously dripped onto the knot. The powers of water are known, not only in terms of floods, or typhoons, or the tsunamis of the Pacific, but also in terms of the regular flow of the creeks and the rivers. I have used words from a history of the Wisconsin River, from a Native American writing about the Rain Dance, and from an account of riverboat living on the Ohio River, all speaking about the power of water or the wisdom of the waves.

"A river tugs at whatever is within reach, trying to set it afloat and carry it downstream. Living trees are undermined and washed away. No piece of driftwood is safe, even stranded high up on the bank, for the river will rise to it and away it will go."
(Harlan Hubbard, Shantyboat)

If one circle has been made and empowered by the group, then those first moments of connection and trust lean, and those first activities of cooperative sit-down and stand-up, have very special meaning. If many circles have been made, then a first connection, and tightening of the water knot, can be accomplished by having each person connect their circle to one that has been previously empowered. I often begin a workshop with a circle that was made in an earlier workshop, or used by another group, so that there is a symbolic spreading of the power to new circles.

Ritual in the Activity Sequence

One of the early activities with the Raccoon Circle is the basic sit-down and stand-up with "sound effects." I usually instruct the group to create a down-sound that brings all the wisdom and warmth of the moment to center, and an up-sound that is a joyous celebration of the group's achievements. Groups enjoy creating their own special "celebratory" cheer as they bring their energy to the top. When the group can do a threefold celebratory, down, up, down, up, down, up, in smooth balance and with vigorous sound effects, they are ready for anything that lies ahead. Then, as the program sequence unfolds, successful solving of a problem or completion of a challenge, means that the group can celebrate with their Raccoon Circle and their group cheer.

There can also be ritual in moving the group from one place to another, or from one activity to another. One teams course instructor told me that she requires everybody in the group to connect to the "power circle" as they walk. This, of course, keeps the group in close proximity, and allows for some spontaneous discussion along the way. The importance of the Raccoon Circle can also be reinforced by appointing one of the group members to be the "Keeper of the Sacred Circle" as they move from one place to another. The group can make a decision after each initiative problem or activity about who should be awarded the honor of carrying the circle to the next station. One teacher reported that she decides on who the keeper will be, and uses that choice to reinforce positive student's behaviors.

A teacher of behavior-disordered students informed me that after their group had become involved with the Raccoon Circle she used it for situations that required some intervention and conflict resolution. When two students were evidencing an interactive problem, they had to sit inside the circle and talk out their problems. This could be done by simply spreading the circle on the floor or ground, or if it wasn't too threatening, by having the rest of the group hold the circle around the involved parties. She noted that the powers of the circle seem to work wonders, as student problems are discussed away before they develop into overt conflicts.

Processing, Debriefing and Reviewing with the Raccoon Circle

Typically, when I am going to facilitate a group on a teams course or a sequence of initiative problems, I will introduce the Raccoon Circle during warm-ups and early group-building exercises. Once the group has learned the basic procedure of "connect up, breathe deep, lean back, breathe-deep, eye-contact, breath deep, and slowly, cooperatively, in silence, sit down," that sequence can be instructed each time there needs to be a processing circle. I usually instruct the group to relax their hold on the webbing, but keep one hand in contact with the powers of the circle. This ritual puts everyone in a close circle, and processing can proceed.

If there is need for a more structured processing the leader may choose to have the group pass the knot around the circle until the command "stop." The person with the knot in front of them, and only that person, must speak. This procedure can be valuable in keeping the more dominating voices silent, and bringing the quieter members of the group into the circle.

One challenge education facilitator, who works with adjudicated youth, told me that he carries two different colors of Raccoon Circles. When the group is functioning smoothly, or has successfully completed the assigned task, the blue circle appears. This means some positive processing and reinforcement of the group's behaviors. When the group has problems, or there is a developing conflict between participants, the red circle appears. The participants learn that the red loop means they have to deal with some problems before they can move on. That leader told me that such "color coding" of the circles brought the group to appropriate mind-set for the processing ahead. He even noted that if the processing circle starts out "red," but the group deals with the issues at hand successfully, he will change the circle to "blue" as the group ends their discussion.

Personally, I think utilizing the Raccoon Circle for initiating the processing circle is it's most valuable contribution to the challenge/adventure sequence. How many times through the years I struggled with questions about how to involve everybody in the group de-briefings, or how to quiet the voices of the more talkative, or how to insure that there was meaningful focus. The magic of the Raccoon Circle is never more apparent than when it is the starting point for group processing.

When I have facilitated a group with everyone creating and empowering their own Raccoon Circle, I find an appropriate time in the sequence of activities to have them find a "special place" to put down their circle, and then sit quietly inside it. They may use this time for journaling, or simply sitting in silence. I have come to appreciate the ritual of silence, for it works for people.

Native tradition speaks of "being able to sit within one's own hoop." The symbol of Buddha lives at the center of the symbolic mandala. Before the group disperses to find their special place, I may

teach them a simple Native American exercise called "Starstretch," to help them focus on their center, or I may instruct them in a simple ritual for silence called "three breaths."

> *"Take three breaths: one to let go of whatever energy charge was commanding us;*
> *one to touch the still mind; and one to ask "now what?" "Inhale—center—*
> *exhale. Inhale—stillpoint—exhale. Inhale—now what?—exhale."*
> (Baldwin, 1994)

I have also used the circle for a special end-of-day experience that is patterned after the Gestalt technique of having each person become "the center of the universe." The group stretches the Raccoon Circle out on the ground and gathers around it. Then, each person has a few moments to lie inside the circle and share thoughts, feelings, reactions, learning's, and reflections on the experiences of the day. I have sometimes used this processing technique after a closing exercise with "Raccoon's Cradle."

Ritual in the Closing Ceremony

When a Raccoon Circle is used throughout a program sequence, its power and symbolic significance seem to grow. It wasn't long after I began using the web circle as a part of facilitating groups that someone in the closing circle discussion asked if the group could cut the webbing into souvenir lengths for everyone to take away. I still remember it clearly, for she noted, "It will be my symbol of people being at their best, and my symbol of hope for the whole world to be like we were today." Since then, I have frequently suggested that groups divide up the circle. I've been informed that foot-long strips of tubular webbing have been tacked to bulletin boards, draped from the mirror of cars, attached to keychains, placed atop desks, sewed to the outside of backpacks, or just carried in pocket or purse.

I have had groups debate the question of cutting the powerful circle, and decide, instead, to simply autograph it and keep it whole. At one corporate center, a team reported that they start each weekly meeting with a basic sequence of activities with their Raccoon Circle; and after the meeting someone

is appointed to be the "keeper of the sacred circle" until the next meeting. A camp director told me that the autographed Raccoon Circles of over twenty groups are now draped over the ceiling beam of the lodge—waiting for that group to come back and share the growth and healing powers of the circle again. At an outdoor education center for special education students, where classes visit five or six times each year, the first activity when the kids get off the bus is to "connect up" to their Raccoon Circle. It brings them to that special place, as if they had not left, and creates a psychological mind-set for the program to unfold.

If everyone in the group has created and empowered their own Raccoon Circle, then there can be interconnecting exercises in the closing. If there has been more than one group operating through the activity sequence, then they can be brought together with the activity called "A Gathering of Raccoons." In any case, there are many possibilities for creation of special closing ceremony after a sequence with the Raccoon Circle.

Conclusion

Special rituals and ceremonies can be very powerful additions to the challenge/ adventure sequence. They can stimulate special awareness and guide our clients to significant understanding of self, others, environment, the Other, and the self-other-environment-Other Oneness. They can help our clients find personal meaning from our experiential challenge/adventure programs. They may even insure that the effects of our programs are not just short-term, but endure on into the future.

References

Baldwin, C. (1998). Calling The Circle. Bantam Books.

Bell, C. (1992). Ritual Theory, Ritual Practice. Harper & Row.

Berry, T. & Swimme, B. (1991). The Universe Story. Harper & Row.

Cahill, S. & Halpern, J. (1992). The Ceremonial Circle. Harper & Row.

Cahill, S. (1994). "Creating Ritual." In Creation Spirituality, Vol.10, No.3.

Clark, R. & Hindley, G. (1975). The Challenge of the Primitives. Little, Brown and Company.

Eliade, M. (1958). Rites and Symbols of Initiation. Harper & Row.

Hays, E. (1988). Prayers for a Planetary Pilgrim: A Personal Manual for Prayer and Ritual. Forest of Peace Books, N.Y.

Huang, A. (1973). Embrace Tiger, Return to Mountain. Real Peoples Press.

Hubbard, H. (1953). Shantyboat: A River Way of Life. University of Kentucky Press.

Johnson, D. & Johnson, F. (1987). Joining Together: Group Theory and Group Skills. Prentice-Hall.

Jung, C. G. (1964). Man and His Symbols. Doubleday.

Keen, S. (1991). Fire In The Belly. Bantam.

LaFontaine, J. (1972). The Interpretation of Ritual. Tavistock, Maine.

Lame Deer, A. & Erdoes, R. (1971). Lame Deer: Seeker of Visions. Pocket Books.

Liebman, V. (1991). Tending the Fire: The Ritual Men's Group. Ally Press.

McGaa, E. (1990). Mother Earth Spirituality. Harper.

McGaa, E. (1993). Rainbow Tribe. Harper/Collins.

Moore, S. & Myerhoff, B. (Eds.) (1977). Secular Ritual. Van Gorcum, N.Y.

Moore, S. & Gillette, D. (1991). King, Warrior, Magician, Lover. Harper.

Myerhoff, B. (1978). Number Our Days. Dutton.

Nadon, S. (1988). Full Bloom. Maplestone Press.

Neihardt, J. & Black Elk. (1972). Black Elk Speaks. Pocket Books.

Noble, V. (1991). Shakti Woman. Harper.

Ortner, S. B. (1978). Sherpas Through Their Rituals. Cambridge University Press.

Rogers, C. (1970). On Encounter Groups. Harper.

Smith, T. (2000). Wilderness Beyond....Wilderness Within.... (3rd Edition). Raccoon Institute. (1st Edition, 1980; 2nd Edition, 1990.)

Smith, T., Roland, C., Havens, M. & Hoyt, J. (1992). The Theory and Practice of Challenge Education. Kendall/Hunt Publishing.

Smith, T. & Quinn, W. (1998). The Challenge of Native American Traditions. Raccoon Institute.

Standing Bear. (1928). My People the Sioux. Reprinted, U. Nebraska Press.

Starhawk. (1987). Truth or Dare: Encounters with Power, Authority and Mystery. Harper & Row.

Starhawk. (1989). Dreaming the Dream. Harper & Row.

Storm, H. (1972). Seven Arrows. Ballantine Books.

Sun Bear, Wabun Wind, & Crysalis Mulligan. (1991). Dancing With the Wheel: The Medicine Wheel Workbook. Prentice-Hall.

Turner, V. (1969). The Ritual Process: Structure and Anti-Structure. Aldine Press.

Turner, V. (1982). "Religious Celebrations." Studies of Festivity and Ritual. V. Turner, Editor. Smithsonian, Washington D.C

A Ritual for the Creation of a Raccoon Circle

Dr. Tom Smith

"If you are involved in the creation of the Raccoon Circle,
it makes the experience more meaningful."
Workshop Participant, April 2002.

Ritual, symbol, and ceremony can be important in teaching and confirming cultural, community, and reference group (family, fraternity, gangs, etc.) values and behavioral expectancies. Experiential and Adventure-based educators can benefit by utilizing rituals when working with groups. Such attention can contribute to heightened achievement of program goals.

It should be noted that the most significant rituals are those created by the people themselves, with words, symbols, objects, and behaviors that are meaningful for them. So it follows that challenge and adventure-based leaders should develop rituals that relates to their clients, their programs, and their own experiences. What will be offered here is meant to be an example of ritual for creation of Raccoon Circles, not necessarily a format for everyone to copy. I have used this ritual with a single group of 10-15 people, and with as many as seven groups of 10-12 people each. I have used it when each working group was to create their own circle for the activity sequence to follow, and when the workshop was designed to have every participant create, empower, and take away their own circle for future use. Sometimes I have begun a training session with the ritual of creation, and then proceeded to experiences. Other times I have facilitated some of the activities with already empowered circles, and then guided the group into the process of creating new circles.

Typically, as the workshop begins, I have the participants sit in a circle. If there is background disturbance and interactive chattering, I instruct the group to close eyes, breathe deeply, come to center, come to this place, in silence. It is the nature of people to follow instructions at the start of a workshop, and a few simple words can bring the group to readiness for the adventure ahead. I usually open with these words from Black Elk:

> *"You have noticed that everything an Indian does is in a circle, and that is because the power of the world always works in circles, and everything tries to be round. The sky is round like a ball, and so are the stars. The wind, in its great power, whirls. Birds make their nests in circles, for theirs is the same religion as ours. The sun comes forth and goes down in a circle. The moon does the same, and both are round. Even the seasons form a great circle, and always come back to where they were. The life of a person is a circle from childhood to childhood, and so it is in everything where power moves."*

I then give brief overview to the workshop, explaining that we will be making and empowering a circle of tubular nylon webbing to create a Raccoon Circle, which will enable us to do many small group activities that involve trust, cooperation, risk-taking, problem-solving, nurturance, healing, and fun. But first, I explain, it would be good for us to share some basic experiences with the Raccoon Circle, so that we all understand its magic, its power, and its potential for ourselves and our work with small groups. I then distribute the appropriate number of loops (one for every 10-12 people) with instruction for everyone to "connect up." When everyone is in a circle with both hands on the loop, I

note that they are holding circles of power that have been created and used by other people at another time. Everyone then shares the basic trust and cooperation sequence of the Raccoon Circle. I have them lean back in trust, breathe slowly and deeply, and, in silence, make eye contact with others in their circle. Then I have them close their eyes and feel the power of the circle, the power of the group, the power of our circle of connection. There is no need for lots of explanation about the powers that are found because the circle speaks for itself.

At the end of the activity sequence (short or long), the group turns to the process of creation of Raccoon Circles. I usually give out 150-foot lengths and explain that the group will have to divide the webbing into 15-foot lengths so that each person (or each group) will have one strip of webbing. This is, of course, an initiative problem for the group. When each group (or every individual) has a length of webbing, I have them sit in their circle of connection and, while holding their web strip, introduce themselves to the group. If time allows, I may also ask them to share their thoughts on the symbolic significance of the circle, or to talk about important circles of connection in their lives. After appropriate time, I announce that we are ready to begin the creation process.

"As we create and empower our Raccoon Circle, we need to attend to the wisdom of the ages. In Buddhism, the symbol of the Mandala is a squared circle, at the center of which one finds personal energy. For Taoism, the circle of Yin/Yang shows how energies move together in balance and harmony. The Native Americans of the great plains spoke of Medicine Wheels, circles for understanding and vision, and for being aware of the connectedness of all that is. But we shall focus on the wisdom of the Ancient Greek Philosophers, who saw the four elements of all that is of the world to be EARTH, AIR, FIRE, and WATER."

I have sometimes had the group discuss the importance of these elements by sharing personal memories. I ask everyone to recall a special time when they touched the earth, planted a tree, walked barefooted on the beach, or rolled in the leaves and to share that memory with their group. I then suggest that we shift the focus to the air, and recall a special time when they flew a kite high in the sky, sailed a boat over the waves, laid under the sun and watched the clouds and the birds, or just stood quietly and took in deep breaths of fresh air. For fire, the stimulus comment is to remember a time when they sat by a campfire, burned fall leaves, shared the warmth of a radiating woodstove or fireplace, extinguished the birthday candles on a cake, or stretched out under that fireball we call the sun. Finally, for water, I have them share memories of wading in a creek, paddling down a river, wading in the rain, or sharing a canteen of water with others. Many groups would talk for hours about these memories, and I often have to cut them short. I note that they seem to understand the importance of the four elements, and so our creation process will unfold with attention to Earth, Air, Fire, and Water.

Earth

I have the group stretch the length(s) of webbing on the ground, running from north to south. Half of the group kneels on the east side, and half the group kneels on the west side. Then all lean forward to press the webbing to the ground, and silently ask for the nurturing powers of Mother Earth to enter the webbing. When the creation process is offered outdoors, I have had participants cover the web strips with leaves or grass, and then press them to the ground again. When inside, I have sometimes carried in leaves, grass, or soil, and had the participants spread it over the web strips.

One can find many words of inspiration to share with the group as they are seeking to bring the powers of Mother Earth to their web strips. For example:

"The old people came literally to love the soil, and they sat or reclined on the ground with
a feeling of being close to a mothering power. It was good for the skin to touch the Earth,
and the people liked to remove moccasins and walk with bare feet on the sacred Earth. The
birds flew into the air and then came back to the Earth, and it was the final abiding place
for all things that lived and grew. Soil was soothing, strengthening, cleansing, and healing."
(Luther Standing Bear)

Air

I shift the group's focus to the air by another favorite passage:

"Now I see the secret of making the best persons.
It is to grow in the open air, and to eat and sleep with the earth."
(Walt Whitman)

I inform the group that we shall take the powers of Mother Earth with the web strips as we seek the powers of the air, the sky, the winds, and the clouds. A favorite stretching and breathing exercise called Roots and Wings, or Raccoon and Eagle, is then taught to the group. It begins on hands and knees, hands pressed to the Earth with fingers and thumbs forming a small frame. The starting position is to lean forward and put the nose into the frame, right on the ground, and then breathe in the wonderful odors of the soil, the grass, the sand, the leaves. Then the person raises head, rocks back on haunches, and slowly stretches arms out and up to the sky, while taking in a deep breath and holding it. Let the breath out slowly as you return to the Earth, and even take a couple of extra breaths of the goodness, while down. Begin the stretch upward while taking in another deep breath, and stretch the arms out like the wings of the Eagle.

I give the group another small initiative problem, having them slide their hands under the webbing, palms up, and then lift it off the ground while keeping it parallel to the ground. When they have done this to satisfaction, and are standing in a line with the web strip stretched across their hands, I have them carefully, cooperatively, toss the web into the air and then catch it in their hands again. There can be significance in having the group hold the web strip(s) while facing the four directions, and asking for the powers and the wisdom of the four winds as overviewed by Native American cosmology and in the teachings of Buddha. When everyone is seeking to create and empower their own web loop, I have them spread out and swing the web-strip high overhead. (If the area is crowded, have them half, or even quarter, the length, so that nobody gets hit.) I usually finish focus on the powers of Air by having participants squeeze open the end of the web strip and breath/blow their own best medicine into the hollow.

The air is all about us. It is the sky, the clouds, the winds of change. Again, there are many words one could share about the goodness of air. For example:

> *"Let us sit down here on the open prairie. Let's listen to the Air. You can hear it.*
> *You can feel it. You can smell it. You can taste it."*
>
> (Lame Deer, Seeker of Visions)

Fire

The powers of fire have been long recognized. The ends of the web strips must be burned to bring those powers to the web circle. (This also has the practical effect of keeping the ends of the nylon web from unraveling.) If there has been a campfire, I might use hot coals for this procedure. However, in recent years, as I have followed the Journey of a Sacred Fire, I have carried coals from that fire to spread over a fire or atop a candle for burning the web strips. Many Native American people carried their fire coals from one place to another, from one generation to another, seeking to maintain the wisdom and energy of their heritage. They also had sacred rituals for the creation of new fires, and a fire was started in 1995, at the International Conference of the Association for Experiential Education, in Lake Geneva, Wisconsin, with guidance from a keeper of the fire for the Ojibway. Coals from that fire have been carried to other fires throughout the world where people have gathered in celebrations of peace and love. My friend Dan Creely, professor at Northeastern Illinois University, has chronicled the journey of this sacred fire and he makes the ever-lengthening report available to all interested.

Ireland's Unification Festival at the end of spring involves a fire that has burned for over a thousand years. The festival focuses on connecting the solar and the lunar cycles. The sun, a ball of fire, symbolizes the heart and the love that supports all of life. The moon symbolizes the mind, always changing, but so often returning to where it has been before. The Unification Festival is a time for bringing balance to the head and the heart of all peoples, and the fire is the connecting force.

It is important to note that the Sun is a ball of fire, and there are many words of wisdom about the power of the Sun. For example:

> *"Turn your face to the sun and your troubles will fall behind you."*
>
> (The Morai)

Many years ago, when teaching folks the stretches and prayers of some Native American peoples, I wrote in my own journal about the sun:

"I am the Sun.
I fill the Earth with Light.
Without me there would be darkness everywhere.
I bring the Earth warmth.
Without me there would be coldness everywhere.
I charge the Earth and all the growing things with energy.
Without me the flowers, the foods, the animals, and the people would not survive.
Is there a time when you do not remember me?
I slide away at night, but I return every morning.
Sometimes the clouds hide me, but I am there with light and warmth.
I warmed the Earth in the years of the dinosaurs.
I sent light and life to the hearts and minds of the very first people.
I smiled on you on the day that you were born.
I am here with you now.
Reach up for the energy and warmth.
I will glow beyond you, and within you, for all your days.
I will glow for you children, and for your children's children.
I give forth energy for living, giving, healing, growing, and becoming.
Reach up for me.
Grab a handful of my sunshine."

When searing the ends of the web strips over flames, I often share words that connect fire to the underlying force of the circle of connection, LOVE!

"Some day, after mastering the winds, the waves, the tides, and the gravity, we shall harness for God the energies of Love. And then, for the second time in the history of the world, man will have discovered FIRE!"

(Teilhard de Chardin)

Water

The focus turns to the final element of all creation, Water, as the web strip is tied into a circle. I show the participants how to tie a water knot for the circle. This is the strongest knot for tying two ends of rope together. While they are working on the knot, I give some input about the strength, safety, and security of the circle they are making. When the knots are in place, they should be watered before tightening. I have had people dip the whole knot into a pail of significant water, from a nearby lake, river, marsh, or well. If there is no nearby source of water, I carry in a jar from a place of geographic significance (e.g., a jar of water from Lake Michigan for a workshop in the suburbs of Chicago; a jar of water from just downstream of the convergence of the Mississippi and Missouri rivers when doing a workshop in Missouri. I have also used melted snow or fresh rainwater, and once carried in water from the torrential rains of a hurricane —- with words about wanting the powers of Mother Nature's storms to charge the new circle of webbing. The knots do not need to be submerged, as a few drops can be dripped onto the knot from a symbolic vile. There are many words on the powers of water, not only in terms of floods, typhoons, and the tsunamis of the Pacific, but in terms of the endless flow of creeks and rivers. I have offered words from a history of the Wisconsin River, from a Native American writing about the Rain Dance, and from Mark Twain's Huckleberry Finn. One of my favorite quotes about the powers of water is from an account of shantyboat living on the lower Ohio River.

"A river tugs at whatever is within reach, trying to set it afloat and carry it downstream. Living trees are often undermined and washed away. No piece of driftwood is safe, even stranded high up on the bank, for the river will rise to it and away it will go."

(Harlan Hubbard)

In order to tighten the water knot, the group must connect up, trust lean, and then do the standard sit-down and stand-up exercise. If one circle has been created and empowered by the group, with attention to the energy, strength, goodness, nurturance, and love of EARTH, AIR, FIRE, and WATER, then this first experience with their new Raccoon Circle has very special meaning for participants. If many circles have been made, I have the group take them in hand, one by one, and then pull the knot tight. The second phase of the final empowerment involves temporarily connecting their new Raccoon Circles to the old (previously created, empowered, and used) Raccoon Circle that they had used for warm-up exercises. This involves wrapping the new circle around the old circle and passing the loop through itself. The group(s) can then connect up to their own circle and do a standard trust lean, and, with community cooperation, they can even do a balanced sit-down and stand-up. When everyone in the group has created a circle, they do not have to tie their new circle to the old circle; they can simply drape the loop over the old circle and then hold the ends in opposite hands.

As the group is proceeding through these final steps of the process for creating and empowering their Raccoon Circle, I point out that even with all the powers and the wisdom of EARTH, AIR, FIRE, and WATER implanted to the circle, there is even greater power, wisdom, energy and love that will be carried there. I speak of the power of the group, which will grow as we share activities that involve trust, cooperation, caring, sharing, risk-taking, problem-solving, and fun. As the group proceeds through the day, their growing power and bonds of connection will enhance the magic, the potency, and the potential of their new Raccoon Circle.

The creation ritual described here was first presented at Indiana State University in April of 2002.

References

Hubbard, H. (1953). *Shantyboat: A River Way of Life.* University of Kentucky Press.

Lame Deer, A. & Erdoes, R. (1971). *Lame Deer: Seeker of Visions.* Pocket Books.

Neihardt, J. & Black Elk (1972). *Black Elk Speaks.* Pocket Books.

Smith, T. & Quinn, W. (2004). *The Challenge of Native American Traditions.* Raccoon Institute Publications.

Standing Bear (1928). *My People the Sioux.* Reprinted, University of Nebraska Press.

Tielhard de Chardin, P. (1951). *The Phenomena of Man.* Harper & Row.

Talking Circles, Talking Sticks and Talking Knots

Thomas E. Smith

T he theory and practice of *Raccoon Circles* now has over a decade of application in challenge/adventure education, therapeutic recreation, leadership training, and small group counseling. Facilitators of small groups in process welcomed publication of *The Book on Raccoon Circles* (Cain & Smith, 2002), and many have created new activities and procedures for using the simple 15 foot long web loop. There are a number of answers to the question, "Why Raccoon Circles?" (Smith, 2004).

A few years ago, after the introduction of *Raccoon Circles,* many experiential education leaders discovered the value of this "circle of connection" for the debriefing or processing phase of the experiential education cycle. When everyone in a small group connects to the circle and in trusting cooperation sits down, they are in a perfect processing circle. No one is apart from the group, and there are no splintered sub-groups. Everyone can look at and listen to everyone else.

Not long after I started advocating the power and potential of the *Raccoon Circle,* other leaders began to share with me the ways they had creatively expanded on my suggestions. I am sorry to say that I do not remember who it was who first suggested using the knot in the circle as the Native American Indians had used the "Talking Stick." Perhaps the parallels were so obvious that a number of experienced leaders explored this special use of the *Raccoon Circle* as a processing tool. In any case, I soon began telling others about the "Talking Knot."

I want to provide more information on the use of the Talking Knot to enhance small group debriefing and sharing circles. As the ideas about the Talking Knot are based, in part, on the historical tradition of Talking Circles and Talking Sticks, let us begin there.

Talking Circles

The Talking Stick is both a symbolic object and a methodology for group discussions that are called Talking Circles, Listening Circles, Wisdom Circles, or Councils. Christina Baldwin, in her book *Calling the Circle: The First and Future Culture* (1998), refers to small group gatherings as simply "circles." Parker Palmer, in his book *A Hidden Wholeness: The Journey Toward An Undivided Life* (2004), writes about "circles of trust" or "trust circles." Other names for groups that gather to enhance the participants psychological, social and spiritual life are "Sharing Groups," "Quaker Circles," "Prayer Circles," and "Personal Growth Groups." In the field of challenge/adventure education, there are the "debriefing," "processing," or "reviewing" groups which are important procedures for fostering people's reflection on experience.

Although the motives and intentions of all these discussion groups vary, there are some common denominators. Words to describe the dynamics of these groups, and the recommended characteristics of the participants, would include: Trust, Sensitivity, Empathy, Acceptance, Tolerance, Compassion, Honesty, and Respect. There are also some important ground rules or boundaries for the group process, which may be written or stated clearly in advance or simply understood by the participants. I think the most important of these ground rules can be summarized as five interrelated concepts:

1. *Guidelines for Speaking.* Everyone in the group has the right to speak their thoughts, and, more importantly, share their feelings; i.e., people should speak from both their head and their heart. People are encouraged to speak truthfully and sincerely. They should "say what they mean, and mean what they say." People should try to use "I" statements as much as possible.

2. *Guidelines for Listening.* Everyone in the group should be heard. People should listen carefully to each other, with open mind and non-judgmentally; i.e., people should listen with their heart as well as their ears. There should be no cross talk and no interruption while someone is speaking, and if there is a "break-in" the discussion should revert to the person who was speaking as soon as possible. People should not be mentally rehearsing what they want to say while another person is talking, for this will prevent them from fully listening to that other person.

3. *Inclusion.* Everyone is an important part of the group, just by being there. Everyone's thoughts, opinions, feelings, and individual differences should be respected. People should have compassion and tolerance, and accept other people as they are — here and now; i.e., people should avoid making value judgments about other people or their behaviors. All members of the group should be encouraged to share thoughts and feelings — but just as everyone has the right to speak, they also have the right to remain silent.

4. *Confidentiality.* What is talked about in the group should stay in the group. People must feel secure in sharing their thoughts and feelings, and have no fears that what is shared will be taken outside the group. Only when there is both trust and trustworthiness will everyone be able to speak all of their personal wisdom, fears and passions.

5. *Guidelines for Facilitators.* Most of these groups are "leaderless," but there may be a "facilitator" to guide the group to appropriate discussion. Facilitators are not there to lecture or preach, but to insure that the process of the group unfolds from within the group. The facilitator also has the important function of protecting all members of the group, and the integrity of the group process. Facilitators should guide people to speak clearly and share their thoughts freely, and to practice good listening; and he/she should also insure that inclusiveness and confidentiality are present at all times. It is also important that the facilitator keeps the group "leaderless," and prevents the aggressive, domineering group member from "taking over."

Experiential education professionals have given considerable thought to the theory and process of reflection (Dewey, 1933; Boud, 1985; Nadler and Luckner, 1992; Knapp, 1992; Priest and Gass, 1997; Luckner and Nadler, 1997; Priest, Gass and Gillis, 1999; Sugerman, et.al., 2000; Greenaway, 2004). The reflective stage of David Kolb's "Experiential Learning Cycle" (1984), which has become a cornerstone of most experiential education theory, has been recognized as extremely important.

The small group discussion circle has become the most frequently used procedure for facilitation of reflection. There are alternatives, such as using experiences of solo and solitude, journaling, or breaking the group down into dyads or triads (Smith, 1987; 1993), but the processing circle is most often the technique of choice. One recommended procedure for the debriefing circle is to ask three questions: What? So What? Now What? (Schoel, et.al., 1989). After completing an experience, the group is circled for discussion about these questions:

1. What just happened? What was that experience all about? How did we function as a group? How did we accomplish it?

2. What did you learn about yourself and the group from the experience? What are the lessons of importance?

3. What do those lessons tell you about what you should do different? Better? What do those lessons tell us about how we should do things in the next activity? How will those lessons affect you tomorrow? In the future?

While these processing circles of experiential education programs are sometimes facilitated to help participants cull significant learning from specific shared experiences, they also result in personal growth and learning. When a small group of people connects and shares experiences and reflective dialogue, something special happens. Christina Baldwin (1998) summarized her thoughts about connecting in circles as follows:

> *. . . Something is called forth within us by these circles. We find strength and renewal. We can be life's faithful pilgrims again, able to touch source, to be grounded in Spirit . . . We have come to this place in time to receive a gift, and to know how to offer that gift back to the world. We prepare the place inside us which will receive, which will give. We go inside and make center, make altared space. Make ready. Clean the cobwebs, light the oil lamps, set the sacred objects into their niches. Hold the place so that the circle may come. And not be afraid to act. And not be ashamed to hope. (pp. 205-206)*

When people connect in *Talking Circles,* the very process of being and becoming is activated. In most cases, the overall goals of challenge/adventure/experiential education sequences can be seen as very similar to that of personal growth groups. I often ask young leaders the question, "Why do we do what we do." Then I answer that question with the following lines.

*Experiential educators facilitate small groups of people through sequences of creative and challenging activities that are designed to promote growth and learning. . . . The intertwined goals of these programs are to enhance each individuals awareness and understanding of self, others, the environment, **the Other,** the self-other interdependency, the self-environment interdependency, and the self-other-environment-Other- ONENESS!*

The Native American Indians, like indigenous peoples about the world, understood the connectedness of all things and the importance of circles: "The American Indian regarded the circle as the principal symbol for understanding life's mysteries, for he observed that it was impressed everywhere throughout Nature" (Meadows, 2002). Many Native Americans danced in circles. They sought understanding of their place in the universe from the Medicine Wheel. They set down their huts and tepees in circles. They drummed in circles. They held council in circles. They knew the value of *Talking Circles, Listening Circles,* and *Wisdom Circles.* They knew the value of discussion circles that followed the ground rules summarized above. And so, somewhere along the line, some Native groups created and adopted the symbolism and procedures of *Talking Sticks.*

Talking Sticks

Determining the authenticity of reports on most Native American traditions is very difficult. (Smith and Quinn, 2004). As there was not written history, and the anthropologists and historians did not begin to study the Native American cultures until the end of the 19th century, it is difficult to determine which of the now-reported traditions began where, and for which of the Native peoples. It must always be remembered that there are many different Native American cultures, and the lifestyle and traditions of the Indians of the Northeast, the Southwest, and the Central Plains were as different as those of the Latvians, the Spanish, the Greeks, and the English of Europe. One must be cautious with statements of generalization about Native American practices with the *Talking Stick.*

Through the years, as I have expanded my facilitators "bag of tricks" by exploring and creating adaptations of various Native traditions, I have found it useful to make distinction between "psychological relevance" and "historical authenticity." When I have taught others how to facilitate challenge/adventure activities that are based in Native traditions, I noted that I was: ". . . neither an American Indian, nor an Native American historian. I have been less concerned with the questions of historical accuracy and authenticity than with the search for exercises and activities which have psychological relevance and can make contribution to programs designed to facilitate personal growth and learning." (Smith, 1990, pg. 95).

Professionals who offer training programs and personal growth workshops often advertise and promote their services with questionably accurate statements about Native American traditions. Thus, one can look up *Talking Sticks* and *Talking Circles* on the internet and find different versions of history and traditional practices. Seldom do these professionals make note of their concern for contemporary groupwork relevance as opposed to historical accuracy. And so, ideas about the traditions of *Talking Sticks* transfer from one website to another without concern for authenticity. It has been in the past couple of decades that many of the "new age" groupwork professionals have become enamored with Native American philosophy and tradition, and focus on *Talking Sticks* is certainly in vogue. I shall overview the symbolism and methodology of *Talking Sticks* with concern for relevance to challenge/adventure growth and learning groups, and I make no claim as to the historical authenticity of these descriptions.

It has been reported that the council meetings of different tribes, such as those of the six nations of the Iroquois Confederacy or the Great Sioux Nation, used the *Talking Stick* to provide order for the group and give everyone a chance to be heard. Council meetings were organized in a circle, and the *Talking Stick* was passed around. Only the person holding the stick was allowed to speak their mind. Other native groups used the *Talking Stick* in tribal councils and small group sessions. The *Talking Stick* became symbolic of the heartfelt wisdom of the speaker, and was also believed to contain the wisdom of the whole group.

Information from the world wide web references practices that parallel the *Talking Stick* among other indigenous peoples of the world, and there are suggestions that other symbolic objects may have been used in similar manner. Rocks, shells, feathers, animal bones, and even the peace-pipe, may have been passed about the circle to give an individual the right to speak. Silent Wolf (2005) talks of an "answering feather" which would be held by the person wanting to have the stick passed to them.

On the internet one can find artists and craftsmen who make *Talking Sticks,* and who can council people about making their own personal one. They give guidelines about decorative colors and symbolic attachments such as feathers, fur, colored beads and ribbons, and good medicine bundles. Some report that a shamanic journey or a vision quest would lead to the creation of the guiding object for the *Talking Circle.* Ross Lew Allen (2005) tells of having "adopted the Hawaiian Huna talking stick in my art and my healing practice." The Hawaiian name for stick is "Paoa," which, according to Allen, means "talking from the tree." Like the Native Hawaiians, the Aboriginals of Australia, and many tribal groups in Africa, most Native Americans did have utmost respect for all things of the environment. Trees held special respect; they gave wood for the fire, poles to build shelters, heartwood for sacred ceremonies, birchbark for canoes, and bark, leaves and roots that were used for medicinal purposes. Sticks were important; they were used to plant corn, to beat drums, to make pipes and flutes, as walking aides, and as weapons. It is certainly understandable that a carved stick, the host of a special spirit, might be decorated and empowered to be used as a *Talking Stick.*

Whatever the symbolic significance of the *Talking Stick,* it is the groundrules for utilization that offer the most potential for the *Talking Circle.* When people gather in *Talking Circles* that incorporate the *Talking Stick,* there are three rules for the speaker and the group:

1. Speak from the heart. This means to speak honestly and sincerely.
2. Listen with the heart. This means to listen attentively and with open-mind.
3. Be lean of expression. This means to speak simply, using as few words, and as little time as necessary to say what you want to say.

Because listening is the key to the success of the *Talking Circle,* I would suggest that there might be an additional groundrule:

4. Speak spontaneously. If you are thinking in advance about what you are going to say, then you are not completely listening to the person who is speaking. It would be better to take silence during the first few moments that you hold the *Talking Stick* to organize your thoughts and decide what you want to say.

This latter groundrule involves respecting silence. Good things happen in small groups even when there is silence. In many ways, Quaker Circles are circles of silence. Only when a member feels moved

from within to speak aloud is the silence broken, and after they have finished nobody responds. The wisdom of silence becomes evident again.

Historically, the leading elder of the council would be the first to hold the *Talking Stick*, but makes personal choice as to whether to speak or not. Some report that when they were finished, they would lay the talking stick at the center of the circle, and someone else could pick it up. More frequently, the stick would be passed clockwise around the circle. Each person could then choose to either speak or pass the stick on. The *Talking Stick* would continue circling until no one had anything more to say. Finally, it would be passed back to an elder for safe keeping until the next gathering of the group.

Talking Knots

It is certainly not surprising that experiential educators who have worked with the theory and practice of *Raccoon Circles* recognized the possibility of using the knot in the web loop in the manner of the *Talking Stick*. As indicated, procedures similar to those of the *Talking Stick* have been followed with other objects. One fourth grade teacher reported that she sometimes had the students "choose various objects from nature as a talking stick." (Cleveland, 2000).

One of the important contributions of the *Raccoon Circle* is that it can provide a thread of connectedness to a whole sequence of challenge/adventure activities. One way it can do that is to become the prop for a "circle of connection" for a debriefing/processing discussion. Groups can begin an experiential education program with basic connections and activities with the *Raccoon Circle*, to experience the joy of trusting and cooperation. A skilled facilitator can frontload the whole program by emphasizing the symbolic significance of the circle and establishing the metaphor of a "circle of connection." Then, after a couple of activities, there can be instruction to "connect up and sit down."

The group is then in a perfect circle for a debriefing discussion. This circle of sharing thoughts and feelings, and listening attentively to others can then be re-created throughout the whole sequence of activities in the program — and even thereafter!

When groups begin by making their own special *Raccoon Circle,* then part of the creation ritual can focus on the symbolic significance of the knot. The knot of the circle can be discussed as having special power to create connections that are filled with trust, cooperation, sharing, caring, and love. Then, when the group sits down for a processing session, the groundrules for use the *Talking Knot* can be laid out. Group members can come to recognize their opportunity to share thoughts and feelings in the safety and security of the "circle of connection."

I have seen the *Talking Knot* used in a number of ways:

1. After laying out the groundrules that only the person with the knot can talk, and all others must listen, the knot can be passed around the circle to each person in turn. While this may seem to be a sort of "forced participation," it should be remembered that when the knot stops in front of a person they have the right to say, "no comment" or "pass" and then move the knot along.

2. Sometimes the knot can be moved about the circle with instructions to "grab it, and then you, and only you, have the right to talk." When the talker is finished, the circle begins to flow again, and the *Talking Knot* moves around the circle until someone else grabs it. When the knot moves completely around the circle two or three times, the debriefing discussion is over.

3. I have observed the facilitator start out with the knot and raise an important debriefing question, and then start the rotation of the circle until someone grabs it and shares an answer.

4. One facilitator shared with me her practice of grasping the web circle so that the knot would stop in front of a particular student. She said that this was her way of involving the reticent or guarded student in the conversation to share thoughts and feelings. It might even be possible to give permission to everyone in the group to grab the webbing to stop the circle in front of someone they wanted to hear from. Again, people should know that they can say, "pass," "I've got nothing to say," or remain silent.

5. I have sometimes taken the opportunity to grab the knot and then take a few minutes of silence. If someone interrupts (and someone usually does), I re-cap the groundrules of the *Talking Knot,* and suggest that they simply "listen to the silence."

I am sure that other leaders who work with *Raccoon Circles* have explored other ways of using the *Talking Knot.* In *THE Book on Raccoon Circles* (Cain and Smith, 2002), I pointed out that: "Each leader, each program, will have to create ritual that is appropriate for their client population, and that fits into their program goals" (pg. 50). This will certainly be the case in applying the wisdom and potential of the *Talking Knot.*

I close this paper with brief comments about eye-contact and somatological experiences. Much of the literature on interviewing, counseling, and shared feelings conversation, stresses the important of establishing and maintaining good eye-contact between talker and listener. I learned a lesson many years ago from Native American elders. They often engaged in conversation with their head down, and when I inquired about that practice they informed me that by looking down, or even closing their eyes, they could listen more attentively. Only after I was finished talking would they raise their head, look at me, and nod. I knew that I had been heard.

There is value in sharing the physical connections that the *Raccoon Circle* and the *Talking Knot* create. When people connect to this simple prop, there is a physical as well as a psychological experience. Thomas Hanna (1993) might say that it is a "somatological" experience, and therefore is registered and remembered by both mind and body. When groups use the *Talking Knot,* they come to the processing circle more completely each time they grasp that symbolic and sacred knot. I have observed people welcome the knot to their grasp, and squeeze it tightly as they share some difficult or exciting awareness. When everyone is physically connected, the debriefing discussion can be more intense. While it takes a little time to introduce the group to the ideas and groundrules of the *Talking Knot,* the time is well spent, for the processing discussions will be very productive. Using *Raccoon Circles* and *Talking Knots* can enhance the growth and learning of all of our students and clients.

References

Allen, L. *www.lewallenjewelry.com/roses/talkstick.* (Retrieved April, 2005)

Baldwin, C. (1998). *Calling the Circle: The First and Future Culture.* New York: Bantam Books.

Boud, D. (1985). *Reflection: Turning Experience Into Learning.* New York: Routledge Farmer.

Cain, J. & Smith, T. (2002). *THE Book on Raccoon Circles.* Tulsa, OK: Learning Unlimited.

Cain, J., Cummings, M. and Stanchfield, J. (2005). *A Teachable Moment.* Dubuque, Iowa: Kendall/Hunt.

Cleveland, P. (2000). "Talking Circles in Fourth Grade." *The Ripple Effect.* Chicago, IL: TEAM @ Northeastern Illinois University.

Dewey, J. (1933). *Experience and Education.* Reprinted 1997. New York: Touchstone.

Greenaway, R. (2004). "Reviewing Adventures." *www.reviewing.co.uk/rva.* (Retrieved January, 2004).

Hanna, T. (1993). *The Body of Life: Creating New Pathways for Sensory Awareness and Fluid Movement.* Rochester, VT: Healing Arts Press.

Kolb, D. (1984). *Experiential Learning: Experience as the Source of Learning and Development.* New York: Prentice-Hall.

Knapp, C. (1992). *Lasting Lessons: A Teacher's Guide to Reflecting on Experience.* ERIC, Clearninghouse on Rural Education.

Luckner, and Nadler, R. (1997). *Processing the Experience: Strategies to Enhance and Generalize Learning.* Dubuque, Iowa: Kendall/Hunt.

Meadows, K. (2002). *The Medicine Way.* San Francisco, CA: Castle Books.

Nadler, R. and Luckner, (1992). *Processing the Adventure Experience.* Dubuque, Iowa: Kendall/Hunt.

Palmer, P. (2004). *A Hidden Wholeness: The Journey Toward an Undivided Life.* San Francisco, CA: John Wiley & Sons.

Priest, S. and Gass, M. (1997). *Effective Leadership in Adventure Programming.* Champaign, IL: Human Kinetics, Inc.

Priest, S., Gass, M., and Gillis, L. (1999). *The Essential Elements of Facilitation.* Dubuque, Iowa: Kendall/Hunt.

Schoel, J., Prouty, D. and Radcliffe, P. (1989). *Islands of Healing.* Hamilton, MA: Project Adventure.

Silent Wolf. *www.geocities.com/RainForest/9637/pg000014.* (Retrieved May, 2005)

Smith, T. (1986). "Alternative Strategies for Processing the Outdoor Experience." *The Bradford Papers Annual,* Vol. 1. Revised and reprinted in Gass, M. (1993). *Adventure Therapy.* Dubuque, Iowa: Kendall/Hunt.

Smith, T. (1990). *Wilderness Beyond . . . Wilderness Within . . .* Cazenovia, WI: Raccoon Institute.

Smith, T. and Quinn, W. (2004). *The Challenge of Native American Traditions.* Lake Geneva, WI: Raccoon Institute.

Sugerman, D., Dougherty, K., Garvey, D. and Gass, M. (1999). *Reflective Learning: Theory and Practice.* Dubuque, Iowa: Kendall/Hunt.

Raccoon Circles and the Transformation of Humankind

Tom Smith

The challenge for humankind is obvious. We must learn to connect with one another in cooperative, tolerant and compassionate ways. We must create a global community devoted to peace and love. We must learn to care for each other, for all creatures great and small, and for our planet. Words like "me," "family," "community" and "country" can no longer be our focus. We must think in terms of "we," recognizing a world "family," a world that is an interdependent "community." We must find balance and harmony in relationships with our fellow beings and with our earth. One can no longer separate concerns for self and country from concerns for others and the world.

We must move forward toward Teilhard de Chardinís *Omega Point,* where a collective consciousness unfolds. Chardin is optimistic about the future, because he senses the evolutional unfolding of humans *"From one end of the world to the other, all people, to remain human or to become more so, are inexorably led to formulate the hopes and problems of the modern earth in the very same terms."* Teilhard was hardly alone in dreaming of a human unity and its chief benefit—peace.

Paradoxically, that very "me" which is becoming increasingly irrelevant is the place where things must begin. Each of us must come to know the joy and the necessity of interactive trust, caring, communication and cooperation. Each of us must discover our need for belonging, sharing, peace and love. The process begins with personal awareness and personal growth, and that can begin with experiences of small group interaction and the reflection that follows. In small group circles of connection, people can find what Marilyn Ferguson calls *transformative relationships. "A transformative relationship is a whole that is more than the sum of its parts. It is synergistic, holistic . . . Experiences of unity, fullness, awakened senses, empathy and acceptance, flow—all of these open us to more possibilities for connection than we had before. As more individuals open up to each other, expressing warmth and encouragement, love is a more available source of approval and energy. We cannot find our growth alone."*

There are many lessons to be learned as our personal transformation unfolds. Each of us must discover new ways of thinking, feeling, believing and behaving. This can begin in small group circles of connection, small experiences where we can learn new dances for moving along the trails of life. In spite of our fears, our loneliness, our disillusionment, and our feelings of hopelessness, we must, as Pablo Neruda suggested in accepting the Nobel Prize in 1971. . . . *". . . dance our clumsy dance and sing our sorrowful song—for in this dance or in this song, there is fulfilled the most ancient rights of our conscience in the awareness of being human and of believing in a common destiny."*

Our journey to the future can begin today if we connect with others in a sequence of activities with *Raccoon Circles.* Like Neil Armstrongís 'one small step' on the moon, which was a giant step for all humankind, connecting with a *Raccoon Circle* may be a small step for today—but it can be a big step for tomorrow!

189

Some Thoughts on Connectedness

Jim Cain

"When the Raccoon looks out from inside, the circle of connectedness of all things of the universe becomes quite evident."

Tom Smith

When I first read Tom Smith's words, I wasn't sure if 'connectedness' was really a word. But lately, this word has been showing up in some pretty interesting places. Most recently, in the published results of the National Longitudinal Study on Adolescent Health. In the Journal of the American Medical Association (JAMA), Resnick et. al reports that parent-family connectedness and perceived school connectedness were factors that protected youths against nearly every health risk behavior measured in the study (See the first article mentioned below for details). Clearly connection between people, between people and the organizations they belong to, to the environment, and to the global community is a valuable thing. The Alameda Study conducted in California in the late 1990's also illustrates that above many significant social factors (such as poverty, access to healthcare, community, substance abuse, and other social pressures) the presence of connectedness within a community has an overwhelming effect on the overall health of the community. Edward Hallowell mentions some of these findings in his book simply titled 'Connect.' I encourage you to read some of these findings the next time you are trying to justify the need for community building activities in your classroom, adventure program, learning community or corporation. The facts are in, 'connectedness' is one of the most outstanding methods for the health of your community - and with Raccoon Circles, you have hundreds of methods for creating connectedness. Good Luck!

Jim Cain

Protecting Adolescents from Harm: Findings from the National Longitudinal Study on Adolescent Health, Resnick, Bearman, Blum, Bauman, et.al., JAMA, September 10, 1997, Volume 278, Issue 10, pages 823-832.

The National Longitudinal Study on Adolescent Health: Preliminary Results: Great Expectations, Klein, JAMA, September 10, 1997, Volume 278, Issue 10, pages 864-865.

Connect: 12 vital ties that open your heart, lengthen your life, and deepen your soul, 1999, Edward M. Hallowell, Pantheon Book, New York, NY USA ISBN 0-375-40357-4

Try using the word 'connectedness' for a Google search on the internet. You'll find dozens of articles, websites and links that are worth researching.

More Thoughts on Connectedness and Belongingness

A popular song from the broadway musical Funny Girl starring Barbara Streisand gave us all some excellent advice: "People who need people are the luckiest people in the world." Unless people address their basic needs to connect to each other, and take on the obligations and responsibilities for belonging to each other and to the earth, our very survival may be endangered.

Tom Smith

In my 1992 book, *The Theory and Practice of Challenge Education*, I wrote a chapter entitled "Philosophical Foundations for Challenge Education." I began by noting that the chapter was not a philosophy OF the evolving methodology, but a collection of ideas about places that people could search FOR some theoretical foundations. I called one of the sections of that paper "Connectedness and Belongingness Theory," and the following information is taken from that section.

It is possible to cluster a number of thoughts about the human being and the world into an overview that could be called a theory of connectedness. Basically, such a theory would rest on two propositions. The first is that all things of the universe are living and are a part of the whole; they are bio-spiritually connected and interdependent. Second, when human beings become aware of this connectedness, their natural tendency is to care for, nurture, and belong to all other things—to actualize the beauty, the wisdom, and the love of this connectedness through belongingness. Many have recognized the connectedness of all things, for example:

"The deeper we look into nature, the more we recognize that it is full of life, and the more profoundly we know that all life is a secret and that we are all united with all life that is in nature. Man can no longer live life for himself alone."

Albert Schweitzer

"Cosmic awareness differs from self-awareness in that it goes beyond being present in the moment and provides an experience of contact with the universe that differs from the one usually presented to the senses—a new way of perceiving the world and one's relationship to it."

John Mann

"A human being is a part of the whole, called by us the universe, a part limited in time and space. He experiences himself, his thoughts and feelings, as something that is separated from the rest—a kind of optical delusion of his consciousness. This delusion is a kind of prison for us, restricting us to our personal desires and to affection for only a few persons nearest to us. Out task must be to free ourselves from this prison by widening out circle of compassion to embrace all living creatures and the whole of nature and its beauty."

Albert Einstein

I was suggesting that Challenge Education should look to the wisdom of those who spoke of "earth consciousness" and awareness of the human-earth interdependency—we cannot survive without knowing that the earth does not belong to us—we belong to the earth. In retrospect, I realize I should have focused in more detail on the human-human interdependency—no one can survive without knowing that each of us is a part of all of us—we belong to each other. I think one might be able to make the case that people need people to become whole, and that there is a biological, psychological, social, and spiritual drive toward connectedness.

Tom Smith

A New Book: The Value of Connection–In the Workplace

Since writing the Book on Raccoon Circles with Tom Smith, I have seen the value of connection through new eyes. In the past year, along with co-author Kirk Weisler, I have been writing a new book, focused on creating an environment of connection in the workplace. This book includes stories of organizations that are working hard to create such environments, and activities for the 'do it yourself' crowd. This book is filled with dozens of activities, stories, resources and ideas for creating a connected work environment, for little cost, but with significant impact. Visit www.teamworkandteamplay.com for more information about this soon to be released book.

Jim Cain

What's Next in Adventure-Based Learning?

Jim Cain, Ph.D.

For 34 years now I've been active in the field of adventure-based learning (and along with it the many other names that this style of education includes, such as: experiential learning, experience-based training, teambuilding, leadership development, ropes and challenge courses, and most recently, active learning). During this time, there has been a flow of ideas, grass root programs, curriculum development, research and general discussion that has allowed this field to mature and proliferate. Adventure-based learning now spans the extremes from collaborative and cooperative games played by children on the school playground and at summer camps, to experiences that test the leadership principles and alter the culture of international corporations in their boardrooms.

With such a rich history, and a strong presence in our modern society, the obvious question is "What's Next?" I believe that in order to answer this question for the future, you must first look at the past.

Ten years ago, an adventure-based trainer or challenge course professional could approach local businesses or schools and mention the word 'teambuilding' and easily attract business. More recently, the focus has changed from teambuilding to exploring leadership issues. Corporations want to take existing employees and help them achieve the skills they need to become leaders within the organization. To this end, many of the activities used for adventure-based teambuilding have been reformatted to focus not only on the team completion of a task, but also on the leadership talents utilized during the project. Even more important in this transition, is the change from simply accepting what a challenge course offered, to corporations requesting facilitators to frame activities and initiatives around a central theme or goal. In many cases, the actual activities used in each of these cases is the same, but the facilitation of these activities has dramatically changed. Corporate audiences have become 'informed consumers' of adventure-based training, and often request specific outcomes for each training session.

For a number of years now, I believe that traditional Human Resources (HR) and Organizational Development (OD) professionals have been looking at the adventure-based and active learning communities, and 'borrowing' some of our best materials, repackaging these in more traditional lecture style formats, and positively impacting their corporate training presentations. It is now time for adventure-based facilitators to borrow the best from the HR and OD fields, and apply it to our programs. By delivering 'content rich' programs, which focus on key corporate initiatives (such as clear communication, creative problem solving, consensus building, decision making, resource management, conflict resolution, teambuilding and leadership), we are able to bring the best training technique known (experience-based education and active learning) to our clients, with confidence that we can help them achieve their training goals.

With this in mind, it is now time to revisit our initial question from above, "What's Next?" While the following opinions and comments are certainly my own, there are an enormous number of authors who agree with me. The reference and resource listings in my upcoming book on this subject contain more than 200 books, publications, journal articles and websites. Many of these references did not exist just a decade ago, and are the result of expanding interest and perceived value in this arena.

I believe, as we go forward, that the next wave in adventure-based programming and active learning will be shaped by the word 'connection.'

Jim Cain

The National Longitudinal Study of Adolescent Health (a study funded near the time of the Columbine High School tragedy a few years ago) had two not-so-surprising results. Students that felt a connection to their families, and students that felt a connection to their schools, were incredibly well insulated from nearly all of the traditional risky behaviors associated with adolescence. Corporations have discovered that employee retention and engagement improves as an employee feels a sense of connection in the workplace. Even our current conventional wisdom on organizational effectiveness shows that there are three things required for highly effective teams:

1. A clearly identified, articulated and worthy task.
2. The opportunity for growth, advancement and building new skills.
3. The opportunity to create connection and maintain relationships with other members of the group. Sometimes referred to as the 'social capital' of the organization.

The third item mentioned above clearly demonstrates the need for connection in the corporate world. The NLSAH results show similar needs in the world of our children. And additional studies, such as the Alameda County Study (1979) by Dr. Lisa Berkman of Harvard University, show that for even the elderly in our communities, personal health and the quality of their lives improve with the amount of connection they have to the other members of their community. For more information about these subjects, see the references listed at the end of this article.

"It is time for us to do what we have always done well - build unity, community, connection and teamwork through activities that utilize a wide variety of life skills and that open the door to meaningful conversations about subjects that matter."

Jim Cain

I would encourage each of you that read this article to find the following information at your local library, on-line or at your local bookstore, and learn how to apply it in your pursuit of the next wave in adventure-based and active learning. And, if you would like a publication that is a bit more specific to the corporate adventure-based learning field, you can review a copy of "The Value of Connection - In the Workplace" by Jim Cain and Kirk Weisler. Available in 2007.

Reference Articles

Connect - 12 vital ties that open your heart, lengthen your life, and deepen your soul, 1999, Edward M. Hallowell, Pantheon Books, New York, NY USA ISBN 0-375-40357-4 Connection improves the quality and length of your life, and here is the information that proves it!

The Value of Connection in the Workplace - You can become the catalyst for building community within your workforce, creating a positive work environment and promoting a culture of connection in your corporation, 2007, Jim Cain and Kirk Weisler "A new classic in creating the kind of unity, community, connection and teamwork in the workplace that you always knew was possible, in an active, fun and productive manner. This book contains the philosophy, research and easy-to-follow activities for anyone to have a positive impact on their organization."

Exploring the Stages of Group Formation Using Adventure-Based Activities, Jim Cain, Teamwork & Teamplay website www.teamworkandteamplay.com

Peer Harassment, School Connectedness, and Academic Achievement, Marla Eisenberg, Dianne Neumark-Sztainer and Cheryl Perry, *The Journal of School Health,* Volume 73, Number 8, October 2003, pages 311-316.

Protecting Adolescents From Harm: Findings From the National Longitudinal Study on Adolescent Health, Michael Resnick, Peter Bearman, Robert Blum, et.al., *Journal of the American Medical Association (JAMA),* Volume 278, Number 10, September 10, 1997, pages 823-832.

The National Longitudinal Study on Adolescent Health - Preliminary Results: Great Expectations, Jonathan Klein, *Journal of the American Medical Association (JAMA),* Volume 278, Number 10, September 10, 1997, pages 864-865.

Circles of Connection: Raccoon Circles in the Design of a Professional Training Conference

Tom Smith
The Raccoon Institute

Jim Doncaster
Presley Ridge

This paper discusses how Raccoon Circles (Cain and Smith, 2002; Smith, 2005) were used in the design, organization, and programing of a professional training conference. The conference steering committee was given the assignment to weave a symbolic thread of connection through the various events of a three-day conference so that participants could sense it as a unified, holistic, complete experience. The web-loop circle was used for small group activities and processing discussions throughout the conference and was also incorporated in the opening and closing ceremonies. The Raccoon Circle provided symbolic meaning and enabled creation of rituals and ceremonies of significance.

The conference was designed for teachers, counselors and family workers of a non-profit social services agency providing special education programs and mental health services for troubled children and their families in Washington, D.C. and bordering states. More than 200 professionals attended the event, representing over 20% of the total employment for this organization.

Challenges of the Steering Committee

As is the case for many professional conferences, preparation began a full year earlier, in the office of the Director of Training. It was recognized that there should be a steering committee to help with the task ahead, and soon six leaders were selected. Early discussions and questions about conference design, goals, and procedures resulted in the identification of several challenges that would need to be addressed by the committee.

Challenge 1 – Can we organize and program the conference with our own internal resources, or should we enlist the assistance of outside resources, presenters, consultants and experts?

Challenge 2 – Can we design a conference that will make every person attending truly connected to everyone else? Even in the best-case scenarios, some conference attendees fail to network and interact with other participants. How can this too often occurring consequence be avoided?

Challenge 3 – Could the majority of conference presentations and events be offered in an active and experiential format? Most conferences deliver content in lecture-based presentations. We would prefer active, hands-on participation. Such presentations would also introduce participants to techniques that they could use in their own education and counseling sessions.

Challenge 4 – How can a multiple day conference be designed so that a thread of connectedness runs through each element of the program? The steering committee noted that they wanted to avoid conference presentations that were disjointed or unconnected to each other.

Challenge 5 – Ritual and ceremony have a significant place in our lives. How can we incorporate such elements into our conference program? A number of professional sociologists, anthropologists, historians, psychologists and critics of contemporary society have suggested that our society's lack of ritual and ceremony may contribute to many of our current psychological, social, and spiritual problems. Ritual binds people to their group and their culture; it helps them make sense out of the nonsense of every day life. Ritual and ceremony can be important in working with troubled youth and their families, and the committee was challenged to include both ritual and ceremony in the conference.

Challenge 6 – Since most of the professional people-workers who would attend the conference work with small groups (*residential living groups, special education groups, wilderness therapy groups, family groups*), the committee was challenged to provide them with a small group experience in which they could improve their skills for working with small groups, educationally and therapeutically. It was hoped that the small group experience would also reinforce basic beliefs in the power of small groups.

Challenge 7 – Could a three day conference be an experience of personal growth, value clarification, and energy renewal for participants? The committee recognized that leadership development involves skill development <u>and</u> ongoing personal growth. Professionals need to have experiences that afford them opportunity to explore personal values and decisions, and which can enhance their personal psychological, social, and spiritual development.

Challenge 8 – The agency's founder, Nicholas Hobbs, had a philosophy and methodology for working with troubled youth often referred to as Re-education of Emotionally Disturbed Children, or Re-ED. Hobbs captured the spirit of Re-ED in his book *The Troubled and Troubling Child* (1982), where he set down twelve principles for working with emotionally disturbed and behavior disordered youth. The steering committee was challenged to design and implement conference experiences that would affirm and reinforce these twelve principles.

1. *Life is to be lived now, not in the past, and lived in the future only as a present challenge.*

2. *Trust between child and adult is essential, the foundation on which all other principles rest, the glue that holds teaching and learning together, the beginning point for reeducation.*

3. *Competence makes a difference; children and adolescents should be helped to be good at something, especially at school-work.*

4. *Time is an ally, working on the side of growth in a period of development when life has a tremendous forward thrust.*

5. *Self-control can be taught and children and adolescents helped to manage their behavior without the development of psychodynamic insight; and symptoms can and should be controlled by direct address, not necessarily by an uncovering therapy.*

6. *The cognitive competence of children and adolescents can be considerably enhanced; they can be taught generic skills in the management of their lives as well as strategies for coping with the complex array of demands placed on them by family, school, community, or job, in other words, intelligence can be taught.*

7. *Feelings should be nurtured, shared spontaneously, controlled when necessary, expressed when too long repressed, and explored with trusted others.*

8. *The group is very important to young people; it can be a major source of instruction in growing up.*

9. *Ceremony and ritual give order, stability, and confidence to troubled children and adolescents, whose lives are often in considerable disarray.*

10. *The body is the armature of the self, the physical self around which the psychological self is constructed.*

11. *Communities are important for children and youth, but the uses and benefits of community must be experienced to be learned.*

12. *In growing up, a child should know some joy in each day and look forward to some joyous event for the morrow.*

Design and Organization of the Conference

With these challenges in mind, the steering committee overviewed the conference. It was decided that many of these challenges could indeed be met by using the theory and practice of Raccoon Circles, although for this conference the web-loops would be referred to as 'Circles of Connection.'

Everyone who attended the conference would be assigned to a small group of 10-12 people at registration. They would have lodging and dining hall assignments with others in their group. Peer leaders from the rank and file of the organization would serve as facilitators for these small groups. As projected attendance at the conference was over 200 people, there needed to be many peer leaders. Peer leaders were nominated by program supervisors throughout the organization.

The peer leaders chosen participated in a training program prior to the start of the conference. They would meet three times for a 2-day training presented by Dr. Tom Smith and the six members of the steering committee, who were referred to as "meta-facilitators." It was decided that the peer leader training program would be an experiential sequence that closely paralleled the projected experience of the small groups at the conference. There were three goals for the peer leadership training program:

1. To development of the leadership skills of those selected, with focus on the skills they would need in their role as small group facilitators during the conference.

2. To teach these peer leaders a repertoire of experiential activities that they could use in their future work with small groups, with focus on activities using the 'circle of connection' which they could use with the conference groups.

3. To familiarize these peer leaders with some of the basic skills necessary for leading small group debriefing and personal growth/value clarification discussions, with focus on procedures for facilitating processing circles with the web-loop 'circle of connection.'

Raccoon Circles and Peer Leader Training

Since the Circles of Connection (*Raccoon Circles*) were to be the major focus for the conference they became the center of the whole training program. The community of peer-leaders in training was divided into three groups for most of the training. They began their training with a basic sequence of Circle of Connection activities. In accordance with the Re-ED principal that states the importance of ritual and ceremony, one of the early activity sequences for these groups involved a ritual for creation of personal Circles of Connection. Each leader made and empowered a web-loop circle which they would later use with their conference groups.

Throughout the training, the peer leaders learned *Raccoon Circle* activities involving trust, cooperation, problem-solving, risk taking and fun. They were also provided with experiences from a variety of standard low-prop / no-prop challenge activities, such as All Aboard, Blind Trust Walks, Group Juggle, Helium Stick and Traffic Jam.

After these activities, groups always joined their Circle of Connection for the debriefing process. Trainers introduced the peer leaders to basic processing techniques, including use of the 'talking knot' of their Circle of Connection.

A significant training manual (over 200 pages) was provided to each of the peer leaders. Sections of the training manual included: principles of Re-ED, basic theory of 'talking circles,' ground rules for groups, techniques for group processing, leadership characteristics and instructions for small group activities.

As the training program wrapped up, these peer leaders were empowered for the task ahead in a final graduation rites-of-passage ceremony involving their Circle of Connection.

Raccoon Circles and the Opening Ceremonies

The opening session of the conference was choreographed to honor organizational dignitaries, the steering committee/peer leader trainers, and organizational teachers and counselors who had been recognized during one of the past twelve months. The opening ceremony was in a large activity field. A circle of banners, each with one of the Re-Ed principles printed on it, circled the field. The conference participants were seated on a hill beside the field as the opening ceremony began. The ceremony unfolded in the following steps:

1. Dignitaries were introduced followed by welcoming statements.
2. Meta-facilitators were then introduced and they walked to the center of the field center carrying a single web circle. This strip would soon become the 'alpha' Circle of Connection.
3. The teachers and counselors of the month were then introduced. After each name was called, one of the twelve principles of Re-Ed was read. These teachers then moved to the center of the field and attached a small laminated card with one of the principles printed on it, to the Circle of Connection.
4. When all twelve principles were attached to the web strip, it was time to create the Alpha circle. As the keynote facilitator for the conference, Tom Smith commented on the circle being a symbol of wisdom, power, peace, love, and hope for many people throughout history. The web strip, which then contained the power of the twelve Re-ED principles and the energy of the twelve honored T/C's, was knotted into a circle. Conference participants were reminded that Nicholas Hobbs had taken a 'string of principles' and connected them to become the philosophical basis of Re-Ed and the organizational programs. Therefore, the web strip was tied into a circle with a very special knot called a "Nick Knot."
5. Tom Smith then facilitated the twelve T/C's in the basic sequence of connection, trust lean, balance, and cooperative sit-down and stand-up sequence. It was announced that the alpha Circle of Connection was now ready for delivering wisdom and power to everyone at the conference.

6. The thirty trained peer leaders were then announced, and they came to center. Each carried their personal Circle of Connection which they had created during the training sequence. Using a caribiner, they connected their circle to the Alpha circle, and then stepped back to the outside. Tom Smith again facilitated the basic trust lean, balance, sit-down, stand-up sequence for the peer leaders, and noted that the wisdom and power of the Alpha circle was being transferred to the 30 circles, and will become available to everyone at the conference.

7. Peer-leaders then disconnected their circle from the center circle and walked to their assigned station by one of the Re-Ed banners. Conference participants were then asked to move to their assigned station and circle up with the peer-leaders.

8. From center, Tom Smith then had everyone "connect up" to their group's Circle of Connection. He facilitated the basic *Raccoon Circle* sequence, followed by some additional activities to quickly bond each group together. There were simple problem solving initiatives (such as pass-the-loop) and the task of each group to create their own special sound effects or group cheer.

9. As the opening ceremony came to an end, the peer leaders had their group connect-up and sit-down for a first debriefing discussion. One of the suggested topics/questions for discussion was "what does a Circle of Connection mean to you?" Peer leaders also facilitated icebreaker activities. Finally, a discussion about the ground rules for the group process completed this first stage of the conference.

Raccoon Circles and the Group Process

Group facilitators were with their groups throughout the conference, including during meals and evening lodging. There were opportunities for solo time and free time, and some evening activities of interaction between the whole conference community, but each group spent most of their time at the conference as a small group in process. They shared many experiential activities, many of which involved using their Circle of Connection. Whenever a group completed an activity, they would always "connect up" for celebration and debriefing.

During the conference, there were six different activity stations which groups visited to share experiences. Each of these stations was a focal point for activities that represented one of the principles of Re-ED. At each of these stations, one of the meta-facilitators was available as a resource. The meta-facilitators sometimes helped the peer leaders with activities, but the peer leaders had primary responsibility for facilitating more *Raccoon Circle* activities, or to use various props and equipment available at the stations.

Whatever the activities, and the front-loaded lessons to be learned, all of the groups periodically experienced the "connect up, sit-down, let's talk" processing discussions. At times the peer leaders focused on discussion about the Re-Ed principles, or on aspects of the particular initiative problem or sharing experience the group just completed. Most often, however, the processing discussions were less structured and free-flowing. As the hours unfolded, some of the groups moved into discussions of personal and professional values, issues and decisions. At all times, the peer leaders had responsibility for insuring that everyone in their group was physically and psychologically safe, satisfied and having a good time.

There were twenty groups in process throughout the conference and each developed and unfolded in its own way. Some of the groups moved rather quickly to a greater psychological depth in their processing sessions and others avoided anything serious. When groups had difficulty taking the group processing discussions serious, some of the peer leaders facilitated the processing by breaking the group into dyads or triads, or taking time in a "special place" for solo reflection. The training program had emphasized that the peer leaders should "follow the group" not "lead the group."

Raccoon Circles and the Closing Ceremony

The conference closing ceremony had three goals. First, to provide opportunity for all of the small groups to debrief their conference experience. Secondly, to offer an experience that would help all conference participants become aware of their connection to the whole of the organizational family. And finally, to take away new knowledge about the value, growth and healing power of Circles of Connection. The closing ceremony unfolded as follows:

1. All of the small groups returned to the activity field and sat in a Circle of Connection with their peer-leaders. From centerfield, Tom Smith facilitated the basic connect-up, trust lean, sit-down and stand-up sequence. Then he announced:

   "Over the past three days we have created our very first Circle of Connection — and used it to empower 20 other circles. These 20 circles have now been impacted by the energy, wisdom, and spirit of all of you."

   "There is much power in our circles. It is time to set the world record for a Circle of Connection."

2. Peer leaders were then instructed to take out their caribiner and connect their circle to the one to the right. This created a large circle approximately 200 feet (61 meters) in circumference. The total conference community was then instructed to "connect up and lean back." Tom Smith then explained that to qualify for a world record, the whole community had to do a three-time sit down and stand up in a flowing sequence — with sound effects. He instructed the group that the appropriate down-up slogan for this large circle of connection would be the name of the organization, or "Presley - Ridge."

3. After the total community Circle of Connection, peer leaders were instructed to unhook their group's circle and sit down for a summary processing of the group's conference experience. As part of that process, groups were instructed to choose someone in their group to become their "Keeper of the Sacred Circle."

4. Groups were then told that it was time to bring all the wisdom, power, energy, and spirit of their circles to center. The original (Alpha) Circle of Connection was brought to center by the meta-facilitators. The twenty conference participants who had been selected by their group as "Keepers of the Sacred Circle" were instructed to bring their circle forward and connect it to the center circle. When all were in place they participated in the basic trust lean, sit-down and stand-up sequence. It was noted that the wisdom and energy of all the groups was now being passed into the Alpha Circle of Connection.

5. The twenty circles were then disconnected from the Alpha circle and carried back to the groups. Groups were instructed to remain silent, connect up, trust lean, make eye contact with each other to silently say thank you, and then to sit down.

6. It was then announced that since the Alpha circle now contains all the power, energy, and 'good medicine' of the whole organizational family, and all the wisdom of the 12 principles of Re-ED, that circle will always be available to help create additional Circles of Connection. The twenty circles that the groups had been using were no longer needed — they have done their job and can be retired. Each group decided what to do with the Circle of Connection they had shared throughout the conference.

   Some of the groups decided to cut the circle into small strips so that everyone could take a symbolic reminder of the conference experience away. Some of the groups autographed their circle and gave it to their peer leader. A conference participant from Hungary was given the Circle of Connection by her group, with instructions to take it back and help the people in her country "connect up." Some students from Portugal also took a Circle of Connection back to their native country.

7. Although the closing ceremony ended, the Circle of Connection for the small groups still existed. Peer leaders had responsibility to judge the group's need for more discussion, or the need to wrap up and move on.

8. After conference participants departed, there was a final debriefing session for the peer leaders and the meta-facilitators. As part of that discussion, the Alpha circle of connection was given to Jim Doncaster, with instructions to keep it at hand for others to use when they want to create and empower Circles of Connection for their work.

Summary

Organizing a training conference with *Raccoon Circles — Circles of Connection,* weaved a thread of continuity into the whole experience. That made the conference a whole event, not a series of disconnected workshops, lectures, and interactions. And, as the Gestalt dictum teaches, "the whole is greater than the sum of the parts."

Using *Raccoon Circles* in the conference addressed people's need for ritual, symbol, and ceremony in their personal and professional life. Perhaps it inspired them toward incorporating ritual and ceremony into their own work with small groups and families. *Raccoon Circles* seemed to reinforce and awaken people's awareness about the power and potential of Circles of Connection.

Finally, using *Raccoon Circles* in the conference seemed to meet people's basic need for connection. There were no people drifting about the fringe of the whole event. *Raccoon Circles* as part of the conference design provided each participant with experiences of small group interaction, where everyone has the opportunity to learn about the wisdom, the power, the joy, the spirit and the love of Circles of Connection.

If you enjoyed this review of using Raccoon Circles in the design and program of a professional conference, you can contact Tom Smith for more assistance at: tsraccoon@earthlink.net

A Little Research

Jim Cain

There is something very familiar and universal about a circle. The sun appears round like a circle. Pizzas are baked in a circle. In geometry, circles are some of the first shapes discussed. The knights of the round table sat in a circle. There are traffic circles, quality circles, literary circles, circles of connection and circles of friends. It seems like there are circles in almost every conceivable part of our lives. In our relationships. In our technology. In our food, and so much more. Perhaps that is why Raccoon Circles have such a familiar and friendly feeling about them.

I was intrigued by these ideas when I decided to conduct a (very) brief research assignment. My goal was to spend just ten minutes searching the internet for references to circles and connectedness. As you can imagine, I found quite a few references. Although I gathered a substantial list in just a few minutes, it easily took the better part of a day to review the sources identified during the search.

So, if you are trying to find a way to make Raccoon Circles work within your own circle of connectedness, try inputting 'circles' and 'connectedness' coupled with your interest area, in your favorite internet search engine or library book records and see what happens!

Here is a partial list of some of the more interesting references I found during my ten minute search:

Concentric Circles of Interfaith Action, by Abra Pollack in the book *Awakening the Spirit, Inspiring the Soul: 30 Stories of Interspiritual Discovery in the Community of Faiths,* Edited by Brother Wayne Teasdale and Martha Howard, 2004, Skylight Paths Publishing, Woodstock, Vermont, USA ISBN 1-59473-039-3. "There is a thirst for authentic connection in our scattered, busy, speed culture . . ."

Coaching Character at Home–Strategies for Raising Responsible Teens, by Michael Koehler, 2003, Sorin Books, Notre Dame, Indiana USA ISBN 1-893732-48-7. The very first chapter is on connectedness.

Stick Your Neck Out–A Street Smart Guide to Creating Change in Your Community and Beyond, John Graham, 2005, Berrett-Koehler, San Francisco, CA USA ISBN 13:978-1-57675-304-0 Definitely worth reading!

Protecting adolescents from Harm: Findings from the National Longitudinal Study on Adolescent Health, Michael D. Resnick, Peter S. Bearman, Robert Wm. Blum, Karl E. Bauman, et. al., Journal of the American Medical Association (JAMA), September 10, 1997, volume 278, Issue 10, pages 823–832. Parent-family connectedness and perceived school connectedness were protective against every health risk behavior measured, except one (history of pregnancy).

Circlemakers   The website for England's crop circle makers. Provides photographs, witnesses, case histories and perpetrator profiles. www.circlemakers.org

The Study Circles Resource Center. Study circles are small-group, democratic, highly participatory discussions in which large numbers of citizens discuss and take action on a problem. www.studycircles.org

Stone Pages (Web guide to Megalithic Europe) Stonehenge, stone circles, dolmens, ancient standing stones, cairns, barrows, hillforts and archaeology of megalithic Europe. www.stonepages.com

Literature Circles. A website sponsored by the Walloon Institute (a summer retreat for educators where Literature Circles and other progressive practices are shared. www.literaturecircles.com

Circles of Light: The Mathematics of Rainbows. Explains reflection, refraction, and how together they make a rainbow. www.geom.uiuc.edu/education/calc-init/rainbow

Suzanne Alejandre: Designs With Circles. If you connect the centers and one of the points where the circles cross and keep drawing new circles at the new intersection points . . . mathforum.org/alejandre/circles.html

Shamanic Circles. A listing of Shamanic Circles around the world. We invite you to post your Circle here and join with other Circles in conversation and celebration. www.shamaniccircles.org/

Circles Network—Building Inclusive Communities. Circles Network is a national voluntary organization based around the key principles of Inclusion. www.circlesnetwork.org.uk

Learning Circles. A description of the Global Learning Circles of the International Education and Resource Network. www.iearn.org/circles

Welcome to the Wisdom Circles Home Page! Self-discovery and community building in small groups. www.wisdomcircle.org

Human Connectedness Research Group. This web site is a complete documentation of the work of the Human Connectedness research group. web.media.mit.edu/~stefan/hc

Synchronicity and Acausal Connectedness—Jim Fournier. This brings us back to the question of general acausal connectedness. Von Franz points out that Jung saw synchronicity as a unique and special phenomenon. www.geoman.com/jim/synchronicity.html

Connectedness. We want to ensure that students engage with real, practical or hypothetical problems which connect to the world beyond the classroom. education.qld.gov.au/corporate/newbasics/html/pedagogies/connect/con0.html

Social Connectedness—Social Report provides information on the overall social health and well-being of New Zealand society. www.socialreport.msd.govt.nz/social-connectedness

5 Ways to Develop Connectedness—Part of your homework for your Wellness Makeover involves strengthening your connections to your family, friends, colleagues, as well as to nature. altmedicine.about.com/od/optimumhealthessentials/a/Tips_Connected.htm

Circles and Lines: The Shape of Life in Early America, James Kirby Martin, Journal of Social History, Volume 39, Number 1, 2005, pages 289–290.

Circles, Sarah L. Schuette, Capstone Press, Mankato, Minnesota, USA ISBN 0-7368-1460-4.

Complex circles: Historiography of African Christian Women's Organizations, Ezra Chitando, Journal of Religion in Africa, Volume 35, Number 2, 2005, pages 232–238.

Moving in Circles: The Dialectics of Selfhood in Religio Medici, Ladina Bezzola Lambert, Renaissance Studies, Volume 19, Numer 3, 2005, pages 364–379.

Circles of Recovery: Self Help Organizations for Addictions, 2004, K. Humphreys, Cambridge University Press, UK ISBN 0-521-79277-0. Reviewed in Psychological Medicine, by Karen Cropsey, Volume 35, Number 1, 2005, pages 146–147.

Collaborative Circles: Friendship Dynamics and Creative Work (review), Randall Collins, Social Forces, Volume 83, Number 1, 2004, pages 433–436.

And a special thanks to Faith Evans, who referred me to the searchable database of quotations at www.quotationspage.com.

"He drew a circle that shut me out —
Heretic, rebel, a thing to flout.
But Love and I had the wit to win:
We drew a circle that took him in."
Edwin Markham*

---

*Outwitted by Edwin Markham. Reprinted by permission of Wagner College.

Section III

Stories of Raccoon Circles in Interesting Places

This section of The Book of Raccoon Circles is a collection of stories from the authors, friends and fellow facilitators. Enjoy!

   With each new printing of the Book of Raccoon Circles, you'll find the newest Raccoon Circle stories in the final section of this book, entitled Recent Additions.

Raccoon Circle Stories from Special Education Teachers

Dr. Tom Smith
Raccoon Institute

Since the 1960's, I have often done training workshops for special education teachers. In the past few years, those workshops have usually involved an introduction to the theory and practice of Raccoon Circles. It warms me greatly when teachers come to me some months or years later to say thank you for introducing them to the circle, and to tell me that they often use it with their students. Most of all, I enjoy hearing about their creative applications and modifications of activities, and their stories about special moments with the Raccoon Circle. This paper summarizes four of those stories.

The Field Trip

Margo is a teacher of 'behavior disordered' junior high students at a day-school program in the Northwest Suburbs of Chicago. She told me that she has found the circle a powerful way to focus the student group for discussion sessions. Early in the school year, she introduces the students to the circle with a sequence of activities, spending some time after each activity in basic 'connect up and sit down.' Then, throughout the school year, she uses the circle whenever there needs to be a group discussion.

Last year, Margo's class had a special field trip to the Field Museum in Chicago. The group did all right at first, but when they went to the lunchroom there was trouble. A boy from another class visiting the museum said something to one of Margo's students, who then responded in kind, and a minor scuffle broke out. Things were quickly brought under control, and the group finished lunch. As they walked out of the lunchroom, Margo reached into her pack and took out the Raccoon Circle. The group immediately knew that they were going to have to deal with the problem that had occurred. They found a spot at the end of a hallway and proceeded to 'connect up and sit down' for discussion. As they were talking, an elderly oriental gentleman stopped near the group, and looked down at them, curious about what was going on. When the group finished the discussion, they proceeded to 'connect up and stand up.' The onlooker walked over towards the group and said, "In China we call it 'Chi Circle,' where the energy of all becomes the energy of one."

Not much more was said, but the students remembered the old man, and wanted to talk about the incident later that week. Their discussion led to the class wanting to know more about 'Chi' energy. In a few weeks, with some help from the schools physical education teacher, Margo's students were starting each day by connecting to the Raccoon Circle, then stepping back to larger circle to do a ten-minute sequence of activities modified T'ai Chi Chu'an. The sequence involved breathing, balance, movement and focus on personal energy. The students liked the time, and Margo found that the whole day went better when they began with the connections, the breathing, and the balance. Of course, Margo's class got the curious eye of many other teachers and students, and some of the teachers have begun to inquire about her methods.

The Little Circle

Rich teaches high school students with learning disabilities. Many of them have a bit of hyperactivity or 'ADD,' and attention span is short. He told me that the basic trust lean and balance connection of the Raccoon Circle is the quickest way he has found to bring the whole group down to order when things are starting to escalate. He said, "I have been trying to figure out how to get some breathing exercises into the daily routine, and the circles are it." He takes out the circle and has everyone connect up in silence and with deep breaths, for 2-3 minutes, and then proceeds to his schedule. Some days, when the group is particularly high strung, Rich may call the group to 'connect up' eight or ten times.

One of Rich's students discovered that by deep breathing and some isometric tension/release (progressive relaxation), he could self-control his hyper-activity much more than he thought he could. After that had started with the circle, Rich worked with the student to try to develop self-relaxation techniques. At first, there did not seem to be a lot of progress, but then one day the student jokingly suggested that he might have to carry a Raccoon Circle in his pocket to use when he was trying to self-control. Rich chuckled at first, but later thought about it more seriously. He took a piece of nylon webbing a little over one foot long, and tied it into a miniature Raccoon Circle, only 4-5 inches in diameter. It was small enough for the student to stuff into his pocket, and big enough for grasping in two hands. The student would hold the circle across his chest, then pull outward to tension as he took deep breaths, and then release the tension and the breath. If he did this 5-6 times, he found that he could take the edge off escalating energy bursts. No doubt he could have accomplished the same with another tension/release exercise, but because of his earlier experiences with the group and the Raccoon Circle he truly believed in the healing power of his own little circle. That belief, no doubt, was an important ingredient in the success of the little circle.

Susan's Nap

Jim teaches a high school class for the mentally retarded. Through the years he has recognized the value of experiential learning methodology for his students. He has been an enthusiastic supporter of the school's program for 'adventure outdoors,' which is offered by a local outdoor education center. The adventure outdoors program is built around the theory and practice of a teams course and a 'high ropes' course, and through the years, Jim has learned to help facilitate his students through those activities. Like many classroom teachers, Jim has found that the Raccoon Circle activities, which can be facilitated in the classroom or the gym, the schoolyard or the park, can create some of the same psychodynamics and group dynamics as the ropes and teams courses. Jim has come to my workshops a number of times, seeking new ideas to use with his students. A couple of years ago he told me this story.

Susan had a diagnosis of Down's Syndrome, but was high functioning and had done well in her early school years. It was the middle of the first semester when her parents moved into the school district where Jim worked. They brought Susan in to meet her new teacher, and told Jim that they were concerned about her adjustment to the new program. They explained that she had been with many of the students in her former class for many years, and was quite upset when they moved after her father accepted a new position with his company. The parents told Jim that Susan, who had always loved school, had now been telling them she didn't want to leave home. Jim could tell by the look on Susan's face that she was unhappy, and quite scared of the new situation, but he welcomed her to his class.

For the first couple of weeks of attendance, Susan would not participate in any of the class activity or lessons. She teared frequently, and was obviously quite depressed, a rather unusual condition for young adults with Down's Syndrome. Jim, and some of the other students, tried to reach out to Susan, but with little success. She did watch with some curiosity when the class would 'connect up' to the Raccoon Circle, but she chose to stay apart from the group. Then one day in the activity room, as Jim had the class doing the Raccoon's cradle activity, Susan moved closer to the group. Jim seized the teachable moment, and asked if she would like to go in the cradle. She agreed, and the group proceeded to rock her gently. Susan let out a big sigh, closed her eyes, and was quite relaxed as the group lowered her to the floor. She did not get up, and although Jim could hardly believe it, she was sleeping. The other students laughed quietly, and went on to other things. It was only a couple of minutes, but Susan woke up smiling, and then spoke to her new teacher and classmates for the first time.

She told them, "Susan went to sleep, and she dreamed a dream. She was being hugged by all her friends, and she liked it very much." Thereafter, Susan made good adjustment and good school progress. Her parents told Jim that she was her old self, happy and loving, at home, and gave him mighty thanks. When he told me this story, Jim had a tear in his eye as he said, "but I didn't do much at all, it was the magic of that wonderful circle, right?" I smiled, gave Jim a hug, and said, "right!"

A Good Medicine Wheel

Barbara and Tim shared this story with me in 1996, when I was first exploring the Raccoon Circle activities. They co-teach an off-campus class of Native American teenagers who live on reservation grounds. Their class is funded under a special project grant from the State of Wisconsin, and the local School District, designed to re-capture students who have dropped out or been kicked out of the high school. Barbara has a teaching degree, and Tim's professional training was in therapeutic recreation. Both of them have some native heritage, and both are long time advocates of challenge education. Their class met in the old community building on the reservation, and they had quite a bit of freedom in curriculum for the students. The core of their whole program was the small group in process, with much experiential/adventure curriculum.

Tim had taken a Raccoon Circles workshop with me, and immediately sensed the value of the circle for working with native youth. He took the idea to Barbara, and she was quite ready to explore the sequence of activities, because they had not had a lot of success in building a group that worked toward their goals. At a therapeutic recreation conference a year or so later, they cornered me to share their story of success. Tim said that he remembered my comments about not having to do a lot of teaching about what the circle is and can do because 'the circle speaks for itself.' So, in the early going, that is exactly what he allowed to happen. He had not talked of connection, or trust, or balance, or empowerment, or healing, he had just had the boys connect up and then proceed through activities with the circle.

"And," said Barbara, with a smile on her face, "the circle sure did speak to them." After a couple of sessions with the Raccoon Circle, the boys began to bond as a group, and Tim and Barbara were enthused. When they shared their joy with one of the tribal elders, they were told, of course it worked, circles are good medicine. The whole project then unfolded with some success. Later in the project, Barbara and Tim offered a whole sequence of teaching and experiences that had basis in the Native American traditions of the Medicine Wheel. As we shared this wonderful story, the three of us laughed as we noted that the little old Raccoon Circle is, indeed, good medicine.

"Raccoon Circles Saved My Teaching Career"

Dr. Jim Cain
Teamwork & Teamplay

In 1998 I had the opportunity to assist the faculty of a new charter school in upstate New York. As part of my work, I created a series of activities that the teachers could share with their students during the first two days of school. The goal was to create a positive learning environment for the students, and begin the new school year, and this totally new educational concept, in perfect form, and Raccoon Circles were a part of it. This particular year, the school had hired some new college graduates as part of the faculty. Since all students, and teachers, were new to the project, it was just the luck of the draw that one of the newest teachers was given the class with some of the roughest and toughest students. This particular school was populated by students in the 5th, 6th and 7th grades. Most of these kids were dangerously close to dropping out of school, and some extremely capable and kind faculty members were going to see that that didn't happen.

I can tell you that during our two days together, there was a great deal of difference between the behavior of some 7th grade boys (at least two of whom had been held back for a year or two), and some of the smaller 5th graders. Fear, is the only word I can think of to describe the look on their faces, as they came to know their fellow "schoolmates." And that fear wasn't just on the face of the students, but at least a few of the faculty as well.

About 2 years later, I happened to meet one of the new teachers, and she told me a story that forever changed how I think about teaching. "You know, Raccoon Circles saved my teaching career," she said. "What do you mean?" I asked, and she said, "I happened to be given one of the toughest classes I had ever encountered. I was at my wit's end most days. But even when I couldn't get through to them directly, I would just stretch out my Raccoon Circle, and say, 'connect up,' and they would. It was the one trump card I held. If all else failed, at least I could get through to them, and talk, and share, with the Raccoon Circle. If it hadn't been for that circle, I probably would not have made it through my first year of teaching."

A Raccoon Circle Story

Jean Berube
Director of Discovery Programs
Gallaudet University
Washington, D.C.

The Gallaudet University Discovery staff has been sharing our challenge education program with interested groups in Russia for the past ten years. Since 1997, we have been giving a four day seminar at the Raoul Wallenberg University in St. Petersburg on the theory and philosophy behind the Discovery Program and sharing activities which give practical application of the program. Interested administrators, faculty and staff, students—both hearing and deaf, and area psychologists and teachers have all attended these seminars. One of the events we always bring to these seminars is our collection of Raccoon Circle activities. In sharing the Raccoon Circle, we always start by talking about the importance of circles in our lives and how we can share our energy with others when we come together in circles. We have talked about how wonderful the Raccoon Circle is as it can bring people together who may not be able, for whatever reason, to touch each other. On past visits, we have left some Raccoon Circles at the University for their use.

This past year, one of the teachers shared a beautiful story with us, and I would like to share it with the challenge/adventure education community. Tanya Zinkevitch-Evstigneeva explained that her professional training was in deaf education and she has been involved in the deaf education program at the University in the past. She and another teacher recently developed a fairy tale therapy program that she takes to schools and orphanages where she works with troubled children. She always begins her therapeutic sessions with the Raccoon Circle.

Recently, a little girl was found at the railroad station in St. Petersburg. This little girl had no language skills and was hard of hearing. She was homeless and without parents. She was brought to a school for the hard of hearing. This little girl would not allow anyone to touch her. Since she had no name, the people at the school gave her the name Sveta. When Tanya would come to the school to do the fairy tale therapy with the children, Sveta would stand in the corner and watch. One day, as Tanya began the Raccoon Circle activities, Sveta came over and joined the group. Each time thereafter, Sveta would come and join the Raccoon Circle as Tanya would begin the therapeutic journey with the children. Then one particular day, as the children were releasing the circle, Sveta held on and when the last child let go, Sveta ran to her room with the Raccoon Circle, and closed the door. Tanya watched through the keyhole to see what Sveta was doing. Sveta began placing the Raccoon Circle on her bed, making

different shapes, almost as if she was trying to build a nest. None of the shapes seemed to please her, so she finally folded up the circle and used it as a pillow. Whenever Sveta left her room, she would wear the Raccoon Circle around her neck as a necklace, or she would hide it under her clothes. Tanya never asked for the circle back. However, she did ask Sveta if she would share "her" circle with the other children. Sometimes Sveta was able to share and other times she was not. The Raccoon Circle became known as "Sveta's Circle." Sveta would suck on the circle, play with it in her fingers, and always loved it.

One day, Sveta left the circle in the play area after the fairy tale session. She did not come back to get if for a couple of days, so Tanya brought it home to wash it, because it had become quite filthy. When Tanya brought the circle back, the children said it was not "their" circle. Tanya assured them it was theirs, and that she had only taken it home to wash it. She finally convinced the children to try the circle. They did, and accepted it again as being their circle, but they made Tanya promise that she would NEVER wash it again.

Tanya Zinkevitch-Evstigneeva and Tanya Grabenko, both teachers in Russia, have written a collection of fairy tales. In the collection, there is a story entitled, "A Magic Circle." The story is based on the story of Sveta and the Raccoon Circle. Anna Golovnia, a Russian Discovery staff person and one of our interpreters, translated the story for me before we returned to the United States. The story begins . . .

> . . . *Once upon a time, there was a little girl. This little girl lived in a big city, but she did not live in a beautiful house with white stone walls, nor in a colorfully decorated wooden house, nor in a king's palace. Her home as a cold and damp dungeon, where water was always seeping from the ceiling, and the floor was covered, not with parquet, but with wet thatch. The little girl slept, not on a feather bed with silk covered pillows, but on slippery, wet stones. At night, the little girl tried to stay warm by wrapping her torn and tattered clothes around her. Her favorite delicacies were dark dry bread and frozen potato peelings which seemed wonderfully sweet to her. The plain boiled water from the leaky tin cup from which she drank was so tasty! She had no nannies nor servants to take care of her. Instead, she had poor homeless people, like herself, who watched out for her.*
>
> *No one could remember how this little girl came to the dungeon. They didn't even know her name, so they called her "Baby." Even in such God forsaken places, wonderful meetings*

can happen. These wonderful meetings would happen for Baby when a lonesome stranger would come and join the group that would be huddled around the fire. He would come and find a place and would be given a cup of water and a rusk that would seem to him to be the tastiest thing in the world. Joy and gratitude would always fill this traveler's heart because these unfortunate people were always willing to share their last piece of bread and give you a place near the fire . . .

The authors have written, "You know, dear friends, that nothing protects us better than the company of nice and friendly people with whom we feel as comfortable as if we were home." The story continues by saying the stranger is now at the fire and Baby is sitting beside him. You might say to me, "so what? A Stranger by the fire." but believe me, dear friends, that nothing in our world happens by chance. Each meeting and each person brings something new and special into our lives. Oh, how lucky we would be not to miss, not to pass by any of those magical gifts. IT would be so wonderful to absorb all these new experiences, and treasure the talents and generosity of those around us, or even feel the bitterness of disappointment. We grow wiser and stronger because of these meetings. But let us go back to Baby and the dungeon and the homeless sitting around the fire...

Here the tired stranger tells wonderful stories of his way which is full of dangers, adventure, happy discoveries and victories. "Oh Granddaddy, where do you get the strength to go over such long roads, to conquer enemies and to find new friends?" asked Baby. He answered, "You know, pretty child, it's true that there were moments when I was losing physical and spiritual strength and when I couldn't believe in myself and in the importance of my chosen way. At those moments my Magic Circle would help me. You know, I always have it with me.

"Will you show me your Magic Circle, please?" asked Baby timidly. The stranger smiled and pulled out of his old bag the Magic Circle. He held it for a second then handed it carefully over to Baby. Trembling, she looked at the ragged band. Yes, yes it was an old and worn and faded band. A tight knot connected its ends, making a circle from it. "Can you tell me the secret of your Magic Circle, Granddaddy?" Baby asked.

"A long time ago, when I was young, I decided to go my way all alone. The way of the Path of Life. It was very important for me to find out what is my strength and what is my weakness, what do I know already and what I need to learn; how I can help and what help I need. It wasn't an easy way. So my friends with whom I shared all the happiness and pleasure of my young life prepared me for the way. One of them gave me a feather and a piece of paper so I could send home messages. The other one gave me a little bag with a handful of soil so I wouldn't forget my Motherland. A third one gave me a dozen wheat seeds so I wouldn't die from hunger. And my closest and most trustworthy friend gave me a blue band. He gave it to me and asked me to tie its ends together with a tight knot. Thus, I had a circle in my hands. And my friends came into the circle and took the band in their strong young hands. And in their hands, the circle became alive. It became a sea and a raft, an abyss and a bridge, a shaft of burning sun and a tent. In my friends hands, this circle became magic. It showed me what difficulties and obstacles were awaiting me on my way, and it showed me how I could overcome them. I keep the band as a most treasured thing. If you could only know, my dear girl, from how many problems this Magic Circle has gotten me out of! I'm strong only because of the precious gift of my friend."

"How lucky you are, Granddaddy! How important it is in life to have such friends and to deserve their precious gifts," Baby said. And suddenly, after saying that, Baby became very sad.

"I came today to your fire to give this blue band to you," said the stranger. "It has the color of your eyes; the color of a dream, the color of a bottomless sea and of an endless sky; and of a most delicate flower, the 'forget-me-not.' Take it, it's yours. The time will come when you, with your tender and strong hands, will tie its ends into a tight knot. And the band will become a Magic Circle that friends will join. They will join it to give you the power of kindness and love, to encourage your dreams and actions, to send you along the great path of knowledge and victory. And I know it will happen soon!" Saying that and leaving her no time to thank him, the old man disappeared.

There in the girl's hands was a blue band and it looked just like the one I have now in mine. What wonderful gifts life gives us. Just yesterday, Baby couldn't even think of happiness, and now, holding the gift from the old man in her hands, she felt strong . . . and the winged dreams started to form her Path of Life.

Many days have passed since then. Baby grew up and became a beautiful young woman. Her life was successful. And though her name wasn't in the newspaper headlines, it was often spoken with a sense of gratitude. She had a wonderful gift of kindness that warmed up the souls of those who needed that. And she kept as a talisman, the gift from the old man who changed her life so magically. And she always shared her story with anyone who would listen. The End.

Tanya told me that she needs to get some new Raccoon Circles since the one she had been using was now Sveta's. She told me that Raccoon Circles make wonderful birthday gifts, because all of the people who are celebrating the birthday can put their wishes for the birthday person into the circle where the wishes will remain forever. With tears steaming down my face, I gave her seven pieces of blue webbing that luckily I had brought with me and told her they represented the seven directions and she was to use them as she needed. With tears on her face, we embraced. All of this happened through interpreters. We never know what gifts we give that will make a difference, what words we say that might leave an impact, or what touch or hug might give confidence and faith. The Raccoon Circle is bringing people together from all over the world, and it is making a difference.

Raccoon Circles or Baboon Circles?

Karl Rohnke

A few years ago Tom Smith and I were working together in South Africa. We were traveling near Cape Town to a game preserve and had stopped at a roadside pull out to stretch our legs and look around. During that time Tom, because of some personal atavistic aura, attracted the attention of a fairly large and inquisitive baboon. During that brief period of joint introspection, Tom, at some level, connected with the primate. Tom commented about and processed at length that simian contact for the remainder of the drive. Do you anticipate what's coming? Baboon / Raccoon! I, of course, suggested that the heretofore Raccoon Circles might be more appropriately called, what else, Baboon Circles. It was a toss up for awhile, but Raccoon Circles it remains and rightly so. Except in South Africa, of course, where Baboon Circles still get the nod.

Raccoon Circles AND Baboon Circles

Tom Smith
Baboon Institute

In the fall of 1997, Karl Rohnke and I traveled to South Africa to meet Bill Quinn. Karl and I were to offer a series of training programs for professionals who facilitated challenge and adventure programs for schools, community agencies, and corporations. Between the programs we had some free time to explore the beauty of the country. This story begins with a climb up Cape Point to look down at the mixing of the Indian and Atlantic Oceans.

Climbing along the rocky trail to the point, our South African friends told us that there were colonies of Baboons in the forest below. Lucky we were, for when we reached the top of the mountain several baboons were moving across the trail. Next came one of those 'I don't understand this' experiences. A large male baboon, who had been sitting atop a large rock formation as a lookout for the others, spotted me. He moved toward me, but then stopped about ten feet away. We looked at each other for a long time, communicating in some special soul-mate language. We stood in silence for five or ten minutes, as all the other baboons moved down the hill into the forest.

When it was time to go, and I turned to start down the trail, he followed me. When I took out a bottle of water to take a drink, he moved quickly towards me and tried to grab the bottle. I walked...he walked. I stopped...he stopped. When I sat down on a rock to look out over the ocean, he sat on a rock a few feet away. Other hikers passed us on the trail, but he stayed near me. What was he trying to tell me? Why was our connection so intense?

He followed me all the way to the bottom of the mountain, but as I moved toward the parking lot, he stopped. I turned around and looked at him to say good-bye. We stared at each other for a few more minutes, and then he turned and climbed back along the side of the mountain to find his colony. As we drove back to Capetown, I pondered the experience, but I could make no sense out of it.

Two days later, we met with some trainers of the EDUCO School of Africa to plan my presentation. One of the trainers pointed out that there are no raccoons in South Africa, and participants might not understand my use of that name for the web circle activities. We kicked around names, such as 'power circles,' 'connection circles,' or 'magic circles.' I noted that a teacher friend of mine had told me that she used the name 'power circles' and that students liked the idea of building their personal power.

The next evening, I was standing under the stars at the Sadawa game farm. Here I saw gazelles, wild dogs, wildebeests, zebras, ostriches and a cobra nearly six feet long. I was simply trying to digest the whole experience in a solo walk outside the compound, when my thoughts returned to my baboon friend. And then it came to me. He had been suggesting that the appropriate name for the web loop activities in South Africa would best be "Baboon Circles."

Of course! Baboons are closely connected in family and extended family colonies. Baboons are playful, and they take care of each other, and they are certainly in touch with Mother Earth. And, after all, wasn't the wisdom given in that powerful book, Ishmael (by Daniel Quinn), presented by a great ape...somewhere between the baboon and humankind on the evolution scale? If the wisdom of that great ape could be passed along to humans, could it not also be passed to baboons? It may well be that my baboon friend had an understanding of the connectedness of all creatures to the Earth, just as I did. Maybe my soulmate knew that learning about the circle of connection was an important awareness for all the people of the world.

Two days later, training young South Africans to facilitate "Play for Peace" workshops for people across their country, I introduced the group to the magic, the power and the 'good medicine' of 'Baboon Circles.' As I have often noted, "the circle speaks for itself." It is the process of people sharing experiences about the circle that is important. It does not matter what they are called. So let the web loops begin to circle South Africa as "Baboon Circles."

Accessibility and Inclusion

Don Rogers

Indiana State University

I've always enjoyed Tom's personal message to me in his book, Wilderness Beyond—Wilderness Within…

> *'If the wisdom of life and living and people, and the Great Spirit, is circular, and all goes round and round—then do you guys on wheels have a head start on the trails to that wisdom?'*

I have known Tom Smith for many years as a friend, mentor and colleague. During these years we have shared adventures together and discussed at length many of the important issues related to experiential learning. Tom has, for as long as I have known him, supported the inclusion of people with disabilities in adventure and experiential learning activities. It would be accurate to say that Tom is an inclusion specialist. Not just because he has found so many ways to include people with disabilities, but more because he works to include all people, period. He demonstrates a keen awareness of the needs of members of his groups and is innovative in how he keeps everyone involved in the group process and keeping the process group centered. In this section, I will discuss some inclusion methods with the Raccoon Circles, as well as some thoughts about the inclusion of people with disabilities and the trails we are on.

Circles and Rituals

While the symbol of the circle that is present in the wheel of the wheelchair represents the medium for achieving greater insight for the person with a disability of themselves and the world around them, as Tom is suggesting, paradoxically this same circle triggers powerful social distancing. Over time, humans have used the circle to separate themselves and as a first line of defense, as with 'circle the wagons', the circled wall around the city, and the 'inner circle' of elite membership. Black Elk said that 'Everything the power of the world does is done in a circle,' which seems true of us as we exert our power over the world and each other. From the same statement about the circle, Black Elk observes, 'Birds make their nests in circles, for theirs is the same religion as ours.' If we can feel such connectedness to animals from other species, why don't we have a much greater bond with all of those from our own? The person using the wheelchair is not so unlike the bird. With wheels as wings, what we want from life is no different than any living thing.

Nietche's observation about human adaptation seems relevant here; 'That which does not kill me makes me stronger.' If that which does not kill you makes you significantly different from those around you, is there something that those around you should be learning as well? The tendency for those who associate closely with a person with a disability, family members (the person's first circle), friends or colleagues, is to develop or redevelop a relationship with the person that views the person first and the disability second. That is not the tendency for others who are outside those inner circles that the person with a disability comes into contact with.

These relationships vary depending on a number of factors. One salient factor appears to be the severity of the disability. As the functional ability of the individual decreases due to impairment, the role of those around them tends to take on more care providing and helping responsibilities. The interdependency dynamic in this type of relationship is unbalanced. Where you would typically see a give-and-take dynamic in healthy relationships, it is difficult for the person with a severe disability to fulfill the reciprocal role. For those outside the close-relationship circle (the inner circle), the person with a physical disability is primarily perceived as deviant. This is particularly true in our society where appearances and physical abilities are highly valued. With impairments that involve communication, emotional, behavioral, and/or intellectual functioning, the interaction skills of the person without a disability may be inadequate to engage in basic, initial socialization, potentially creating an uncomfortable situation for both individuals. This phenomenon has been referred to as disabling the able. The more different the person is as a result of disability, the more different that makes the other person in an interaction. The interaction skills of the person without a disability also seem inadequate for the situation. Getting past this initial barrier to getting to know each other is critical to the inclusion of people with disabilities, and the Raccoon Circle provides an ideal technique for accomplishing this.

Tom has written much about the value of Ritual in the adventure experience. He invites facilitators to incorporate rituals in the Raccoon Circle process. Indeed, in many groups I have facilitated, rituals have been an important part of the experience, either through conscious planning, as an emergent quality, or spontaneously as when some unique group behavior results in a powerful, unexpected outcome.

Though rituals are reported as lacking in our contemporary society, there are in fact many behaviors that we engage in that constitute rites of passage or stepping-stones to greater personal and social growth. Consider behaviors associated with high school proms, college fraternities, and workplace expectations. Subtler, yet no less significant to group membership, are things like body language, a firm handshake, eye contact, and minimal verbal responses during conversation. Most people without disabilities take these behaviors for granted. That is not to say they don't think about them, or that they all perform them with ease. Instead, I mean these behaviors are part of a set of expectations that most people leave the house with everyday. In fact, the most common rituals are an integral part of how we evaluate ourselves within our social roles.

It is a substantial challenge for many people with disabilities to participate in these and other rituals. The difficulty may rise from environmental inaccessibility or the physical or psychological inability to perform the ritual due to impairment. There is also the issue of social exclusion, which amounts to attitudinal inaccessibility. At the root of attitudes are beliefs that, in this case, form the content of how disability is understood.

There is much to say about the social construction of disability. In this limited space let's consider the process as one based on relatively universal beliefs that result in similar attitudes and behaviors across many cultures. There is substantial literature to support this perspective. This consistent approach to defining and understanding disability constitutes a ritual of how people relate to disability in a social context. The tragedy is that instead of people with disabilities being participants in rituals, they become objects of ritual.

Another important concept regarding ritual and disability is Dignity of Risk. Risk exists when there is doubt about the outcome of some behavior. Therefore, risk taking is a part of life. Attempts to develop relationships, live independently, pursue an education, compete for a job, share one's ideas, and to be one's self are risky behaviors. We all know how difficult it can be to move confidently through the mainstream of society. As such, we share the same basic risks, and we respect each other as a result of our efforts. This respect fosters dignity in knowing that you are recognized as a member of this society having engaged in the universal struggles. What about people that do not have access to these struggles? Are they viewed as second-class citizens? The sharing of risk, regardless of outcome, is a powerful catalyst for inclusion.

People with disabilities may experience many situations that serve to diminish the potential for them to encounter risk in their lives. These situations include over-protective parents or guardians; institutional living; the influence of the medical model; media-driven stereotypes; and the well-intentioned, but often solicitous behavior of the general public. There are two ideas to consider as to why this occurs. First is the general notion that people with disabilities need to be protected from risk because they are predisposed to failure and lack the ability to adapt to typical life challenges as a result of having a disability. Second is the 'right with the world' idea, which believes that it is fair to make the lives of people with disabilities easier, even if it means sacrificing the needs of others, because they have been unjustly treated by having a disability.

These beliefs, however well intentioned, undermine the attempts of people with disabilities to be included in meaningful group roles. The adventure learning process has tremendous potential to recreate how disability is understood. As presented by Tom, Raccoon Circles are meant to be humanistic and inclusive, building on Carl Rogers' approaches to human growth. Genuine communication, unconditional positive regard, and mutual respect are effective in both de-constructing how we know disability and people with disabilities and re-constructing new, healthy understandings.

When working with diverse groups and rituals are planned or they somehow become part of that group culture, take responsibility to facilitate the creation of rituals that include and value all people. This is particularly important when rituals communicate and perpetuate group values and interpersonal behavior. The interactive experiences of Raccoon Circle activities will greatly influence how group members relate to and evaluate each other. At the core of experiential learning is the idea that what we do with each other, coupled with what we think, feel, and say about it, has more impact on individual and group growth than conversations detached from experience. If there are members who are not participating or they are engaged in minor, relatively meaningless roles, this will shape their identity in the group on that day, and possibly reinforce those same roles in other situations. Encourage rituals that provide all members with opportunities to be involved in each activity in a meaningful way. Meaningful involvement suggests that each person has a role in the group process that contributes to achieving the goals of the individual and group.

Preparing for Inclusion

Assessment

If it is known ahead of time that a person with a disability is going to be part of the Raccoon Circles program, it is important to identify the needs and abilities of that person in order to plan for effective inclusion. The information collected will be used to guide decisions of individual and group safety needs, activity selection, activity adaptations, equipment needs, and various accessibility concerns. This information will also impact staffing considerations, program logistics, and facilitation strategies. Assessment information is meant to provide support for inclusion and not be used as justification for limited involvement. For this reason, be sure to focus on identifying individual strengths and abilities instead of what a person cannot or may not be able to do.

There are numerous ways to assess an individual or group. The methods selected will depend on many things, including cost, time constraints, staff availability, assessment skills, and access to participants. Regardless of the difficulties associated with the assessment process, it is too important to forgo it in favor of the 'assumptions model.' That is when a program assumes or intuits the needs and abilities of a group without having specific, valid information about them. In fact, the minimal use of pre-program assessment may be the weakest component in the field of experiential learning, particularly with programs that do not do client assessment and then promise to help clients improve or change in some specific way. Without an appropriate assessment or other acceptable way of knowing the needs of the group, the program plan becomes a template for 'that kind of group.' Templates have very limited helping potential.

One method of assessment is to observe clients in their 'natural environment' prior to their arrival. This provides opportunities to evaluate social, communication, behavioral, and physical skills, as well as current activity levels and assistance needs. It may also helpful to engage in one-to-one interviews and even some self-report, written assessment tools. When identifying areas to assess, consider the following topics. For a more detailed explanation of these topics, see the reference document at the end of this article.

1. Mobility and Physical Functioning
2. Communication
3. Cognitive Functioning and Understanding
4. Adaptive Equipment Needs
5. Medications
6. Daily Living Needs
7. Dietary Needs

Accessibility

An area of concern that impacts all areas of program inclusion is accessibility for participants with disabilities. When access is compromised, it can result in more than inconvenience. Accessible facilities, environments, and program components have implications for safety and inclusion, and may be the single most important variable in the quality of a person with a disability's experience. A group can interact and devise ways of being inclusive in spite of incompetent leadership, but if they consistently encounter accessibility problems, then the person with the disability becomes more dependent on the group for mobility, safety, and communication than he or she needs to be.

There are standards for accessibility that can be found in the Americans with Disabilities Act Accessibility Guidelines (ADAAG) and in other guidelines being developed for inclusion in ADAAG, such as playgrounds (12/00), trails, beach areas, and recreation areas. These areas have valuable suggestions for making the kind of environments and facilities we utilize in adventure programming more accessible. The guidelines for facilities, such as restrooms, doors, parking, and information areas are very straightforward and can be readily applied to facilities that support our programs. In fact, any facility providing programs, services, or facility usage to the public is required to comply with ADAAG. It is important to note that programs and services as well as the physical facilities are covered by a variety of accessibility legislation, including the Americans with Disabilities Act (ADA). It is advised that programs consult with specialists in the area of accessibility, particularly those who have experience in similar environments and with similar programs before committing to major renovations or new designs. When trying to create program access for an individual with a disability, it is critical to involve that person in the planning process.

Concepts for Inclusion

Inclusion of all group members in the growth process requires efforts from the beginning that establish inclusion as something that the group understands and values. An initial discussion with the

group about inclusion is a good place to start. Have them talk about the value of inclusion to them, what are the inclusion needs within the group, how will they work to meet those needs, and something I like to ask is "When you are including everyone, what will it look like?" They may not be able to be too specific at this point, but that is okay. This early discussion will provide a foundation for future strategies and debriefing issues.

A discussion of this nature, particularly at such an early stage of group development, may be difficult for some individuals. That is okay too. It is best not to push, but instead let the group find its own level of comfort on the topic. At the same time, a superficial discussion of the topic will not benefit the group. This is where direct, honest intervention by the facilitator will be helpful. If the group is still reluctant, then move on to early activities that will bring the inclusion question out in the open again.

It may be the case that the person with a disability is the one who is most uncomfortable with the topic. That too is understandable, because now it seems like we are talking about them. That is one of the biggest challenges of inclusion; to make it work and learn from it without making individuals with differences feel like they are at the center of the work being done, or that the work is being done to them or because of them. Keeping the process group-centered is very important for the group learning about inclusion. The following are some ideas for facilitating inclusion.

1. Be sure everyone has a chance for input. This includes asking questions about the task at hand, having input into the decision making process, and during the debriefings. People that have difficulty with communication may need more direct opportunities, such as go-rounds that let everyone take a turn, or direct inquiry from the facilitator. As a group goal, they should be working to make sure that everyone is heard, however that has to happen.

2. Establish the values of effort and involvement. Not everyone will be able to do activities the same way or to the same degree. Emphasize that getting involved and contributing to the group process in meaningful ways are essential building blocks of teams and communities.

3. Assign specific roles within the group for some activities. These responsibilities can be assigned in pairs to encourage relationship building.

4. Be aware of the terminology you are using, but do not be apprehensive about using 'everyday' terminology with the group. For example, do not be afraid to say "let's walk over here", to a person who cannot walk, or "see what I mean?", to a person who is blind. There is such a thing as appropriate terminology and it should be part of an agency's training program.

5. Analyze activities well in advance for possible difficulties that individuals might have. This analysis should look at the physical, intellectual, emotional, and social demands of the activities. It may be necessary to adapt an activity in order for the entire group to participate. It is often effective to provide the group with options regarding rules, boundaries, and equipment, and then let them decide on the level of challenge and inclusion. The choices they make and the outcomes of those choices will provide excellent reflection material.

6. Be sure that activities, adaptations and discussions maintain the dignity of all group members. Experiences that, to an extreme, expose weaknesses, break people down emotionally, or set the group up for failure, may humiliate individuals and irreparably damage the group.

Raccoon Circles Inclusion

The first concern with any attempts to include a person with a disability, as with any participant, is safety. Safety is concerned with guarding against the potential damaging effects of an activity. These effects span human domains of physical, emotional, psychological and social functioning. There are things to know about people with disabilities that have significant ramifications in all of these areas that are often not the case for a person without a disability.

Someone using a wheelchair may have extremely sensitive skin in some places that the Raccoon Circle might irritate. There are also issues of urinary drainage systems, colostomies, illiostomies, and pressure sores. A concern for many people with paralysis is the level of self-consciousness associated with a group physically handling their atrophied limbs and the very real possibility of the uncontrolled passing of bodily gasses (you know, flatus). If you are not sure about the safety of an activity, consult with the person with a disability or others who may have tried the activity that way before, or possibly with someone who knows the health and safety needs of the person with a disability. Given that some or most of the resistance for inclusion originates from psychological or emotional concerns, the best advice may be to press the group cautiously and let them encounter these concerns as they become more comfortable and trusting of each other. If the resistance is persistent, then an open discussion that identifies specific behaviors might be necessary.

There is not one way to adapt an activity that works for all people. In fact, finding new ways to adapt and include people with disabilities is exciting, synergistic, and fun! When groups independently find ways of successful inclusion, it can be an important catalyst for growth. The remainder of my comments here will provide some ideas for including participants with disabilities in Raccoon Circles activities, but remember there are many other options to discover.

Gripping and making contact with the Circle

Arms curled up with webbing between forearms and chest

Arms over webbing with the webbing placed between triceps and chest

Tie a loop in the webbing using a simple overhand knot on a bight. Should be large enough that the person's hand, wrist or forearm will release easily if needed. Do not in any way bind the person to the Circle.

Girth-hitch a separate webbing loop to the main circle that is large enough for the person to loop around the back of the shoulders, and under the arms. Never around the neck!

Some people have orthopedic devices that may be able to grip or 'hook' the webbing with little or no adaptation. Again, be careful that the device releases easily from the webbing if needed.

A person that uses a wheelchair may suggest that the webbing can be attached to the chair. This can work well in some cases, allowing the person full use of his or her hands to move the chair and apply substantial pressure to the webbing. Depending on the activity, be careful that the chair is not in a position that will allow other participants to come into hard contact with it.

Consider breaking activities into smaller groups (2 or 3) and letting those groups find their own ways of adapting the activity. This method may be transferable to the larger group.

Movement activities with the Circle

Down and Up- depends on the person's balance, flexibility, grip strength, and range of motion. The person can reach down as far as possible using the webbing for balance. The people on both sides need to provide firm support. Talk about supporting each other and test techniques as part of first event(s).

Pulling out (trust lean)- wheelchairs facing the circle will be pulled toward the circle in a full trust lean, even with brakes applied. The person can move inside the circle and lean back against the webbing with the webbing across the lower shoulder blades. From the outside, a person in a wheelchair or with balance difficulties can turn sideways and hold the web with one hand and lean to the opposite side, away from the web. The free hand can be a stabilizer either on the outside chair wheel or holding on to someone or something stable.

Lofting or lifting activities with the Circle

Getting in and out of a wheelchair can be difficult for some people, depending on their level of functioning. Most people will be able to tell the group what kind of assistance they need. It is critical in any activities where the person will get out of the chair and onto the ground or the webbing that there is a plan the person agrees with and adequate spotting is provided. Be very careful when assisting with transfers that the person's hips, butt, and legs do not come into hard contact with edges, points, or any hard surface. Also be careful that the surface is not too hot, too cold, or has splinters, etc.

For some participants a tighter weave of the webbing will provide added support.

Placing a doubled blanket, sleeping bag ground mat, or a larger mat over the webbing will help provide extra support and alleviate concerns of skin problems.

For more information about accessibility and inclusion, read:

Universal Facilitation Training Manual, 2000, Don E. Rogers, Alpine Towers International Publishing, Jonas Ridge, NC, USA. Phone (800) 706-0064 Email: info@adventurehardware.com

Happiness Runs in a Circle

Clare-Marie Hannon
TLC Training Resources

"Happiness runs in a circular motion. Love is like a little boat upon the sea. Everyone is a part of everything anyway. You can be happy when you let yourself be . . ."

Recently I had the opportunity to work with a Job Corp Center that was struggling to change its culture. Although many of the young people who came to this residential education and vocational training center left their communities to get away from the behaviors and environments that were keeping them from succeeding, there was a tendency to bring those same behaviors with them and create the same negative environments at the Center. A lack of empowerment and mutual support pervaded. A significant number of students left the program in the first sixty days because they felt alienated and disappointed. Gang activity was the dominant form of groupwork that was evident.

I was part of a team of outside trainers brought in to create a leadership retreat for sixty of the 250 students as a way of beginning the change process. Participants were selected for their leadership power, both positive and negative on the Job Corp site. The leadership retreat took place at a beautiful camp set on a lake. As a part of the introductory activities, we had all sixty students and the faculty together by the lake around raccoon circles. It was a beautiful day and although there was plenty of skepticism there was also a door open to hope. We worked on trust and support using the circle and then used activities to explore how working as a team, we could accomplish goals. We did the Grand Prix Racing activity and some basic trust balances. Among the activities we did was Inside Out, which I often call 'Out of the Loop' (a group of participants step inside the circle and then have to get all the members of the group to the outside of the circle by going underneath the webbing, without using their hands, arms or shoulders.) It was amazing the burst of energy that came from each group as the last person escaped the loop. We talked about all the different ways groups and individuals found to help each other 'out.' Later that day when I had the students in small groups, one of them talked about how they were all caught in a loop that they couldn't seem to get out of. Other students began to share methods they could use to help each other 'just like in the activity.' They talked about things they could do while they were still in the loop and how important it was to stay connected even after they were out of the loop to help the rest of the group.

We ended that day with a campfire, and after an opportunity to laugh through a number of skits and songs, we sang a song about happiness and being connected to each other and then we talked about the circle we had started the day with and how being happy and successful was dependent on our ability to support one another. I placed the circle around the campfire and used the fire to represent a reflection of who we were as a group—that we could either feed it or let it die. Students were invited to come forward to add their own personal fuel to the fire and share what they would contribute. I admit, I didn't know what to expect. These were not a group of people used to sharing their feelings or making public commitments. I guess I hoped that if a few students would come forward and serve as role models, it might help the others feel more empowered. Much to my surprise, for well over an hour, students came forward and added their sticks to the fire in our circle and shared what the support of other students and the Job Corp program meant to them and what they would commit to helping others succeed. Near the end of the campfire, three leaders of major gangs on campus came forward to make a commitment 'together' to try to end the gang activity and turn their

energy to helping other students successfully 'get out of the loop'. When we finally brought closure by gathering the whole group around the circle with one last song, no one wanted to leave, no one wanted to let go. There was such power in the moment.

The balance of the retreat focused on developing skills and specific strategies and plans for creating a culture of support and mutual success but I'll never forget the power in the moment when this group believed they could do it. Thanks, Tom and Jim, for giving us a tool that could surface so much power and bring so much hope!

Raccoon Circles in Texas—In Three Parts

Jennifer Steinmetz
Rocky Top Therapy Center

(Part 1)
Dear Dr. Cain,

I hope you have a few minutes to offer some advice. I am the Challenge Course Director at Rocky Top Therapy Center in Keller, Texas. Our core business centers around hippo-therapy and various equine assisted psycho and physical therapies. One of our programs is in conjunction with our local school district, working with at-risk youth to develop life skills using horses. This is a twelve week program, two hours per week; our kids range in age from 10 to 16. The groups are typically same gender and are always in the same age group. So one day we might have 10 year old boys and the next day we might have 14 year old girls. Group size varies from 6-12, but the average size is 8.

Last year we completed a small low ropes challenge course and we are learning how to incorporate initiatives and elements into our program. I have been reading through the facilitators guides to the Raccoon Circle that you so generously posted. I love the versatility (and the low cost) of this element. What I'd like to figure out is how I could use the Raccoon Circle with these groups each week, so they would have something familiar, something to anchor the group week after week. Not the same activity, but always the same tool, so that each week they would know that we are going to do something with the circle. I would ideally want the Raccoon Circle to come to symbolize the growing bond in the group, and the safety that the group offers. I hope this makes sense.

Any ideas, suggestions or cautions would be greatly appreciated.

Thank you!
Jennifer

(Part 2)
Dear Dr. Cain,

Thanks so much for sharing. The Raccoon Circles have been extremely useful for us. We are using them with all of our groups. We have used Team Balance and Grand Prix Racing with all of our recent groups. With the younger kids, this has been a great tool to demonstrate the impact of each team member on the whole group. We are able to get them focused and functioning as a team very quickly. We also use the Raccoon Circles throughout the day to process; passing the knot, again amazing success with focus and participation.

But the high point so far was with a group of 'at-risk' 13 & 14 year old girls. We played "A Knot Between Us." We talked about the Raccoon Circle as our life's road, and the knots as the problems we encounter. The girls named their knots, and worked collectively to untie them. They learned so much about themselves and working together; asking for help, getting help without asking, passing their problems on to a friend, taking ownership of their own problems, letting someone else solve your problem, sometimes well meaning friends make things worse when they try to help you, etc. Dr. Cain, I had goose bumps! SO ... for me, and for these kids, I thank you!

Never settle for less than your dreams!
Jennifer

(Part 3)
Dear Dr. Cain

As I have mentioned, at Rocky Top Ranch we offer a program called The Right Trail in concert with our local school district, where we use horses and our challenge course program to teach life skills such as trust, integrity, communication skills, etc. This is a powerful program and the Raccoon Circles have become an integral element in our tool kit. I have another favorite story that I would like to share with you about using Raccoon Circles with our students.

Recently, one group of 4th grade girls had a surprise visit by their principal, who is quite a large man. He had just dropped in to observe some of our activities and to see how the girls were doing. They insisted that he play Trust Lean with them; assuring him that they would keep him safe. And do you know what? They did it!

There are other great stories and new ones waiting to happen. We love Raccoon Circles!

Jennifer Steinmetz

One Day in Virginia
Memories of a Blessed Raccoon Circle

Dear Dr. Tom,

I was in your Raccoon Circles workshop at the VCOAE conference in Virginia last month. I just wanted to write you a note and tell you how much I enjoyed the workshop and let you know how I ended up using the Raccoon Circle that we blessed that day.

My brother was killed in a car accident on the Sunday morning of the conference. I had to leave early and drive home with my car still packed from the conference. He was only 36 years old, and left his wife, two loving sons, his parents, siblings, and friends all devastated.

The significance of the Raccoon Circle stayed with me as I tried to comfort my family during those next sad days. When we had the family viewing at the funeral home, it included 18 people, 9 of them children, and I took out the circle. I used it as we were taught, and had everyone connect to it. All of us felt its power, and we were all clinging to the comfort and hoping that the communal strength put into it would be ours. We held on to that circle and I talked about our connection to my brother, to each other, and to the universe. I talked about how this circle represented our strengths. No one wanted to let go when I was finished. All of us kept holding on, grieving and gathering in the strength of our connection. Finally, it ended, and we buried that Raccoon Circle with my brother.

It was a short but powerful life for my Raccoon Circle. Soon I will make and bless another one. Thank you for the circle, as it provided a meaningful, strengthening ritual that my family will always remember.

Students Up Against the Wall
Thoughts from a Teacher

Dear Tom,

I used the Raccoon Circles with my students today at the start of our session at a local challenge course—and we had a great day. I'm not sure that junior high school students with behavioral disorders truly understand the symbolic significance of circles, but getting them connected to the webbing did seem to create some magic.

Our group was scheduled to do the wall in the afternoon, and they had quite a bit of trouble with it. Our facilitator thought we should call it off, but I asked the group to 'connect up and sit down,' talk about the problems, and develop a plan that would work. For the first time this year, it seemed like they were really talking to each other... and listening. After the circle, they went back to the wall, and everyone made it over. We ended up with another connection to the circle, and the group let out a mighty cheer.

The whole experience seemed to bring the group together for the first time. I hope the magic stays with them. I plan to keep the Raccoon Circle on my desk at school and use it whenever I can. Thanks Tom.

Believe It or Knot

Mike Anderson

A few years ago I was asked to facilitate a program for staff members of the New Jersey Juvenile Justice Commission. The program would bring the AM and PM staff together for the first time. I was asked to present activities that would allow interaction between staff members while limiting the perceived physical risk that seems to be associated with the adventure-based learning field.

My good friend Anthony Capone introduced the Raccoon Circle to the group and facilitated a great version of Grand Prix, which he called the Raccoon Circle Races. Afterwards, we wanted to take some time allowing everyone in the group the opportunity to learn a little bit more about each other. Believe It or Knot just came to me, out of the blue. There were three groups, each holding onto their own Raccoon Circle. I told them that the knot was to act as the 'talking stick' and whomever the knot was closest to would have the opportunity to share something about themselves that they think others in the circle would not know. Each person in the group would have an opportunity to share. I realized I had set the stage for some fantastic interaction if I could only explain that the level of information to be shared was a choice to be made by the individual. I was able to explain to the group that their level of participation in this activity was up to them, they can share very personal or more superficial information depending on their comfort level within the group. I told them the entire days activities would be based on this philosophy. I also explained that the day was about making choices and taking risks. This spur of the moment creation was to become one of my favorite activities. I explained to the group that this was not an opportunity for discussion, but a time to listen and proceeded to read Emerson's poem 'Listen' to the group.

It was not until about half way through the activity that I discovered the value in this type of interaction. I had created an environment where each individual was afforded the opportunity to open up if they wished. I also realized that there was a need for some closure, and decided to add another component to the infant activity. I explained to the group that some people may have shared some things that sparked interest in others. I told them that part two was to give each person an opportunity to ask one question of one other person in the circle, but the question had to relate to what was shared earlier. It occurred to me that this was good for finding things in common with one another but also a useful tool for inviting group members to enter their growth zone. Imagine that you shared something very dear to your heart, but held back just enough to make the sharing comfortable. You may have been asked a question that allowed you to share a little bit more information, possibly information you were not ready to share sooner.

The activity as originally created was used with almost every program we did for six months without a name. Over lunch one day, a variation to this activity was created that harked back to another favorite of mine; Two Truths and a Lie. The name Believe it or Knot was tossed out and it stuck. Today, the name Believe It or Knot is used with both versions.

A Sacred Circle Experience

Brian Brolin
The Saint Francis Academy
PREPARE Program
Picayune, Mississippi

A small band of young offenders bumped their way along the nighttime trail, stumbling from moonlight splash to moonlight splash. Some were there for theft, some for fighting, some for property destruction-but not tonight. Tonight they were nervous. Some even scared. Tonight they were not seeking destruction, they were headed for unity.

"I've heard stories of secret 'Raccoon Circle' places in the woods; a spot where raccoons come together on moonlit nights like this and dance a peaceful, playful dance in an open clearing." The scoffers scoffed, the wonderers wondered, and the scared just shivered silently. Mumbled references to Blair Witches and psycho killers were quickly squelched. "A Raccoon Circle is a safe place. Bad things don't happen there." Scoffers and Wonderers and the Scared shuffled on a little further in silence. One Wondrous Scoffer (with a quiver in his voice) suddenly said "What's that ahead?!" The trail ahead widened, and the moon cast a spotlight on an unusual sight; The thick pine straw had been strangely disturbed to form a circle in the clearing. "This must be it," was whispered by a now Wondering ex-Scoffer. Individuals wandered around and inspected the circle and the surrounding trees and brush. "Here's an animal path that crosses the trail!" "Here's another one going this way." "It looks like an intersection of paths-I'll bet they come from all around!" The excitement was thick. "I found a den!!" The young band all scrambled to the discovered hole, peering inside to see if any secret dancers were still around. The group re-gathered at the Circle, being careful to not disturb the formation.

"It is a tradition in many cultures to have a flame in the middle of a special place like this." A candle lantern was ceremoniously lit, accenting the form of the group sitting around the Circle. Then a special piece of colored webbing was produced. The young wonderers watched in the flickering light as it was carefully tied to form a ring, and spread out before the group. Following instructions, a sort of dance ensued; the group in unison standing, leaning, sitting-imitating the sounds of the wildlife around them. This continued until the midnight chill began to settle on the clearing. Again sitting quietly in the flickering candlelight, the knot was passed to each participant, and they shared thoughts and feeling of the moment. Tomorrow they would each receive a piece of the webbing, the edges seared in a campfire that would become an extension of this sacred Circle place. The group stood, and respectfully moved from the place, now leaving their own imprint of their own secret dance.

The small band bumped their way once again along the nighttime trail, a new sense of Community instilled in their heart, found at a secret Raccoon Circle place in the woods.

World Wide Webbing

Jim Cain

Teamwork & Teamplay

In the past four years, there have been more than 16,000 copies of the Raccoon Circle documents downloaded from the Teamwork & Teamplay website. My web browser only records the top 10 countries each month, but already there have been downloads in thirty different countries. In some cases, facilitators are translating the contents into the local language. In other cases, educators are using rope, heavy cloth and other creative materials if a local source for tubular nylon climbing webbing cannot be found. Suddenly a gift from the heart, that came from the northern central part of the United States is literally and figuratively 'circling the globe.' I wonder if that is why the part of the country where Tom and I are both from, and the Raccoon Circle originated, is called the 'heartland.'

For those 16,000 plus folks who now have in their hands a tool that can help them build community in their own corner of the world, who would have guessed that 'connect up' would have a modern day internet equivalent.' Truly, the Raccoon Circle has become the 'world wide webbing!'

To download a copy of the most recent Raccoon Circles document from the internet, visit:
www.teamworkandteamplay.com/raccooncircles.html

The Best Raccoon Circle of All

William J. Quinn

Northeastern Illinois University

Most people right now, and to many more people once this book about "Raccoon Circles" has been published, understand Raccoon Circles to be a series of clever and well thought out activities centered around the use of a continuous circle of nylon webbing. These activities serve as a catalyst to build relationships between people in a positive and enjoyable way. Originally called "Smith Circles" and sometimes known as Baboon Circles in the southern hemisphere, the activities using the circular strap have evolved and have now been collected in one volume. However when I think about Smith / Raccoon / Baboon circles something different comes to mind.

The first Raccoon Circle I was involved in occurred sometime in the mid eighties in a circular tree house Tom had built at his home in Cazenovia, Wisconsin. A small group of educators were invited to participate in a "think tank" concerning issues pertaining to experiential / challenge / adventure education. Unknown to me a new friendship with a person who would become a trusted confidant and allied professional was born. Since then I have been a witness to the creation of Raccoon Circles of influence in many settings and circumstances.

Tom's circle of influence has extended to dozens of students in my classes that have camped on his property over the past decade. Tom sat around the campfire among us and read Robert Service poems in the wintertime, he spoke about the foundations of adventure education, told jokes and played "two truths and a lie" with everyone. He offered his home, his philosophy and his kindness innumerable times. I watched Tom guide corporate executives during team building sessions. We presented workshops together at Bradford Woods, Association for Experiential Education Regional and International conferences, at TEAM conferences in Chicago and for Play for Peace in South Africa. Tom was ever-present and fully engaged in the development of all those he spoke to. The above mentioned occurrences are merely some of the occasions I have had the privilege to work with Tom. Examples of his professional involvement can go on and on and on....

Whether Tom was acting as a facilitator in China during his trips there or as a "wilderness psychologist" in the Boundary Waters with orphans and sexually abused children from Maryville Academy, he has always spread his goodness, intelligence and healing abilities in ever widening circles. However, even including his books, awards, and commendations for all the known and unknown number of people's lives the Ol' Raccoon has in some way transformed, there is one circle that tops them all.

During "Raccoon Fest"(an annual family and friends reunion on Labor Day weekend), I was fortunate enough to be there with my family in the best "Raccoon Circle" of all. I looked at Tom sitting around a campfire with his six grown children and their children while he did one of the most inspired renditions of "I'm Going on a Lion Hunt" possible. The beautiful glow in the eyes of a beautiful man said it all. And yet that glow was superseded by the affection in the eyes of his children, grandchildren and Charlotte, his wife of fifty years. Thanks Tom, for all the Raccoon Circles you have created.

From the Great White North

Tim Pearson
Anchorage, Alaska

Hello Tom and Jim,

We met in Portland, Oregon at the ACCT conference this past January. I wanted to let you know that I've had great fun using the Raccoon circles with Inupiat and Yupik Eskimos here in Alaska. My only problem has been that there are no raccoons in the Arctic. People here have heard of them, but groups give me a sort of blank look when I talk about raccoons.

My work-around: I remembered Tom's baboon story from South Africa, so I decided that some artistic license would be permissible. Traditionally, rope in the Arctic was made out of the skins of the bearded seal, so the Arctic name was a no-brainer: "Seal Circles." I really like the double OO's of the Inupiat word for bearded seal (oogruk), but "seal circle" is more alliterative sounding in English. I thought you'd enjoy the Arctic update. Cheers and best wishes!

According to the Alaska Department of Fish and Game: The bearded seal (Erignathus barbatus) is the largest true seal normally found in the seas adjacent to Alaska. It inhabits areas of the Bering, Chukchi, and Beaufort seas where sea ice forms during the winter. Eskimos who speak the Yupik language refer to this seal as mukluk, and Inupik-speaking Eskimos call it oogruk. Oogruk is the most common name. Residents of western coastal villages depend upon bearded seals and other seals for hides and a large part of their food. Bearded seal meat is the most desirable of the seals, and the hides are necessary for boat covers, raw-hide line, boot soles, and numerous other uses.

The term mukluk has, apparently by accident, come to mean a certain type of footwear made of skins. The story was told that when white men first came to western Alaska, someone asked a local resident what he was wearing on his feet. The Eskimo, thinking he was being asked what his boots were made from, said that they were mukluk (meaning from a bearded seal). Today almost all types of eskimo-made footwear are called mukluks. http://www.state.ak.us/adfg/notebook/marine/brd-seal.htm

Notes

from Dr. Tom Smith

In the 1960's I studied with and about the Native Americans. I spent time during the summer camping and teaching pow-wows in Wisconsin and Minnesota, and on my third visit I was given (and I took) the name "Raccoon." It was suggested by the elders, and after some soul-searching and dialogue, I began to understand why it was an appropriate name. I did not use my native name for the next twenty years, but when I stared presenting training workshops for challenge and adventure educators and other professional groups in the 1980's, I sometimes used the name. When I retired in 1987 to develop my own consulting and training business, I called it the "Raccoon Institute."

It was also in the early 1960's, and every summer thereafter for 25 years, that I organized and facilitated 10-12 day outdoor adventures for groups of adolescents and adults. Participants were told that they would share a small group experience involving a 'personal growth journey to the wilderness.' The trips involved camping, climbing, caving, and a 4-5 day canoe trip in the Boundary Waters on the Minnesota-Canada border. Although my professional academic training was as a clinical psychologist, I had evolved through time to become an experiential educator and personal growth facilitator. By the 1970's my business card announced that I was a "psychologist/wilderness guide." I had come to realize the importance of the connection between the 'wilderness beyond' and the 'wilderness within.'

In the mid-1970's I learned about rope and team course methodology. I built my first teams and high rope course in 1975, and thereafter my adventure group sequence included experiences on that course. I had come to recognize the value of teams course experiences in the personal growth journey.

However, in the early 1980's, I heard voices from teachers, youth workers, counselors and corporate trainers asking for activities that they could use in classrooms, schoolyards, and corporate centers. They sought experiential activities that might create the same individual and group dynamics as the ropes course and/or the wilderness adventure—trust, cooperation, communication, risk-taking, commitment, empowerment, problem solving, etc. I began to develop my personal 'bag-of-tricks' with which I could create those dynamics. I drew on my experiences with the Human Potential Movement, New Games, Sensory and Somatic Awareness, and the Native Americans. Like many other leaders of challenge and adventure experiences, I prided myself in being able to facilitate two and three day training sessions with just the contents of my backpack—no ropes or teams course, and no outdoor adventure to the 'wilderness beyond.' I especially prized those activities that were simple and portable but still guided participants to explore the 'wilderness within.' Like most facilitators, I was always adding new ideas to my 'bag-of-tricks,' and sometimes replacing or discarding ideas that seemed less effective.

Then, in the early 1990's, I discovered the magic, the simplicity, and the power of a sequence of activities using only a length of tubular nylon webbing. At the time, that web loop became just another carry along for my 'bag-of-tricks.' I'm sure that other challenge and adventure leaders had explored activities with web loops or rope circles before that, as I have learned that nothing we think of as 'new' really is!

Then, in 1994, I was asked to co-facilitate the opening celebration of Northeastern Illinois University's T.E.A.M. conference with Karl Rohnke. I passed out twenty circles of webbing and there were twenty groups of people sharing the joys, the dynamics, and the healing powers of the web loops. Karl was taking pictures from high above, and after we finished he asked me what the circle of webbing was called. I informed him that I just called them "web circles," and he, with a second from my friend, Bill Quinn, suggested that a nice name for the activities would be "Raccoon Circles."

That was nearly a decade ago. Boy, time does fly when you're having fun! The web loop and the associated activities that became "Raccoon Circles," can now be found in the bag-of-tricks of many facilitators and adventure educators. Over 1500 copies of my little booklet of instructions have been distributed, and probably double that amount copied over the years. Jim Cain recently placed a handbook for facilitators of Raccoon Circles on the Teamwork & Teamplay website, and reported that the website had experienced thousands of downloads around the world. Shortly after this, Jim and I decided to collaborate on this project. His enthusiasm, knowledge of adventure-based activities, and writing style; and my work with the ritual, ceremony and philosophy of circles seemed like a natural partnership, and it has been a joy working together. We hope you enjoy the fruits of our labors. We certainly have.

A Visit to the Library

Jim Cain

On a somewhat humorous basis . . . while presenting at an adventure-based facilitation conference in Boulder, Colorado a few years ago, a staff member from the University of North Carolina–Wilmington campus library told me that "The Book on Raccoon Circles" had become the 'most stolen' book from the campus library, replacing "A Sand County Almanac" by Aldo Leopold.

From the Hills of North Carolina

Craig Smith

Jim, I enjoyed the Raccoon Circle workshop this past Thursday. I wanted to let you know that when I stopped back by the conference center on my way to get two more raccoon circles, as I was coming up the driveway I saw a pair of eyes reflecting in my headlights. As I got closer, I saw a raccoon move off the side of the road and begin climbing a tree. Is somebody trying to tell me something?

Raccoon Circles on the Challenge Course

Jordan Rimmer

I have found Raccoon Circles to be so useful that I never do a teambuilding program or workshop without them. To add some variety to the ropes course experience, I sometimes throw random props into an activity just to see how a group might creatively use them. Here are a few of the activities I have used Raccoon Circles with on the challenge course.

Mohawk Walk—I have given groups several Raccoon circles at the beginning of this event. Sometimes the group relies more on the Raccoon Circle than they do on one another. This can make for an interesting teachable moment to process at the completion of the activity.

Nitro Crossing—A group that has a Raccoon Circle for a tool can typically retrieve the swinging rope more quickly and easily.

TP Shuffle—The Raccoon Circle can be used by the group to make a hand rail (or guard rail) to help support members changing position on the log or horizontal telephone pole.

High Courses and Climbing Walls—Tether two climbers together for a partner climb or to keep two participants close together on a high ropes course. You can also use a knotted Raccoon Circle as a 'flag' that each participant can take just a bit farther up the climbing wall or tower.

Portable Activities, Games, and Ground Level Initiatives—Raccoon Circles make colorful boundary markers.

Metaphors for the Raccoon Circle

I like to use object lessons and metaphors with groups to help them understand concepts presented during an adventure-based learning lesson. Here are a few I have used with Raccoon Circles.

Community—With everyone holding onto a Raccoon Circle, I explain that in a community, the attitudes and actions of people effect one another. If one person begins to pull in any direction, it is felt by the entire group. This metaphor works well with the activity 'A Circle of Cooperation' found in Section II of this book.

Knots—Just like individuals and groups, knots react differently to pressure. Some knots can slip under pressure. Some get tighter. With a Raccoon Circle, we use a water knot because it gets stronger when the pressure is applied. This is a wonderful opportunity to discuss how individuals and groups react to challenge, set-backs, stress and pressure.

Connection—Here is a colorful variation of a closing activity often performed with a ball of string or yarn. Give each participant in the group an unknotted Raccoon Circle. Invite them to share something from their experience today. When they are done, they hold one end of their Raccoon Circle and pass the other end to another person in the group. When the entire group is finished, there will be a wonderful tapestry woven by the group, showing the connection that everyone has created with each other.

Raccoon Circles in Unusual Places

Jim Cain

A few years ago, I was scheduled to present a one hour community building program for the entire staff of a collegiate food service program. After a morning of presentations, nearly 150 participants were ready for the program. The biggest challenge of the program was the room in which the program was to be held. It was an auditorium, filled with seats fixed to the sloping floor. The aisles were very narrow, and in short, there was little room left for movement. No problem! Enter an entire collection of Raccoon Circle activities.

In small groups of 8 people, connected by various color Raccoon Circles, participants were able to stand on different levels, stretch over chairs and seats, and yet perform nearly a dozen different activities (many of which are mentioned in this publication). There were even a few folks seated at two circular tables near the front of the room, also able to participate, while seated, holding onto their own Raccoon Circle. Next time you host a program in a restricted space, think about using some Raccoon Circles.

Raccoon Inspiration

Mike Anderson

I first met Dr. Tom Smith in 1998 while facilitating an MBA Orientation program for the Professional Development Center (PDC) at Indiana University. Delivering programs for the PDC was a real treat for me. As a young facilitator, I was given the opportunity to work side by side with industry leaders, professors and authors, not to mention the great food and extra pay that was afforded.

For this program, there were twelve facilitators, all with varying levels of experience and various sized 'bags of tricks.' I was carrying a duffel bag with bandannas, poly spots, soft throwables, Raccoon Circles and judging by the size of the bag I'm sure tons of other stuff. This program was to be my first with the PDC so I shared space with other facilitators in case I needed to be thrown a lifeline. I shared a big grassy field known as the 'Old Swimming Pool' with Tom Smith. Picture two groups, walking down a sidewalk, one being led by a guy with a huge duffel bag that can hardly be lifted and the other being led by a man with a fanny pack that has three soft foam balls, a bandanna and two Raccoon Circles. We spent the next four hours working in our small groups. Every once in awhile I had the opportunity to catch a glimpse of what Tom was doing with his group. I never did see the foam balls or the bandanna come out of the fanny pack!

After the program ended for the day, we had the opportunity to talk a while. Tom told a group of about thirty people about the Raccoon Circle and the meaning behind it. He shared a ton of ideas and listened to stories of how others used the Raccoon Circle. Before the night was over he sat at the table with me and offered feedback about my day. I had only been working as a facilitator for a couple of years at that point so meeting Tom was a real treat for me. The first team building activity I ever experienced utilized a Raccoon Circle; little did I know that a few years later I would be sitting side by side at a dinner table with the creator that wonderful idea. Thank you for everything Tom.

Section IV

Technical Information, References, Resources, Quotes, Thoughts and Photographs from the World of Raccoon Circles

This fourth section of The Book of Raccoon Circles is filled with technical data, webbing suppliers, reference books, photographs, quotes, random thoughts and all the other valuable Raccoon Circle information that we have collected over the years, but that didn't seem to fit in any of the first three sections of this book. If you can't find the information you need here, write us and we'll be glad to help you.

Technical Information
Tying A Water Knot
Supplies of Tubular Webbing
Additional Books from the Authors
Quotes, Thoughts and Photographs
References & Resources

Raccoon Circle Technical Information

The Basics

A Raccoon Circle consists of a single piece of tubular nylon climbing webbing, which can typically be purchased in a variety of colors and patterns from outdoor sporting goods stores, and specifically those outdoor stores that carry rock climbing gear. There is a list of several suppliers of tubular webbing at the end of this section. While a variety of other belt materials (such as those found at horse tack shops, pet stores, arborists catalogs and sewing supply stores) and even rope can be substituted, the 1 inch (2.5 cm) wide tubular climbing webbing is recommended. Tubular webbing is extremely strong (breaking strength typically exceeds 4000 pounds tensile loading), comfortable to hold, colorful and can be easily washed when necessary. Tubular climbing webbing does not stretch, which is also helpful for many activities.

Most of the activities in this book are performed with a Raccoon Circle that is 15 feet (4.6 meters) in length. If you wish to accommodate larger groups, you can either join a few Raccoon Circles together with a water knot or use a single, long Raccoon Circle.

As a general rule, you'll need about 15 inches (38 cm) of length for each member of the group. Remember that the water knot and tails also take up about 1 foot (31 cm) of the total length.

Water Knot Tying

For many Raccoon Circle activities, it is necessary to form a circle or loop. While a variety of knots can be used, the water knot is one of the strongest and best. The "water knot" is so named because river rafting guides use such a knot with flat webbing, so that even when wet, the knot can easily be removed.

A favorite explanation of how to tie a water knot comes from fellow facilitator and friend Kirk Weisler. See the illustration below for details. Start by tying a simple (but loose) overhand knot in one end of the Raccoon Circle webbing, with a short tail (less than 2 inches is fine). Because of the flat webbing, this overhand knot will remain very flat. This first knot is called the "teacher" knot.

Next travel the length of the webbing, unwinding and untwisting the webbing as you go, and hold the opposite end of the webbing. This end is the "student" end of the webbing. The student does everything the teacher does, they just happen to do it backwards. This means that (first) the student looks directly at the teacher (each tail end of the webbing nearly touches). Next, the student "doubles" the teacher by following the same path as the teacher backwards. This involves following the webbing, and finally tucking the student end of the webbing into the teacher knot, leaving about a 1 or 2 inch long tail. Now simply pull the opposite sides of the knot to secure it.

Tying the Raccoon Circle with a Water Knot-Method 1—Teachers & Students

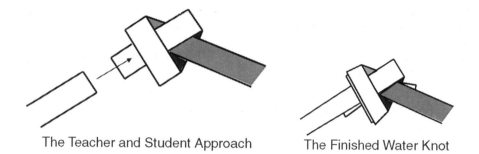

The Teacher and Student Approach   The Finished Water Knot

A second technique for teaching the water knot relies on a slightly different metaphor. Begin by tying the teacher knot so that the black stitching typically found running down the middle of most colorful webbing can be seen. This dashed line looks a bit like the line found running down the middle of many roads. The student end of the webbing is now seen as an automobile (or race car for faster knot makers) which drives down the middle of the road to complete this knot.

Tying the Raccoon Circle with a Water Knot-Method 2—Race Cars and Expressways

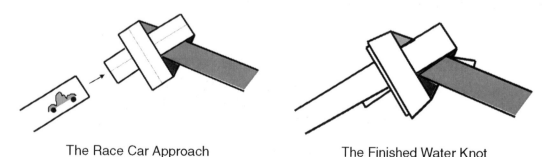

The Race Car Approach   The Finished Water Knot

Untying a Water Knot

Occasionally, the water knot in your Raccoon Circle might become tightly knotted and seemingly impossible to untie. Once, at a first year orientation program for a local college, forty different groups of ten students each tied their group's 15 foot long Raccoon Circles into a giant circle, using the school's colors of green and white for alternating pieces of webbing. After forty minutes of ceremony and activities, the efforts of 400 students pulling on 600 feet (184 meters) of webbing was especially noticed when it became time to untie the knots. While you can resort to the manufacturer's method of a hot knife tool, or even scissors to remove the knot, this technique gradually reduces the size of your Raccoon Circle.

A better technique, and one that will not permanently effect the length of your Raccoon Circle is to use a rubber mallet (hammer) to gently pound the knot while working the webbing material and pinching the tail ends of the webbing to slide these back through the knot. Although this is not a quick method, it does eventually yield success in untying even the most stubborn water knot in your Raccoon Circle.

Decorating your Raccoon Circle

For those creative folks wishing to decorate or embellish the look of their Raccoon Circle here are a few possibilities.

Permanent Marker—This technique is easy and allows autographs, pictures, numbers, debriefing questions and other drawn shapes and graphics, and the circle can still be washed without disturbing the design.

Sewing and Embroidery —Some of the newer computer programmed sewing machines can sew patterns, words and symbols even on thick materials such as tubular climbing webbing. Or, consider hand sewing the names of the group members into your Raccoon Circle. Check with your local sports award or trophy shop for other sewn designs for your Raccoon Circle.

Fabric dye, tie dye and marbling—These techniques can be used to alter the color of a Raccoon Circle but it is best to begin with a light color of webbing such as white or yellow.

Fingerpainting—Begin with a light color Raccoon Circle. Invite individual members of the group to dip their hands in different color fingerpaints and then grab the webbing. They now have 'marked their spot' on the webbing and can always return to the same spot in the group.

Fabric paint, decals, stickers, duct tape, electrical tape, jewelry with fasteners or studs—These options are not recommended for a Raccoon Circle that you plan to use, but are fine for display, keepsake or memento segments of a Raccoon Circle that you plan to hang on a wall or bulletin board.

Keeping your Raccoon Circle Clean

The tubular nylon webbing used for Raccoon Circles can be washed in a standard washing machine, with ordinary detergent. To avoid wrapping the long webbing around the washing machine agitator, place your Raccoon Circle in a mesh bag first. Avoid bleach and fabric softener. Do not dry clean. Hang dry in a well-ventilated area.

The Strength of Tubular Webbing

In strength tests performed at the University of Rochester in 1996, three samples of new 1" tubular webbing loops, knotted with a water knot, were stretched in a tensile testing device, and found to fail at an average pulling strength of 5700 pounds of force. Manufacturers of such webbing typically list tensile strengths in the range of 3000 to 5000 pounds. Basically, this information means than 1 inch tubular nylon climbing webbing is sufficiently strong for many activities. In the event that your Raccoon Circle becomes nicked, sliced, cut, abraded, contaminated, deteriorated, melted, frayed or otherwise damaged, retire it! You can always use small pieces for non-critical activities where the strength of the webbing is not a factor, or give these away to participants as mementos.

Raccoon Circle Questions & Calculations

How many Raccoon Circles are enough? The standard 15 foot (4.6 meter) Raccoon Circle when tied into a circle can host a maximum of 10 adults, or about a dozen children. As a general rule, the length of the Raccoon Circle should be 15 inches (38 cm) per participant. Remember that the water knot and tails also take up about 1 foot (31 cm) of the total length.

How many Raccoon Circles can I expect to make from one standard roll of tubular webbing? Nylon tubular webbing typically is supplied in 300 foot (92 meter) long rolls. These rolls appear to contain approximately 20 Raccoon Circles, each 15 feet (4.6 meters) long. But be careful! Manufacturers of tubular webbing commonly allow a number of splices on each roll (some manufacturers even mark the number of splices on each roll). This means that you may end up with unwanted splices, or short segments of webbing. To be sure to get the most out of a complete roll of webbing, try unwinding the entire roll first, looking for splices (which are typically placed together with masking tape), and then measuring and marking where to cut each Raccoon Circle to obtain the maximum utilization of your webbing.

What can I do with all those short segments of leftover webbing? You can make a regulation length Raccoon Circle from shorter webbing segments, by simply connecting them using water knots. This approach will still work for many of the activities listed in this book, with the exception of those activities that use a single water knot as an "arrow" or "pointer." There are also several activities that utilize shorter pieces of webbing, such as Minefield, A Knot Right Now, and A Knot Between Us. Or, you can create your own Gordian Knot Ball, using short segments of webbing tied and knotted together to form a soft multi-colored ball, that can be used for group games. In the debriefing section of this book, you'll find a reviewing technique known as 'worms' where you can use short segments of webbing. Finally, you can keep a supply of short segments around to give away to participants as souvenirs and keepsakes from their adventure experience.

What is the best way to cut tubular webbing? Tubular webbing is a woven material, which means if you simply cut it with a pair of scissors or knife, the material will unravel and fray. To avoid this, manufacturers use a hot knife, similar to a soldering gun with a heated blade to melt through the webbing, rather than cutting it. This technique melts the webbing, preventing fraying and providing a clean edge. If you prefer to cut the webbing by hand using a knife or scissors, seal the ends of the webbing carefully using the flame from a small candle.

What if I want to use old climbing rope instead of tubular webbing for Raccoon Circle activites? Many challenge courses have a nearly continuous supply of retired climbing ropes that can be used for many Raccoon Circle activities. You can make these ropes the exact length you need for any particular activity, but you will need another knot to tie the ends of the rope into a circle. The traditional water knot used for flat webbing doesn't work very well. A double fisherman knot is one possible choice. Consult a knot book for more possibilities.

Suppliers of Tubular Webbing for Raccoon Circles

The following organizations can supply pre-cut, custom lengths and often spool lengths (about 300 feet (92 meters)) of tubular webbing in a variety of colors and patterns.

Teamwork & Teamplay
468 Salmon Creek Road Brockport, NY 14420 USA
Phone (585) 637-0328
Email: jimcain@teamworkandteamplay.com   Website: www.teamworkandteamplay.com
Equipment, publications, staff training and the most recent Raccoon Circle activities on the web!

Adventure Hardware
120 Coxe Avenue
Asheville, NC 28801 USA
Phone (877) 269-3999   Fax (828) 733-3505 USA
Email: info@adventurehardware.com   Website: www.adventurehardware.com
Raccoon Circles and many other small, portable adventure-based learning props, resource books and more.

Training Wheels
7095 South Garrison Street
Littleton, CO 80128 USA
phone (888) 553-0147 or 303-979-1708   Fax (888) 553-0146
Email: Info@training-wheels.com   Website: www.training-wheels.com
Raccoon Circles and other equipment, including processing & debriefing tools and training.

Sportime
3155 Northwoods Parkway   Norcross, GA 30071 USA
Phone (800) 283-5700   Fax (800) 845-1235
Email: orders@sportime.com   Website: www.sportime.com
Offers the Raccoon Circle under the name "Group Loop" and features activity guides on their website.

Adventureworks! Associates, Inc.
34 Plaza Dr. P.O. Box 63012   Dundas, Ontario, Canada   L9H 4H0
Phone (905) 304-5683   Fax (905) 304-0386
Email: info@adventureworks.org   Website: www.adventureworks.org
The source for Raccoon Circles, adventure equipment, publications and training in Canada.

Country Wide Sales
1431 Cedar Lane   Wooster, Ohio 44691
Phone (330) 262-6112   Fax (330) 262-6317
A wide variety of webbing, including Raccoon Circles.

On Rope 1
5940 Highway 58, Suite C   Harrison, TN 37341
Phone (423) 344-4716   Fax (423) 344-9089
Raccoon Circles, plus webbing, climbing and caving harnesses and safety gear.

Robertson Harness
P.O.Box 90086 Henderson, NV 89009-0086
Phone (702) 564-4286 Fax (702) 564-4287
Email: kdm@robertson-mtn.com   Website: robertson-mtn.com
Raccoon Circles, climbing harnesses, flexible webbing trolleys and the webbing grid (known as the Corporate Maze).

Challenge Course Builders and Equipment Suppliers
Many challenge course builders sell tubular climbing webbing as part of their equipment services. You can find lists of challenge course builders and equipment providers at the following websites: www.acctinfo.org and www.prcainfo.org

Additional Books, Articles, Writings and Publications from the Authors

"Filling a bookcase is like gathering a social circle."
May Lamberton Becker

By Jim Cain and Tom Smith

Jim Cain and Tom Smith, 2007, The Revised & Expanded Book of Raccoon Circles – A Facilitator's Guide to Building Unity, Community, Connection and Teamwork Through Active Learning, Kendall / Hunt Publishing, Dubuque, Iowa USA Phone (800) 228-0810 or www.kendallhunt.com, ISBN 0-7575-3265-9. The revised and greatly expanded book of more than 200 Raccoon Circle activities, stories and ideas for groups. 282 pages.

Jim Cain and Tom Smith, 2002, THE BOOK on Raccoon Circles, Learning Unlimited Publishing, Tulsa, Oklahoma USA Phone (888) 622-4203, ISBN 0-9646541-6-4, The original commercial publication of the book of Raccoon Circle history, ritual, ceremony, activities and resources. Out of print, as of 2007. If you have a copy, it is a collector's item! 272 pages.

By Jim Cain

Jim Cain and Kirk Weisler, 2007, The Value of Connection – In the Workplace. You can become the catalyst for building community within your workforce, creating a positive work environment and promoting a culture of connection in your corporation. Visit the Teamwork & Teamplay website at www.teamworkandteamplay.com for more information about this book.

Jim Cain, Chris Cavert, Mike Anderson and Tom Heck, 2005, Teambuilding Puzzles, FUNdoing Publications, ISBN 0-9746442-0-X. 100 puzzles and activities for creating teachable moments in creative problem solving, consensus building, leadership, exploring diversity, group decision making, goal setting, active learning, communication and teamwork. 304 pages.

Jim Cain, Michelle Cummings and Jennifer Stanchfield, 2005, A Teachable Moment, Kendall / Hunt Publishers, Dubuque, Iowa, USA Phone (800) 228-0810 or www.kendallhunt.com, ISBN 0-7575-1782-X. A Facilitator's Guide to Activities for Processing, Debriefing, Reviewing and Reflection. 282 pages.

Jim Cain, "The Evening Dance Program at Camp," Camping Magazine, American Camping Association, May/June 2002, pages 38-41. Phone (800) 428-CAMP

Jim Cain, "Raccoon Circles – A Handbook for Facilitators," in Horizons Magazine, The Institute for Outdoor Learning (UK), Number 17, Spring 2002, pages 16-25. Email: horizons@outdoor-learning.org

Jim Cain, several activities in 50 Ways to Use Your Noodle (ISBN 0-9646541-1-3) (1997), and 50 More Ways to Use Your Noodle (ISBN 0-9646541-5-6) (2002) by Chris Cavert and Sam Sikes, Learning Unlimited Publishing, Tulsa, Oklahoma. Phone (888) 622-4203 or www.learningunlimited.com

Jim Cain, Raccoon Circles – A Handbook for Facilitators, an annually updated and free PDF download at www.teamworkandteamplay.com/raccooncircles.html Dozens of activities for making the Raccoon Circle a popular part of your programs.

Jim Cain, 1999, "Resources for Adventure Programming," in Adventure Programming by John C. Miles and Simon Priest, Venture Publishing, State College, PA. Phone (814) 234-4561 ISBN 1-892132-09-5

Jim Cain and Barry Jolliff, 1998, Teamwork & Teamplay, Kendall / Hunt Publishers, Dubuque, Iowa Phone (800) 228-0810 or www.kendallhunt.com ISBN 0-7872-4532-1 Award winning adventure-based and active learning activities, resources, references and instructions. 417 pages.

By Tom Smith

Tom Smith, 2006, 100 Books: Recommended Reading for Experiential Education, Raccoon Institute Publications, Lake Geneva, Wisconsin, USA. Phone (262) 248-3750. 209 pages.

Tom Smith, 2005, Wilderness Beyond . . . Wilderness Within . . ., 25th Anniversary Edition, Raccoon Institute Publications, Lake Geneva, Wisconsin, USA. Phone (262) 248-3750. 225 pages.

Tom Smith and Clifford E. Knapp (Editors), 2005, Exploring the Power of Solo, Silence and Solitude, Association for Experiential Education, Boulder, Colorado USA www.aee.org

Tom Smith, 2005, Raccoon Circles: A Book of Readings, Raccoon Institute Publications, Lake Geneva, Wisconsin, USA Phone (262) 248-3750. 100 pages.

Tom Smith and William J. Quinn, 2004, The Challenge of Native American Traditions, Second Edition, Raccoon Institute Publications, Lake Geneva, Wisconsin, USA. Phone (262) 248-3750. 258 Pages.

Tom Smith, Bert Horwood, Mike McGowan, Steve Proudman and Stuart Shepley, 2004, Issues of Challenge Education, Second Edition, Raccoon Institute Publications, Lake Geneva, Wisconsin, USA Phone (262) 248-3750. 180 pages.

Tom Smith, 1996, "Therapeutic Potentials of Challenge/Adventure Experiences," in Issues in Therapeutic Recreation, by D. Compton, Sagamore Press, Sagamore, Illinois USA

Tom Smith, 1996, Shaman Beyond . . . Shaman Within, Raccoon Institute Publications, Lake Geneva, Wisconsin, USA Phone (262) 248-3750.

Tom Smith, 1996, "Fresh Start: An Experiential Outdoor Program for Sexually Exploited Youth," in Experience and the Curriculum, Edited by Bert Horwood, Kendall / Hunt Publishers, Dubuque, Iowa USA. Phone (800) 228-0810 or Kendallhunt.com

Tom Smith, 1994, Incidents of Challenge Education: A Guide for Leadership Development, Kendall / Hunt Publishers, Dubuque, Iowa USA. Phone (800) 228-0810 or Kendallhunt.com Out of Print. New Edition in preparation. 315 pages.

Tom Smith, 1993, "Alternative Methods for Processing the Adventure Experience," in Adventure Therapy, by Michael Gass, Kendall / Hunt Publishing, Dubuque, Iowa USA Phone (800) 228-0810 or Kendallhunt.com

Tom Smith, Chris Roland, Mark Havens and Judy Hoyt, 1992, The Theory and Practice of Challenge Education. Kendall / Hunt Publishers, Dubuque, Iowa USA. Phone (800) 228-0810 or www.kendallhunt.com Out of Print. Contact the Raccoon Institute for Information. 284 pages.

Tom Smith, 1991, The Story of Sundrop: A Storybook, A Coloring Book, and A Guide for Educational And Environmental Awareness Activities, Raccoon Institute Publications, Lake Geneva, Wisconsin, USA. Phone (262) 248-3750

On a recent trip to Ireland, I spent some time at a couple of The Ancient Stone Circles left by the Druids. Although there is debate about the exact purpose and significance of these stone circles found about England and Ireland, the huge stones are indeed arranged in circles. I could not resist packing the wisdom of ages gone by into one of my Raccoon Circles, so I knotted a length of webbing and placed the circle atop the center stone. I sat back and reflected on the wisdom of circles for a time, and then I picked the Raccoon Circle up. It is in my pack for use in creating other Raccoon Circles and facilitating other groups in the journey of personal growth and learning.

Tom Smith, April 2006

Raccoon Circle Quotes, Thoughts and Photographs

"When the Raccoon looks out from inside, the circle of connectedness of all things of the universe becomes quite evident."
Tom Smith

"Tom Smith has been fooling around with tied loops of webbing for years."
Karl Rohnke

"Every time we encourage people to 'circle up,' move through a series of activities and initiative problems and gather in the debriefing circle to share thoughts and feelings, we are giving them an opportunity to understand the need, the value and the joy of being fully human in connection with other people."
Tom Smith

*When asked about having invented the Raccoon Circle, Tom said,
" 'Invented' is a funny word. I tied a knot in a piece of webbing!"*
Tom Smith

"The circle speaks for itself."
Tom Smith

"Raccoon Circle activities teach about the value of discovering trust, balance, cooperation, connectedness and belongingness. The learning may be in our muscles and bones, and it may be unconscious. The symbolic and real meaning of circles of connection have been part of the collective unconscious of humankind for eons and may be awakened or re-learned by each person who 'connects' to a circle with others. Participants may not verbalize that they have come to sense and understand the importance of trust, balance, peace and love after a Raccoon Circle connection—but the lesson has been learned in parts of their total somatic being."

Tom Smith

"A whole challenge course in a tiny backpack."
Tom Smith

"The Raccoon Circle – Profound Simplicity."
Tom Smith

"My favorite Raccoon Circle activities? Wrapped Around My Finger, Pizza Flipping, Where Ya From—Where Ya Been?, Believe it or Knot, The Missing Link, Get the Picture, Grand Prix Racing and Inside Out."
Jim Cain

"In the past 6 years, more than 20,000 people from around the world have downloaded the Raccoon Circle documents from the Teamwork & Teamplay website, and are already changing the way their 'community' interacts. Who would have guessed that 'connect up' would have a modern day internet meaning."

Jim Cain

Raccoon Circles have become the world wide webbing!'
Jim Cain

"God is a circle whose center is everywhere and circumference nowhere."
Voltaire

*"Until he extends his circle of compassion to include
all living things, man will not himself find peace."*
Albert Schweitzer

*"When our eyes see our hands doing the work of our hearts, the circle of
Creation is completed inside us, the doors of our souls fly open,
and love steps forth to heal everything in sight."*
Michael Bridge

*"He drew a circle that shut me out—
Heretic, rebel, a thing to flout.
But Love and I had the wit to win:
We drew a circle that took him in."*
Edwin Markham

*"I imagine good teaching as a circle of earnest people sitting down to ask each
other meaningful questions. I don't see it as the handing down of answers."*
Alice Walker

"We dance in a circle and suppose, while the secret sits in the middle and knows."
Robert Frost

"Filling a bookcase is like gathering a social circle."
May Lamberton Becker

"Gathering in circles is an ancient practice being revived in our time."
Parker J. Palmer

"In a circle of trust, we learn an alternate way to respond, centered on the rare art of asking honest, open questions—questions that invite a speaker to reach for deeper and truer speech."
Parker J. Palmer

"The need to literally make a circle is essential. We cannot understand the circle if we are sitting in rows, being lectured at. Even when our minds have forgotten the power of the circle, our bodies remember. . . ."
Christina Baldwin

*"I hear people express their longing to know what to do, how to apply
personal consciousness to the world in some helpful way. . . . Great power
lies within us. What has been missing is the mechanism for organizing this
power. . . . I believe the mechanism of empowerment and action is the circle."*

Christina Baldwin

*"We may, if we keep to the circling process, be able to provide the living fuel for what will
be known as one of the most profound revolutions of all time. . . . To build a renewable,
sustainable culture is to find our way back into the Sacred Hoop."*

Sedonia Cahill and Joshua Halpern

*"We Indians think of the earth and the whole universe as a never-ending circle,
and in this circle man is just another animal. The Buffalo and the Coyote are our
brothers, the birds our cousins. We end our prayers with the words
'All My Relations' —and that includes everything that grows, crawls, runs,
creeps, hops and flies."*

Jenny Leading Cloud

"There are lessons from history. From my first writings about the theory and practice of Raccoon Circles, I have quoted Black Elk about "everything an Indian does is done in a circle." I do not doubt that Black Elk gave us that famous quotation, but I recently discovered a quite similar statement made some years earlier. In her book, Stars Above – Earth Below, editor Marsha C. Bol quotes Thomas Tyon, a Lakota from the Plains: *"The Oblala (Lakota) believe the circle to be sacred because the Great Spirit caused everything in nature to be round . . . The sun and the sky, the earth and the moon, though the sky is deep like a bowl. Everything that breathes is round. . . Everything that grows from the ground is round like the stem of a tree. . . For these reasons the Oglala make their tipis circular, their camp circle circular, and sit in a circle in all ceremonies."*

"She references that quotation to a paper by J. R. Walker, published in the Anthropological Papers of the American Museum of Natural History—back in 1917!!!"

Tom Smith

References, Resources and Information

References, Books, Articles and Suggested Readings

Anderson, M., Cain, J., Cavert, C. and Heck, T., 2005, Teambuilding Puzzles, FUNdoing Publishers (www.fundoing.com) ISBN 0-9746442-0-X 300 pages of team puzzles that explore valuable life skills.

Baldwin, Christina, 1998, Calling the Circle: The First and Future Culture, Bantam Publishers, New York, NY USA

Boud, D., Keogh, R. & Walker, D., Editors, 1985, Reflection: Turning Experience Into Learning, Nichols Publishers, New York, NY.

Cahill, A., 1994, "Creating Ritual," Creation Spirituality, Volume 10, Number 3.

Cahill, Sedonia and Halpern, Joshua, The Ceremonial Circle, 1992, Harper, San Francisco, CA USA

Cain, J., 2001, Raccoon Circles – A Handbook for Facilitators, a free PDF download from the Teamwork & Teamplay Website at www.teamworkandteamplay.com/raccooncircles.html. Dozens of activities for making the Raccoon Circle a popular part of your programs.

Cain, J., "Raccoon Circles – A Handbook for Facilitators," in Horizons Magazine, The Institute for Outdoor Learning (UK), Number 17, Spring 2002, pages 16-25. Email: horizons@outdoor-learning.org

Cain, J., Cummings, M. and Stanchfield, J., 2005, A Teachable Moment, Kendall / Hunt Publishers, Dubuque, Iowa, USA Phone (800) 228-0810 or www.kendallhunt.com, ISBN 0-7575-1782-X. A Facilitator's Guide to Activities for Processing, Debriefing, Reviewing and Reflection.

Cain, J., and Jolliff, B., 1998, Teamwork & Teamplay, Kendall Hunt Publishers, Dubuque, Iowa ISBN 0-7872-4532-1 417 pages of award winning adventure-based and active learning activities.

Cain, J. and Weisler, K., 2006, The Value of Connection – In the Workplace, (for more information visit: www.teamworkandteamplay.com)

Cavert, C., 2001, Lines and Loops – Community Building Activities with Webbing – 22 pages of activities, illustrations and references. chris@fundoing.com www.fundoing.com

Cottom, J., 1994, Freedom Circles – An Experiential Tool for Group Development. Jay "Mike" Cottom 912 East 10715 South Sandy, Utah 84094 49 pages of activities that explore respect, celebration, balance, play, competition, listening and sharing.

Csikszentmihalyi, M., 1990, Flow: The Psychology of Optimal Experience, Harper & Row Publishers, New York, New York. ISBN 0-06-016253-8

Gass, M., 1993, Adventure Therapy. Kendall/Hunt Publishers, Dubuque, Iowa.

Greenaway, Roger, 2002, Reviewing with Ropes, *Horizons* Magazine, Institute for Outdoor Learning, Number 18, Summer 2002, pages 23-26. www.outdoor-learning.org

Grigg, A., 2001, Creative Idea for Team Work – Using Old Ties.

Alf Grigg 394 Woodsworth Road #48 Willowdale, Ontario, Canada M2I 2T9

Phone (416) 444-7550 Email: 3griggs@sympatico.ca

Heck, T., 2006, The Group Loop Training CD – 27 Fun Teambuilding Activities presented with video clips of actual groups, color photographs and printable directions. Includes two special bonus audio interviews with team building experts Sam Sikes and Jim Cain. www.teachmeteamwork.com Phone (828) 665-0303

Huang, A., 1973, Embrace Tiger – Return to Mountain, Real Peoples Press, San Francisco, CA.

Jackson, T., 1993, Activities that Teach, Red Rock Publishing, Cedar City, UT ISBN 0-916095-49-5

Jackson, T., 1995, More Activities that Teach, Red Rock Publishing, Cedar City, UT ISBN 0-916095-75-4

Johnson, D.W. & Johnson, F.P., 1997, Joining Together: Group Theory and Group Skills, Allyn & Bacon, Boston, MA ISBN 0-205-19750-7

Jung, C. G., 1964, Man and His Symbols. Doubleday, New York, NY

Knapp, C., 1992, Lasting Lessons: A Teacher's Guide to Reflecting on Experience. ERIC, Charleston, WV

Kolb, D. A., 1984, Experiential Learning: Experiences as the Source of Learning and Development, Prentice Hall, Englewood Cliffs, New Jersey. ISBN 0-13-295261-0

McGaa, E., 1990, Mother Earth Spirituality. Harper, New York, NY

Nadler, R. and Luckner, J., 1992, Processing the Adventure Experience. Kendall/Hunt, Dubuque, Iowa

Neihardt, J. and Black Elk, 1972, Black Elk Speaks. Pocket, New York, NY

Palmer, Parker J., 2004, A Hidden Wholeness: The Journey Toward an Undivided Life, Jossey-Bass, San Francisco.

Putnam, R.D., 2000, Bowling Alone, Simon & Schuster, New York, NY ISBN 0-684-83283-6

Rogers, C., 1970, On Encounter Groups. Harper Books, New York, NY

Roland, C., Wagner, R. and Wigand, R., 1995, Do It and Understand: The Bottom Line on Corporate Experiential Learning. Kendall/Hunt, Dubuque, Iowa

Schwarz, R. M., 1994, The Skilled Facilitator: Practical Wisdom for Developing Effective Groups, Jossey-Bass Publishers. ISBN 1-55542-638-7

Sidle, Clinton C., 2005, The Leadership Wheel – Five Steps for Achieving Individual and Organizational Greatness, Palgrave Macmillan, New York, NY ISBN 1-4039-6919-1

Smith, T., 1990, Wilderness Beyond... Wilderness Within... Raccoon Institute, Lake Geneva, WI

Smith, T., Roland, C., Havens, M., and Hoyt, J., 1992, The Theory and Practice of Challenge Education. Kendall/Hunt, Dubuque, Iowa

Smith, T., 1993, "Alternative Methods for Processing the Adventure Experience," in Gass, M., Adventure Therapy, Kendall/Hunt, Dubuque, Iowa

Smith, T., 1996, "Therapeutic Potentials of Challenge/Adventure Experiences," in Compton, D., Issues in Therapeutic Recreation, Sagamore Press, Sagamore, IL

Storm, H., 1972, Seven Arrows. Ballantine Books, New York, NY

Storm, H., 1994, Lightningbolt. Ballantine Books, New York, NY

Sun Bear and Wabun Wind, 1980, Medicine Wheels, Prentice-Hall, New York, NY

Sun Bear, Wabun Wind and Mulligan, C., 1991, Dancing With the Wheel. Prentice-Hall, New York, NY

Watts, L. J., 2002, Mandalas – Spiritual Circles for Harmony and Fulfillment, Hermes House Publishers, London ISBN 1-84038-973-7

Website and Internet Resources

www.reviewing.co.uk	Roger Greenaway's reviewing website, filled with useful information.
www.teamworkandteamplay.com	Jim Cain's adventure-based website, with activities, information, and the newest Raccoon Circle activities in downloadable PDF files.
www.sportime.com	A wide variety of sporting equipment, and nearly all of their equipment has printed instructions which are available at the Sportime website.
www.teachmeteamwork.com	Tom Heck's website filled with teambuilding ideas.
www.adventurehardware.com	Raccoon Circles, adventure equipment, books, and training.
www.training-wheels.com	Michelle Cumnming's website filled with processing and debriefing tools, and more.
www.fundoing.com	Chris Cavert's website of adventure-based ideas.
www.kendallhunt.com	Publishers of books by Jim Cain and Tom Smith
www.kirkweisler.com	Interesting ideas, suggested reading and more.
www.aee.org	The Association for Experiential Education, publications, regional and international conferences, and an experiential education focused listserve on the web.
www.acctinfo.org	The Association for Challenge Course Technology, information, standards, conferences, job listings, references and resources related to challenge courses and adventure-based learning.
www.prcainfo.org	The Professional Ropes Course Association, information related to standards and other challenge course references and resources.
www.ropesonline.org	The ROPES Website, discussion list and general information

Resources

For more information on experiential & adventure-based programs, and Raccoon Circle activities contact:

Dr. Tom Smith, Raccoon Institute N2020 Cty. H, South #570 Lake Geneva, Wisconsin 53147 USA
    Phone (262) 248-3750
    Email: tsraccoon@earthlink.net

Dr. Jim Cain, Teamwork & Teamplay 468 Salmon Creek Road Brockport, New York 14420 USA
    Phone (585) 637-0328
    Email: jimcain@teamworkandteamplay.com Website: www.teamworkandteamplay.com

Tom Heck, Teach-Me-Teamwork P.O.Box 1831 Asheville, NC 28802
    Phone (828) 665-0303 Fax (828) 670-7631
    Email: tom@teachmeteamwork.com

Jay "Mike" Cottam 855 South 500 East Pleasant Grove, Utah 84062
    Phone (801) 756-8518
    Email: cottmi@alpine.k12.ut.us

Michell Cummings, Training Wheels, 7095 South Garrison Street Littleton, Colorado 80128 USA
    Phone (888) 553-0147 or (303) 979-1708
    Email: Info@training-wheels.com Website: www.training-wheels.com

Chris Cavert, FUNdoing Inc.
    Phone (928) 526-6386
    Email: chris@fundoing.com Website: www.fundoing.com

Clare-Marie Hannon, 321 Bouldercrest Way Woodstock, GA 30188
    Phone (770) 516-1977
    Email: claremarie_h@earthlink.net

Alf Grigg 394 Woodsworth Road #48 Willowdale, Ontario, Canada M2I 2T9
    Phone (416) 444-7550
    Email: 3griggs@sympatico.ca

Kirk Weisler, Chief Moral Officer 100 Olivia Court Fayetteville, Georgia 30215 USA
    Phone (801) 360-5648 or (678) 817-6404
    Email: kirk@kirkweisler.com
    Website: www.kirkweisler.com

Don Rogers, Indiana State University, 5 Gardendale Road Terre Haute, Indiana
    Phone (812) 237-3210 or (812) 877-3867 or (812) 249-0286
    Email: rcdonn@scifac.indstate.edu

Mike Anderson, Petra Cliffs Climbing Center, 105 Briggs Street, Burlington, Vermont 05401 USA
    Phone (802) 657-3872
    Email: mike@petracliffs.com
    Website: www.petracliffs.com

For a list of suppliers of Raccoon Circle Materials (webbing, books, manuals & training), see the Technical Information chapter here in Section IV.

For additional references and resources, see the article entitled "A Little Research" found at the end of Section II in this book.

Jim Cain

Dr. Jim Cain is the author of five adventure-based teambuilding texts: Teamwork & Teamplay, which received the Karl Rohnke Creativity Award presented by the Association for Experiential Education (AEE); Teambuilding Puzzles; A Teachable Moment; The Value of Connection - In the Workplace; and this book, The Book of Raccoon Circles. He is the owner and creative force behind the active learning company Teamwork & Teamplay, a Senior Consultant to the Cornell University Corporate Teambuilding Program, and a former Executive Director for the Association for Challenge Course Technology (ACCT). Jim makes his home in Brockport, NY. He holds four engineering degrees including a Ph.D. in Mechanical Engineering from the University of Rochester. Dr. Cain frequently serves as a visiting professor and staff development specialist on subjects ranging from experiential education using adventure-based and active learning activities to corporate leadership, recreational dancing and games leadership, and from structural engineering and chaos theory to his Ph.D. research topic, powder mechanics. In the past 10 years he has presented programs and workshops in 44 states and 12 countries and generally has more teambuilding toys and a library of adventure-based and active learning books larger than that of many developing nations. His publications, including the internet edition of Raccoon Circle activities, have been used around the world to build unity, community, connection and teamwork.

Jim Cain, Ph.D.
Teamwork & Teamplay
468 Salmon Creek Road
Brockport, NY 14420 USA
Phone (585) 637-0328
Email: jimcain@teamworkandteamplay.com
Website: www.teamworkandteamplay.com

Tom Smith

Dr. Tom Smith is the founder and director of the Raccoon Institute, which offers consultation and training in the theory and practice of challenge education. His academic training was as a clinical psychologist, but experience and professional development, which included some study with Native American elders, leads him to describe himself as a personal growth facilitator, wilderness guide, and challenge/adventure therapist. He has 50 years of experience working in universities, community mental health centers, special education programs, and as a consultant for professional training and development.

Tom is the author of eight books and has published over 100 professional papers. He is a frequent presenter at regional, national and international conferences on humanistic psychology, experiential education, special education, therapeutic recreation, corporate training and leadership development. His orientation has always been toward exploration of alternative methodologies for facilitation of personal growth and learning, and he has long explored the potentials of outdoor therapy and challenge/adventure education. In 1997, Dr. Smith was honored with the Association for Experiential Education's Kurt Hahn Award, recognizing him as an important and life long leader in the field. In 2005, he was again honored by AEE and presented with the Karl Rohnke Creativity Award, for his significant work with Raccoon Circles.

In 1995, Tom began presenting workshops with web loops, which have now become known as "Raccoon Circles." This simple experiential training methodology has been recognized by hundreds of challenge and adventure-based educators and leaders as a powerful tool for facilitating small groups, and exploring issues of trust, communication, cooperative problem solving and positive interactive dynamics. While Tom's first book on this subject was entitled "THE BOOK on Raccoon Circles," Tom notes that words cannot adequately describe the magic, the power, and the healing potentials of the "circle of connection." One has to experience the sequence of small group activities with the Raccoon Circle to know its' meaning . . . as "the circle speaks for itself."

Tom Smith, Ph.D.
The Raccoon Institute
N2020 Cty. H South #570
Lake Geneva, Wisconsin 53147 USA
Phone (262) 248-3750
Email: tsraccoon@earthlink.net

Contacting the Authors

Dr. Jim Cain and Dr. Tom Smith are available for conference presentations, facilitator training sessions, workshops, educational events, teambuilding programs and adventure-based and active learning sessions. You are welcome to contact them at the addresses shown below.

Jim Cain
Teamwork & Teamplay
468 Salmon Creek Road
Brockport, NY 14420
Phone (585) 637-0328 Fax (585) 637-5277
Email: jimcain@teamworkandteamplay.com
Website: www.teamworkandteamplay.com

Tom Smith
The Raccoon Institute
N2020 Cty. H South #570
Lake Geneva, WI 53147
Phone (262) 248-3750
Email: tsraccoon@earthlink.net

If you would like to share your Raccoon Circle experiences, activities, photographs, ideas and stories, you are welcome to submit them electronically to the Email addresses shown above. You can also download the latest Raccoon Circle articles and activities online at:

www.teamworkandteamplay.com/raccooncircles.html

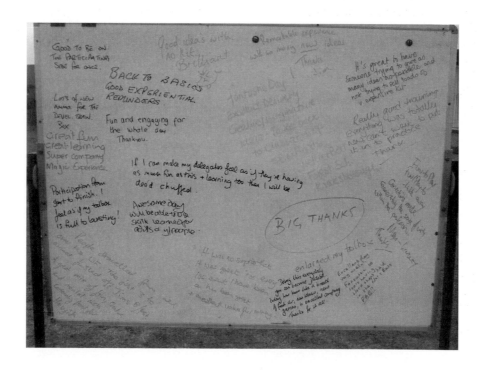

Also From Kendall/Hunt Publishing

Teamwork & Teamplay—The award-winning guide to cooperative, challenge and adventure-based activities that build confidence, cooperation, teamwork, creativity, trust, decision making, conflict resolution, resource management, communication, effective feedback and problem solving skills. 417 pages of teambuilding activities, games, challenges and resources.
ISBN 0-7872-4532-1

A Teachable Moment—A facilitator's guide to activities for processing, debriefing, reviewing and reflection. 282 pages with more than 130 different techniques for facilitating groups.
ISBN 0-7575-1782-X

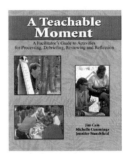

The Revised and Expanded Book of Raccoon Circles—A facilitator's guide to building unity, community, connection and teamwork through active learning. 282 pages of activities, stories and resources for working with groups.
ISBN 0-7575-3265-9

Kendall/Hunt Publishing Company
4050 Westmark Drive
P.O.Box 1840
Dubuque, Iowa 52004-1840 USA

Phone 1-800-228-0810 or (563) 589-1000
Fax 1-800-772-9165 or (563) 589-1046

www.kendallhunt.com

Index

This index should help you locate all of the Raccoon Circle activities, stories, and major topics printed in this book. Though many of the Raccoon Circle activities are contemplative and serene, some are very energetic. These are noted with an asterisk (*).

Recent Additions to the World of Raccoon Circle Stories and Activities

Almost every time a group of Raccoon Circle enthusiasts gather together, some new activity or variation is invented. Since the first edition of the Book on Raccoon Circles over 100 new activities, stories, techniques and ideas have been created, recorded and enjoyed by audiences around the world.

Each year author Jim Cain shares the most recent Raccoon Circles activities and stories together with a few favorites from the past in his annual internet edition of Raccoon Circle activities, which you can download for free at: www.teamworkandteamplay.com/raccooncircles.html

You are welcome to add your own Raccoon Circle activities in the blank pages that follow. In future printings of this book, new activities and stories will be added to these pages.

As an example of what you can expect, here is one of our favorite new Raccoon Circle activities.

W.A.M.F. (Wrapped Around My Finger)

W.A.M.F. stands for Wrapped Around My Finger, and pretty much explains this entire activity. Begin with an unknotted segment of webbing. One person in the group begins wrapping the webbing around their index finger, and while doing so, provides the group with some information about themselves (where they were born, family members, school experiences, childhood pets, dreams, goals, favorite foods, etc.) The goal is for this person to continue talking until the webbing is completely wrapped around their finger. When they reach the end, they allow the webbing to unwind and pass it along to the next person in the group.

This particular activity provides a bit more time for folks to talk about themselves, and also provides a kinesthetic activity coupled with a verbal activity for exploring multiple intelligence opportunities and whole brain learning possibilities. There is also a popular theory that for folks that may be a bit shy about speaking to even a small group in public, the action of wrapping the webbing around their finger occupies that portion of the brain where nervousness occurs. By wrapping and rapping at the same time, the speech center becomes less inhibited and the person talking is less stressed. It is also surprising what participants discuss during this wrapping and rapping session. The 15 foot length of the Raccoon Circle allows more than a minutes worth of communication, which means you'll learn quite a bit more about a person than just their name and where they are from.

This activity is also known by the names: The Strap Rap, Wrap Rap, and Wrapping & Rapping.

Something New

Facilitators, teachers and trainers have been telling us for years that they like the portability of using Raccoon Circles. River rafting outfitters and wilderness guides like the fact that Raccoon Circles can get wet without damage, can be carried into the back country because they are lightweight, and can be used for many different team activities.

For those that enjoy the Raccoon Circle, we have a new collection of team activities that you can carry with you anywhere. The Ropework & Ropeplay collection of team activities, contains a unique variety of ropes and instructions, packaged together in a rugged backpack, all weighing less than four pounds! You'll find some Raccoon Circles in there, plus a variety of other useful ropes with which you can perform more than 200 different team challenges, games and initiatives. Also included is an extensive manual, filled with instructions for leading the 200+ activities compiled so far (with more coming in the future).

For more information about this unique and portable team activity collection, contact:

Jim Cain, Ph.D.
Teamwork & Teamplay
468 Salmon Creek Road
Brockport, New York 14420
Phone (585) 637-0328
Email: jimcain@teamworkandteamplay.com
Website: www.teamworkandteamplay.com

Raccoon Circles

Making Teamwork as Easy as Teamplay